A Passion for
Natural History

This review of the life, interests and collections of the 13th Earl of Derby was inspired by the late Sir Richard Foster DL, Director of National Museums & Galleries on Merseyside 1986-2001. It was published in 2002 to coincide with 'The Earl & the Pussycat', an exhibition commemorating the 150 years since the foundation of the Liverpool Museum. Many of the items in this account were included in the exhibition.

Book production by The Bluecoat Press, Liverpool
Book design by March Design, Liverpool
Printed by Midas

Front cover Mongoose Lemur by Joseph Wolf (K).
Back cover Tin plate. Royal Academy of Arts, London.

ISBN 1 902700 14 7

CHRISTIE'S

STEAM PACKET COMPANY

Acknowledgements

Contributors Text by: Amanda Askari, Xanthe Brooke, Alan Crosby, John Edmondson, Clemency Fisher, Tim Flannery, Errol Fuller, Stephen Guy, Christine E. Jackson, Peter Jones, Janet Kear, Alex Kidson, Loraine Knowles, Malcolm Largen (assistant editor), Edward Morris, E. Charles Nelson, Robert McCracken Peck, Alyson Pollard, Andrew Renton, Gordon Rowley, Sam Segal, Ian Wallace, Kathie Way, Arline Wilson.

Additional research by David Barnaby, The Rt. Hon. The Earl of Derby, The Rt. Hon. The Countess of Derby, John Edwards, Amberley Moore, Richard Schodde, the late William Stearn, the late Martin Suggett, Lucy Wood.

Research Assistants Ann Bridson, Daniel Mangan, Antony Parker, Philip Witter.

Lenders The Earl of Derby and The Earl of Derby's 1929 Heirlooms Settlement; Eton College, Windsor; Liverpool City Libraries; Liverpool Museum; The National Portrait Gallery, London; The Natural History Museum, London; Private Collections; Royal Albert Memorial Museum & Art Gallery, Exeter; Trinity College Library, Cambridge; The Walker, Liverpool; Yorkshire Museum, York.

Sponsored by The Earl of Derby, Knowsley Safari Park, Christie's International plc., Sea Containers Irish Sea Operations (Isle of Man Steam Packet Company), E.C. Chelsea, The Linnean Society of London, The Society for the History of Natural History, The British Ornithologists' Club, The John Fairclough Charitable Trust, Robert Fleming Holdings Ltd., Alan and Martha Armstrong.

Acknowledgements also to: The Academy of Natural Sciences (Philadelphia), Mark Adams, The American Museum of Natural History (New York), The American Philosophical Society (Philadelphia), Tomas Anfält, Alan Armstrong, Tabitha Barber, David Bolton, Graham Boxer, Hilary Bracegirdle, The British Iris Society, The British Ornithologists' Union, Gavin Bridson, Brenda Burgess, John Collins, Louisa Connor, Liz Cowdy, Rob Cox, Philip Cribb, Ann Datta, Ray Desmond, Gina Douglas, Michael Dudley, EDM Ltd., Brent Elliott, Cheshire Record Office, Mike Fitton, John Harvey, Richard Harbord, Martin Harker, John Hawkes, Oliver Impey, Andrew Ingersoll, Charlie Jarvis, Paula Jenkins, Leo Joseph, Knowsley Safari Park, Mark Laird, Lionel Lambourne, Walter Lack, Alan Leslie, Arthur Macgregor, the McIver family, Ann Meyer, Amy Meyers, Sue Minter, New York Botanical Garden, Vivien Noakes, Mark and Nancy Ritchie-Noakes, The Royal Horticultural Society, Lady Jean O'Neill, Storrs Olson, Philip Oswald, Robert Prŷs Jones, Sandra Raphael, John Rogers, Richard Sabin, David Scrase, The Smithsonian Institution (Washington), Gordon Stowell, Johnny Strand, Ruth Stungo, Ann Sylph, Charles Truman, Michael Walters.

Major repositories of manuscripts relating to the 13th Earl of Derby
Lancashire Record Office, Preston. Mainly local history and estate manuscripts.

Liverpool Record Office, Liverpool City Libraries, William Brown Street. The largest collection of the 13th Earl of Derby's manuscripts, the full reference for which is LVRO 920 DER (13) [number as listed], unless otherwise stated.

Archives Department, NMGM. Mainly copybooks of letters written to the 13th Earl of Derby.

Zoology Section Archives, Liverpool Museum, NMGM. Mainly lists of specimens, some botanical.

Knowsley Hall. Family papers.

Special credit is due to the many members of NMGM staff who have been involved in this project, in particular the members of the Working Party (1996-2002) and of the exhibition production team.

A Passion for Natural History

The Life and Legacy of the 13th Earl of Derby

Edited by Clemency Fisher

The 13th Earl of Derby in 1837 by William Derby. At the age of sixty-one, for twenty years past a widower, the Earl is shown surrounded by the trappings of his greatest interests. One of the rolls of paper is inscribed 'Drawings, Nat. History, by Edward Lear' and another 'Plan of the Diversion of Roads in the Township of Knowsley' (K).

CONTENTS

List of abbreviations

BMNH: The Natural History Museum, London. **Houghton**: Houghton Library, Harvard University, Cambridge, Mass.
K: Knowsley Estate, nr. Prescot. **LM**: Liverpool Museum. **LM D**: specimen from the 13th Earl of Derby's zoological
collections. **LM ZDA**: Liverpool Museum, Zoology Dept. Archives. **LRO**: Lancashire Record Office, Preston.
LVRO: Liverpool Record Office, Liverpool City Libraries. **NMGM**: National Museums & Galleries on Merseyside, Liverpool.
NPG: The National Portrait Gallery, London. **RAMM**: Royal Albert Memorial Museum, Exeter. **V & A**: Victoria and Albert
Museum, London. **YCBA**: Yale Center for British Art, New Haven, Connecticut. **YORYM**: Yorkshire Museum, York.

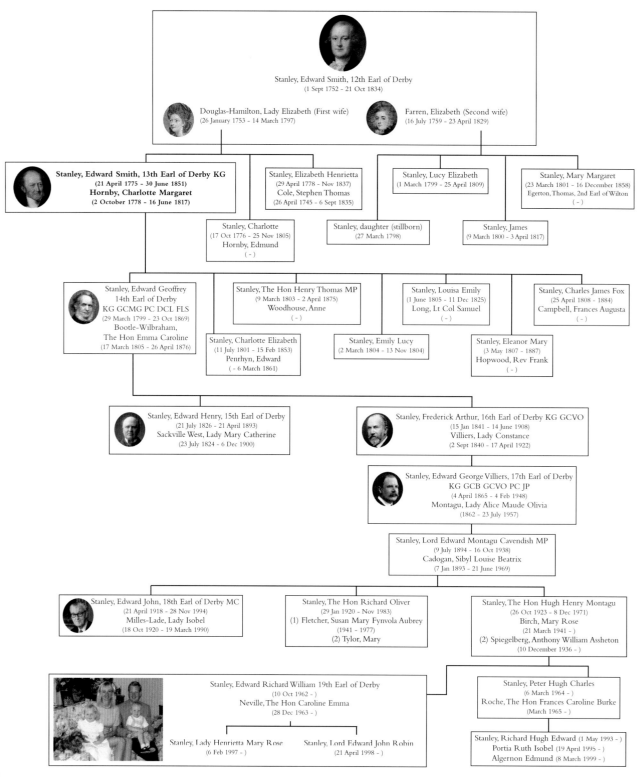

Stanley, Edward Smith, 12th Earl of Derby
(1 Sept 1752 - 21 Oct 1834)

Douglas-Hamilton, Lady Elizabeth (First wife)
(26 January 1753 - 14 March 1797)

Farren, Elizabeth (Second wife)
(16 July 1759 - 23 April 1829)

Stanley, Edward Smith, 13th Earl of Derby KG
(21 April 1775 - 30 June 1851)
Hornby, Charlotte Margaret
(2 October 1778 - 16 June 1817)

Stanley, Elizabeth Henrietta
(29 April 1778 - Nov 1837)
Cole, Stephen Thomas
(26 April 1745 - 6 Sept 1835)

Stanley, Lucy Elizabeth
(1 March 1799 - 25 April 1809)

Stanley, Mary Margaret
(23 March 1801 - 16 December 1858)
Egerton, Thomas, 2nd Earl of Wilton
(-)

Stanley, Charlotte
(17 Oct 1776 - 25 Nov 1805)
Hornby, Edmund
(-)

Stanley, daughter (stillborn)
(27 March 1798)

Stanley, James
(9 March 1800 - 3 April 1817)

Stanley, Edward Geoffrey
14th Earl of Derby
KG GCMG PC DCL FLS
(29 March 1799 - 23 Oct 1869)
Bootle-Wilbraham,
The Hon Emma Caroline
(17 March 1805 - 26 April 1876)

Stanley, The Hon Henry Thomas MP
(9 March 1803 - 2 April 1875)
Woodhouse, Anne
(-)

Stanley, Louisa Emily
(1 June 1805 - 11 Dec 1825)
Long, Lt Col Samuel
(-)

Stanley, Charles James Fox
(25 April 1808 - 1884)
Campbell, Frances Augusta
(-)

Stanley, Charlotte Elizabeth
(11 July 1801 - 15 Feb 1853)
Penrhyn, Edward
(- 6 March 1861)

Stanley, Emily Lucy
(2 March 1804 - 13 Nov 1804)

Stanley, Eleanor Mary
(3 May 1807 - 1887)
Hopwood, Rev Frank
(-)

Stanley, Edward Henry, 15th Earl of Derby
(21 July 1826 - 21 April 1893)
Sackville West, Lady Mary Catherine
(23 July 1824 - 6 Dec 1900)

Stanley, Frederick Arthur, 16th Earl of Derby KG GCVO
(15 Jan 1841 - 14 June 1908)
Villiers, Lady Constance
(2 Sept 1840 - 17 April 1922)

Stanley, Edward George Villiers, 17th Earl of Derby
KG GCB GCVO PC JP
(4 April 1865 - 4 Feb 1948)
Montagu, Lady Alice Maude Olivia
(1862 - 23 July 1957)

Stanley, Lord Edward Montagu Cavendish MP
(9 July 1894 - 16 Oct 1938)
Cadogan, Sibyl Louise Beatrix
(7 Jan 1893 - 21 June 1969)

Stanley, Edward John, 18th Earl of Derby MC
(21 April 1918 - 28 Nov 1994)
Milles-Lade, Lady Isobel
(18 Oct 1920 - 19 March 1990)

Stanley, The Hon Richard Oliver
(29 Jan 1920 - Nov 1983)
(1) Fletcher, Susan Mary Fynvola Aubrey
(1941 - 1977)
(2) Tylor, Mary

Stanley, The Hon Hugh Henry Montagu
(26 Oct 1923 - 8 Dec 1971)
Birch, Mary Rose
(21 March 1941 -)
(2) Spiegelberg, Anthony William Assheton
(10 December 1936 -)

Stanley, Edward Richard William 19th Earl of Derby
(10 Oct 1962 -)
Neville, The Hon Caroline Emma
(28 Dec 1963 -)

Stanley, Peter Hugh Charles
(6 March 1964 -)
Roche, The Hon Frances Caroline Burke
(March 1965 -)

Stanley, Lady Henrietta Mary Rose
(6 Feb 1997 -)

Stanley, Lord Edward John Robin
(21 April 1998 -)

Stanley, Richard Hugh Edward (1 May 1993 -)
Portia Ruth Isobel (19 April 1995 -)
Algernon Edmund (8 March 1999 -)

FOREWORD

$\mathfrak{Knowsley}$
$\mathfrak{Prescot}$
$\mathfrak{Merseyside}$
L34 4AF

It is very humbling to look back at what my forebears have achieved over a great many centuries. The Stanley family has followed closely the course of British history in a variety of roles, from soldiers to diplomats and to patrons of Shakespeare. Henry IV (1405) not only knighted John Stanley (from whom the Earls of Derby are descended) but gave him sovereignty of the Isle of Man. They have held many cabinet positions in the British parliament, including those of Prime Minister and Secretary of State for War.

One member of the family who earned a very different distinction was Edward Smith Stanley, 13th Earl of Derby (1775-1851). He was the son of a passionate sportsman, after whom 'The Derby Red' (a famous fighting cock) was named, and who founded both 'The Oaks' and 'The Derby' horse-races. In spite of (or perhaps because of) this environment, the 13th Earl became a passionate ornithologist and pre-eminent natural historian. His thoughts on the breeding of animals and their conservation are remarkable when one considers that Darwin's *On the origin of species by means of natural selection* was not published until a decade after this Earl's death.

As a young man, Lord Stanley stood as a Whig candidate for Preston in 1796. He used his 21st birthday party to promote this cause and thus became a Member of Parliament at a very tender age. In 1832 he was called to The House of Lords, as Baron Stanley of Bickerstaffe. Although he served for 36 years as an MP, it has to be admitted that Knowsley was his first love. The 13th Earl was delighted to hand over politics to his son, who became Prime Minister three times.

The 13th Earl of Derby was a tall, elegant man with a kind and thoughtful personality. In 1798, he married his cousin, Charlotte, daughter of the Reverend Hornby. She died in 1817, having given birth to three boys and four girls between 1799 and 1808. The youngest of these was called Charles James Fox Stanley, which gives a clear indication of his father's political sympathies.[1] Lord Stanley enjoyed a very happy marriage and family life, living at Knowsley with his father, stepmother and half siblings.

He started his very remarkable involvement in natural history by buying museum specimens of birds in the early years of the nineteenth century. From this point his interest became ever deeper, and he held the position of President of both the Linnean Society and the Zoological Society of London. Artistic interests led him to employ Edward Lear, who both painted the animals in Lord Derby's aviary and menagerie and wrote his famous nonsense rhymes for the children at Knowsley.

Opposite Family tree of the Stanley family; the portraits indicate successive Earls of Derby since the 12th Earl and his wives.

LATHOM HOUSE.

The original home of the Stanley family; Lathom House, near Ormskirk. The manor of Knowsley became the property of the Lathom family by marriage in the thirteenth century and the house was the principal residence of the Stanleys until Cromwell demolished it after a long siege in the Civil War (Lancashire County Library, Preston).

Crayon and chalk drawing of Edward Lear by Holman Hunt, 1857 (The Walker).

Right Engraving of the southeast view of Knowsley Hall in 1839, by G. Pickering (LM).

It was only after his father died and he became the 13th Earl of Derby at the relatively advanced age of fifty-nine, already rather deaf and partially paralysed, that he was able to set about the building of an extensive aviary and menagerie at Knowsley, and extending the Park. The 13th Earl's energies were not confined to the estate, as he is reputed to have spent during his lifetime the enormous sum of £100,000 in building churches, vicarages and schools. Despite all this, and his duties as Lord Lieutenant of Lancaster, he also found time to add greatly and wisely to the family collection of works of art. On the 13th Earl's death, his son was already a member of the cabinet and on the point of becoming Prime Minster, so the speedy dissipation of the natural history collections was inevitable. The 13th Earl of Derby's Will provided for the establishment of the Derby Museum, now the Liverpool Museum, National Museums & Galleries on Merseyside. It is the 150th anniversary of his death and the birth of the Museum, that we are now celebrating with NMGM's *Into the Future* and *The Earl and the Pussycat* exhibition.

My wife and I are delighted that we are continuing the long history of family involvement with NMGM. It is a great honour that Her Majesty The Queen is to visit the exhibition in this, her Golden Jubilee Year.

[1]Charles James Fox (1749–1806), was the force behind the Whig party in the late eighteenth century.

Derby.

The Earl of Derby
May 2002

PREFACE

National Museums & Galleries on Merseyside is celebrating the 150th anniversary of the bequest of the 13th Earl of Derby's bird and mammal collections, upon which the Liverpool Museum - part of the NMGM group - was founded. Lord Derby's zoological collection is held in enormous scientific regard throughout the world, as is the natural history art he bought or commissioned and which remains at Knowsley Hall. We are delighted to be marking the anniversary by re-uniting much of this material in an exhibition, *The Earl & the Pussycat*, and by publishing this review of the life of Lord Derby, his interests and his collections.

On behalf of the Chairman and Trustees of NMGM, I would like to thank the present Earl and Countess of Derby for their generous and unstinting support of *The Earl & the Pussycat* exhibition, for which they have kindly loaned many works of art, and for their assistance with this catalogue.

I should also like to record our thanks to Clem Fisher, who has put in a tremendous amount of work in bringing about the exhibition and catalogue. We are very grateful to the Editorial Board, the many authors of scholarly articles and the members of the production team, without whose contributions the publication of this catalogue would not have been possible.

David Fleming
Director, National Museums & Galleries on Merseyside

INTRODUCTION

The original proposal, considered by the Council of the Borough of Liverpool on 16th July 1851, that the 13th Earl of Derby's Museum be given to the people of Liverpool (K).

The 13th Earl's collections were first housed in the Union Newsrooms in Upper Duke Street, and the building was opened as the first public library (1852) and museum (1853) in Liverpool. Photograph, derived from a watercolour by W. G. Herdman (LVRO).

Liverpool Museum owes its foundation to the bequest in 1851 of the 13th Earl of Derby's natural history collection to the Corporation of Liverpool. After his father's death in June of that year, Edward Geoffrey, the 14th Earl of Derby, wasted no time in writing to the Mayor of Liverpool about his father's wishes for his collection.

> 'It was the anxious wish of my dear and lamented Father, as it is my own that the very extensive and valuable collection of stuffed Birds and Animals which it was the labor[sic] of his life to form, should not after his death be dispersed, but rendered as far as possible available to the Amusement and instruction of his countrymen and neighbours'.[1]

The 13th Earl had initially considered bequeathing them to the British Museum,[2] but because this would have meant dividing the collection, he changed his mind. He instead decided:

> '… that this Museum should be placed in the care of a body of Trustees after the Model of the British Museum to be placed in the Town or environs of Liverpool hoping that the public authorities there may think it fit to erect some building for its reception which might perhaps with advantage be placed in connexion with the Collegiate Institution already in this Town … I would further add my wish that it should bear the name of its original founder as some memorial of the interest I have from boyhood felt in the study of Natural History, and my earnest wish to make that which has formed a constant pleasure during my own life as far as possible conducive to the welfare and gratification of my fellow countrymen and neighbours …'.[3]

A Library and Museum Committee already existed, and at a meeting of the Town Council on 9th November 1850 it had been agreed that 'An Act for enabling Town Councils to establish public Libraries and Museums' be referred to this Committee.[4] The original intention behind seeking a Bill had been to enable the transfer of the collections of the Royal Institution of Liverpool to the Corporation. However, for various reasons, the Royal Institution scheme had been abandoned by June 1851, so the offer of the 13th Earl of Derby's collection was most opportune.

In response to the 14th Earl's letter, a sub-committee, chaired by Mr Samuel Holme,[5] was set up to confer with the new Earl on the matter. The main issues for discussion were the conditions associated with the gift: that Trustees of the collection should be appointed[6] and that the Corporation should provide funds:

> 'for the proper maintenance of the collection in an efficient state to the satisfaction of the Trustees whose jurisdiction shall be confined to securing the fulfilment of the intentions of the Earl of Derby in presenting his collection to the Public'.[7]

The next problem was to find a suitable site for housing the museum. Negotiations with the Royal Institution were resumed, with the hope of acquiring a sufficiently large site in Colquitt Street to accommodate the Derby Museum, the Library, the Royal Institution Museum and the Gallery of Art, and manage them together. In the interim, given that obtaining an Act of Parliament might take some time, and that there was an urgent need to accommodate both the Derby collection and the Library, the Corporation decided to purchase the Union Newsrooms in Duke Street and thus allow more time for the development of the grander scheme.[8]

The staff of the Free Public Museum of Liverpool in about 1890. Thomas Moore had moved from Knowsley with the 13th Earl's collections in 1851 and eventually became the first Director (NMGM).

Fig. 1. Group of Museum Workers about 1890

J. Chard	F. P. Marrat	*Unidentified*	P. Entwistle
	H. H. Higgins	T. J. Moore	

The Act to establish the 'Public Library, Museum and Gallery of Arts at Liverpool' was passed on 3rd May 1852. Admission to the museum was to be free, and it was to be open at least four days a week and a further one day a week by appointment. The money from any objects sold could only be applied to the purchase of further specimens. None of the specimens in the Derby collection could be sold, and any additions to the collection were to be clearly marked to distinguish them from the originals. Any disputes between the Trustees and the Council were to be referred to the Head Curator, or relevant Keeper, at the British Museum in London - whose decision would be final.[9]

The Derby Museum was formally opened in Duke Street on 8th March 1853;[10] it consisted of just two rooms. Fortunately, it was not long before it became possible to put into progress a much grander scheme in a different part of town. Mr William Brown, the MP for south Lancashire, offered to pay for a new Free Library and Museum building to be built on Shaw's Brow (which was subsequently renamed William Brown Street), adjacent to the recently completed and grandiose St. George's Hall. The foundation stone of the museum was laid on 15th April 1857, and the building opened to the public with great civic ceremony on 18th October, 1860.

It took a year to transfer all the specimens from Duke Street to the new building. William Brown himself was aware that ships trading out of Liverpool to all parts of the world would provide great opportunities 'for adding to the museum much that is valuable'.[11] He was absolutely right in his prediction. The development and evolution of Liverpool Museum into National Museums & Galleries on Merseyside owes much to Liverpool's history – particularly as an important international port - but equally to the 19th century triumvirate of donors, the 13th Earl of Derby, William Brown and Joseph Mayer. These

11

benefactors provided the founding collections of science and humanities, and a building worthy of an ambitious Victorian town which recognized that self-improvement and learning was fundamental to the future prosperity of its citizens. One hundred and fifty years later, after early 20th century expansion and post-Second World War Blitz reconstruction, Liverpool Museum is greeting the 21st century with renewal and greater space for galleries. We are very pleased to be marking this significant anniversary by honouring Edward Stanley, 13th Earl of Derby, whose gift has indeed conferred 'a lasting benefit upon the educational resources of the people'.[12]

Loraine Knowles
Keeper of the Liverpool Museum

N.B. We have tried to refer consistently to Edward Smith Stanley, later 13th Earl of Derby, according to the different titles he held at various stages in his life. This is complicated by the fact that his father, the 12th Earl of Derby, was also Edward Smith Stanley. The titles we have used for our subject are, chronologically:

1775-1776. The Hon. Edward Stanley
1776-1834. Lord Stanley [between 1832 and 1851 he was also Baron Stanley of Bickerstaffe]
1834-1851. The 13th Earl of Derby

[1]Letter from the 14th Earl to John Bent Esquire, Mayor of Liverpool, dated 'June 8th' 1851, which was read at a special meeting of the Council on 16th July 1851. The date of the letter must have actually been 8th July 1851, as the 13th Earl did not die until 30th June. [2]Letter from D W Mitchell, Secretary of the Zoological Society of London, to Lord Derby dated 30th October 1847 (LVRO 1/118/23). [3]Quoted in letter, op. cit. [4]LVRO 352 MIN/LIB 1/1, 9th November 1850. [5]Samuel Holme had been Chairman of the St. George's Hall building committee and his firm was responsible for building the County Sessions House (now part of The Walker) and the Municipal Annexe in Dale Street. [6]The 13th Earl had proposed as Trustees two members of the Derby family; his friend and steward Richard Earle, the Mayor of Liverpool and two Rectors of the Town of Liverpool, and had also suggested that the incumbents of Knowsley and Huyton should be ex-officio members. [7]LVRO 352 MIN/LIB 1/1, 21st August 1851. [8]Ibid, 2nd September 1851. [9]The Liverpool Library and Museum Act, 1852. [10]Report of the Library & Museum Committee to Liverpool Town Council, October 1853. On average, nearly 5,000 people a week visited 'The Museum of Natural History' in the first six months. [11]The *Illustrated London News* for 27th October 1860: 405. [12]Letter from Mitchell, op. cit.

The Upper Horseshoe Gallery of the Liverpool Museum, opened in 1906 and photographed in 1936. Many of the animals shown were from the 13th Earl of Derby's collection (NMGM).

The Upper Horseshoe Gallery after the museum was firebombed in May 1941. Only those specimens which had been moved to safer locations were spared (NMGM).

Funded by the Heritage Lottery Fund, the NMGM *Into the Future* scheme will double the size of the museum (NMGM).

THE 13TH EARL OF DERBY'S CHILDHOOD, EDUCATION AND FAMILY LIFE

LORAINE KNOWLES

The young Edward Stanley's character could be said to have been formed in reaction to that of his parents, who were members of the somewhat racy Whig set of the late eighteenth century. The 12th Earl's reputation as a gregarious friend and a generous host was firmly established before he succeeded to the Earldom in 1776 and continued until his death in 1834. In 1774 he became engaged to Lady Elizabeth (Betty) Hamilton, the only daughter of the sixth Duke of Hamilton. The elaborate engagement party, held just two weeks before their June wedding, was one of the most talked about events of the time. It involved specially constructed marquees in the grounds of The Oaks, the Derby family's Surrey home near Epsom which later gave its name to the famous horse race.

> 'He gives her a most splendid entertainment tomorrow [June 9] at his villa in Surrey and calls it a fête champêtre. It will cost five thousand pounds. Everybody is to go in masquerade, but not in mask. He has bought all the orange trees round London, and the haycocks, I suppose, are to be made of straw-coloured satin'.[1]

The couple spent their honeymoon at The Oaks because their London home, Derby House in Grosvenor Square, which had been commissioned from Robert Adam, was not yet finished.[2] It was completed later that year and became their home whilst Parliament was in session; Lord Stanley had been elected a Whig Member of Parliament for Preston in 1774. The London house became an important venue for entertaining during the season, which began in late October with the opening of Parliament and ended in June with the summer recess. Time spent at Knowsley, at least a day's carriage drive away, would have been largely restricted to the summer recess and Christmas and Easter holidays.

Edward Smith Stanley was born on 21st April 1775, within a year of Lord Stanley's marriage. Less than a year later Lord Stanley succeeded his grandfather as 12th Earl of Derby. Edward Smith's birth was celebrated in style; a regatta was held on the River Thames on 23rd June 1775 (bad weather forcing its postponement on three previous occasions). The race, from London Bridge to Westminster Bridge and back, was accompanied by a flotilla of boats and barges decorated in Venetian style, which carried the large number of guests who afterwards wined, dined and danced until dawn at the fashionable Ranelagh pleasure gardens in Chelsea.

Edward's sister, Charlotte, was born on 17th October 1776. Thus, within two years of the marriage which it was claimed Lady Betty had entered into with some reluctance,[3] she found herself with two babies and a husband who, when he wasn't attending Parliament or socialising at one of his clubs (he was a member of White's and the Jockey Club, and later Brook's) was pursuing his passion for horse-racing or cock-fighting. Two years later, signs of strain in the marriage became public for the first time. The country was mobilising its defences against the threat of a French invasion, but the Countess declined to accompany her husband to the south coast to join his militia unit. In February 1778, France had entered the American War of Independence on the side of the Americans. In defence, the government set up camps at Coxheath in Kent and Warley in Essex.[4] Although the Whigs supported the colonists, the 12th Earl at first followed the

The fête champêtre for the engagement party of Lord Stanley (later 12th Earl of Derby) and his first wife, Elizabeth Hamilton, by Antonio Zucchi, 1774 (K).

The third drawing room of Derby House in Grosvenor Square in 1773 (K).

Edward Smith Stanley as a baby with his parents, by Angelica Kauffmann, c.1775 (K).

Opposite The 12th Earl of Derby, by Thomas Gainsborough, undated (K).

15

Edward Stanley (later 13th Earl of Derby) aged five, with his sister Charlotte aged three, by George Romney, 1780 (K).

Engraving dated 1780, after the original portrait by Joshua Reynolds (which was probably destroyed), of Elizabeth Hamilton, first wife of the 12th Earl of Derby (K).

Portrait of Elizabeth Farren, second wife of the 12th Earl of Derby, by John Hoppner, undated. She was an actress whose grandfather was a Liverpool publican (K).

lead of his uncle, General Burgoyne, and supported the policy of Lord North and the King's party, which was to continue fighting. However, following Burgoyne's defeat at the battle of Saratoga, both he and Derby withdrew their support from Lord North's Government and joined the Whig opposition, led by Charles James Fox.

Amidst all these happenings, Lady Derby must have felt neglected. Her head was turned by the attention she received from the Duke of Dorset, whom she met at a cricket match at The Oaks. Lady Mary Coke saw them together in June 1778 and wrote in her diary:

> 'Lady Derby, like the Duchess of Devonshire, has bad connections which lead her into many things that she had better not do, and for which I am sorry ...'[5]

In December 1778, Lady Derby left the family home and her children. Edward was not yet four and Charlotte two. It was rumoured that Lady Derby was pregnant by the Duke of Dorset. 'Now for the news', wrote Mrs Delany to a friend on 7th December 1778; 'I have heard that Lord Derby announced to his Lady on Friday last that their divorce was begun in the Commons which news threw her into fits.'[6] In February 1779 Lady Sarah Lennox wrote to her sister, Lady Susan O'Brien:

> 'It is no scandal to tell you it is imagined the Duke of Dorset will marry Lady Derby, who is now in the country keeping quiet and out of the way. There is a sort of party in town of who is to visit her and who is not ... I am told she has been and still is more thoroughly attached to the Duke of Dorset, and if so I should suppose she will be very happy if the lessening of her visiting list is the only misfortune; and what with giving up her children, sorrow for a fault, and dread of not preserving his affections, I think she is much to be pitied'.[7]

Alas, divorce and remarriage was not to be. The Earl did initially consider divorcing her - he must have been considerably humiliated by her behaviour - but he changed his mind for reasons that remain unclear; perhaps because of the birth of Elizabeth Henrietta on 29th April 1779. In any event, Lady Derby was consigned to social ostracism. Only marriage to the Duke of Dorset would have ensured her being accepted back into society but their relationship did not survive the strain of the scandal. The Duke of Dorset's reputation, on the other hand, did not suffer. The Countess had overstepped the mark by making her indiscretion public.

The Earl is said to have erased all traces of her from his life, and is even reputed to have burned Reynolds' portrait of her.

How did all this marital discord affect the young Edward? Although the children (Edward and Charlotte) remained with their father (in the 18th century the father was automatically given custody of his children) they were not denied access to their mother until the 12th Earl, in a deed of separation dated February 1780, formalised his future relationship with his wife. He agreed to pay the Countess £2000 per annum maintenance for her and her daughter, Lady Elizabeth Stanley (born soon after the Countess left her husband). In return her father, the 6th Duke of Hamilton, had to agree to indemnify the Earl against any debts the Countess might accrue and she was instructed to live abroad for two years. Access to the children was not mentioned.[8] Whether they saw their mother between 1780 and 1782 is uncertain but letters from Lady Derby to her mother suggest they did not. However, by early 1783, after the Countess returned to England, Lord Derby was sufficiently concerned about how 'they [the children] were sent for by her Ladyship more frequently than usual', to take legal advice on how this might be viewed in a court of law. The answer was:

'… as some improper and insidious use may possibly be made of the indulgence of the frequent company of the Children, I think it would be more prudent to withold it for the future, for though it certainly would not of itself amount to any proof of a reconciliation, it might operate with other circumstances, in case any such fact should afterward be pleaded'.[9]

Letters between the Countess and her mother reveal that she had indeed been urged by friends to seek a reconciliation, but she herself thought it unwise to do anything to unsettle the agreement with her husband.

'Certainly the best and only thing I can do is to stay the time he wish'd, and be as careful as I can of my conduct'.[10]

In July 1782 she wrote from Vienna:

'Since I have been abroad, I am more certain than ever of Ld. D. determination of our continuing separate … I have taken more than one occasion to write to Him, and one letter in particular which if he had not fully determined not to allow himself to feel or think about me he would at least have answered me … But he has been as silent to that as to all my other Letters'.[11]

Her instinct was correct. The 12th Earl's affections had been captured by another woman, the actress Elizabeth Farren, introduced to him by his uncle General Burgoyne. In 1793 Horace Walpole remarked:

'I went to town on Friday … In the evening we went together to Miss Farren's, and besides her duenna-mother [chaperon] found her at piquet [a card game for two players] with her unalterable Earl. - Apropos, I have observed of late years, that when **Earls** *take strong attachments, they are more steady than other men'.*[12]

Walpole's observation was prophetic but their long courtship continued for another four years; they were married three weeks after the Countess' death from tuberculosis in 1797.

Most details of the young Lord Stanley's childhood are sketchy. Whether a lack of contact with his parents caused him to be reliant on his own resources, or whether he was naturally studious and that time on his own fostered his interest in natural history, can only be surmised. Lord Stanley did not go to Eton until he was fourteen; before that he was presumably educated at home.

The earliest Eton school list on which Lord Stanley is recorded is dated July 1789. He would have followed a mainly classical curriculum, with algebra and Euclid and some geography. French could be learned out-of-hours and pupils could also take dancing, fencing and drawing lessons. The school day was divided into four periods; from eight to nine, from eleven to twelve, from three to four, and from five to six. The hours in-between were for recreation or private study; by the middle of the 18th century, with books being cheaper, a tutorial system was favoured. There were no lessons on Tuesdays, and only for half a day on Thursdays. On Saturday there was 'play at four'. School work was frequently interrupted by Saints' days. There were three school holidays a year - a month at Christmas, a fortnight at Easter and a month in August.[13] Lord Stanley would have spent at least two of those holidays at Knowsley.

As his father had done, Lord Stanley went up from Eton to Trinity College, Cambridge, arriving in 1792. He matriculated on 17th December 1793. He would

'A Peep at Chrysties, or Tally ho, and his Nimeney-pimmeney taking the Morning Lounge', coloured engraving by H. Humphrey after J. Gillray., 1796. Caricature of the 12th Earl of Derby and Elizabeth Farren, with snide reference to their respective heights (K).

A section of a page from the pre-printed 'The Naturalists' Journal', produced by Daines Barrington. Lord Stanley, aged about 19, has used the journal to make copious notes about some caterpillars he was keeping; what they looked like, what their pupae looked like and what they ate (LVRO).

17

A sensitive portrait of Edward Stanley, aged about 12, by Thomas Lawrence (K).

Edward Stanley, an Eton 'leaving portrait', by Thomas Lawrence, 1792 (Reproduced by permission of the Provost and Fellows of Eton College, Windsor).

Edward Stanley at Cambridge University, by an unknown artist, 1793 (The Master and Fellows, Trinity College, Cambridge).

Right Charlotte Hornby, first cousin and wife of Lord Stanley (later 13th Earl of Derby), shortly after their marriage in 1798, by Thomas Lawrence (K).

have studied mathematics and classics. As a nobleman he enjoyed different rights and privileges to the rest of the students, eating at high table and wearing a hat rather than an academic cap. In 1795 he graduated M.A. as of right, without examination, on the payment of 16 guineas in fees.[14] The University's reputation at that time was not favourable:

> *'Hunting, Racing and Profligacy of every Sort is, and has long been, the Staple Commodity of this once flourishing University.'*[15]

However, from what we know of Edward Smith Stanley's character later in life, it seems unlikely that he would have conducted himself in this manner. Despite the lack of written evidence about his time at Eton and Trinity, there are a number of portraits. There is a small watercolour (artist unknown) painted in 1792 ; a leaving portrait of him at Eton and a matriculation portrait in the Trinity College archives.

Shortly after leaving Trinity, Lord Stanley was elected MP for Preston, a seat he held until 1812. He was appointed the first Colonel of the 2nd Regiment of the Lancashire Militia, which was raised in 1797, and an army Colonel in 1798. Both positions reflected his social standing. On 30th June 1798, a year after he attained the age of majority, Edward married his cousin, Charlotte Margaret Hornby. She was the daughter of the Reverend Geoffrey Hornby, who was Rector of Winwick in Lancashire.

CHARLOTTE HORNBY. WIFE OF 13TH EARL OF DERBY

After their marriage, Edward and Charlotte lived for much of the time at Knowsley. Edward's sisters had both married: Charlotte in 1796 (to her cousin, Edmund Hornby of Dalton Hall, Westmorland) and Elizabeth Henrietta in 1795 (to Stephen Thomas Cole of Stoke Lyne, Oxfordshire). Father and son, both newly wed, shared the family home and their children grew up together. The two families between them produced eleven children between 1798 and 1808. The 12th Earl and Elizabeth Farren had four children, but only one, Mary Margaret, reached adulthood. Their first daughter was stillborn, Lucy Elizabeth (born in 1799) died aged ten and James Smith (born in 1800) died aged seventeen. Edward and Charlotte also experienced the pain of losing children. Emily Lucy (born in 1804) only lived for eight months. Their fifth child, Louisa Emily (born in 1805) died within a year of her marriage in 1825 to Lt. Col. Samuel Long.[16] However, five lived longer: Edward Geoffrey (born in 1799) succeeded as 14th Earl and was three times Prime Minister; Charlotte Elizabeth (born in 1801); Henry Thomas (born in 1803); Ellinor Mary (born in 1807) and Charles James Fox (born in 1808).

Large households full of young children were very usual at this time, as was infant mortality, and one can imagine the mix of happiness and sadness that must have prevailed at Knowsley during these years. The various marriages between the Derbys and the Hornby family extended the family still further; the 12th Earl's sister, Lucy, had married Geoffrey Hornby (of Scale Hall, Lancashire) in 1772 and they had thirteen children. The 12th Earl also assumed responsibility for the four illegitimate children of his uncle General Burgoyne, following his death in 1792.

'To complete the Knowsley menage there were endless numbers of visitors for overnight and even for days and weeks; and to these must be added a vast array of others - tutors, governesses, cooks, butlers, maids, valets, gardeners, grooms, gamekeepers, artisans and labourers.'[17]

The later censuses show the extent of the Knowsley household. In 1841 only seven family members were present in the Hall, but there were 49 household servants and nearly as many again on the estate. In 1851 there were sixteen members of family present and 67 servants in the Hall alone. Some insight into

Section of a page from a book of riddles and other games, with a riddle written by Lord Stanley (later 13th Earl of Derby) The answer to riddle 81 is 'Farewell' (K).

The 13th Earl of Derby in 1837 by William Derby. See enlargement on page 4 (K).

Left Miniature of Edward George Geoffrey Smith Stanley (later 14th Earl of Derby and Prime Minister), aged about two in c.1801, by Mrs Anne Mee (K).

Right Cartoon by Edward Lear entitled 'Adieu to Knowsly'. A large family with large parcels (probably the Stanleys) queue up for a rather small carriage manned by long-suffering horsemen. Lear himself says goodbye (is he already in the coach?); an owl, a Crowned Crane and an Orinoco Goose in full 'puff'[ed] breeding display add their farewells (Private Collection).

family life at Knowsley during the 12th Earl's lifetime can be gained through the writings of Thomas Creevey, a fellow Whig and MP for Thetford. In October 1812, he visited Knowsley:

> 'We sat down 22 to dinner, all of them Hornbys, except 4 Hortons, 2 Ramthornes, young Ashton and myself. My Lord was in excellent spirits, and for such company it went off all very well.'[18]

Creevey returned in December 1822:

> 'We all dined at Knowsley last night … I must say I never saw a man or woman live more happily with nine grown-up children. It is my Lord Derby [the 12th Earl] who is the great moving principle.'[19]

A book of charades and riddles composed at Knowsley between 1804 and 1815 gives an insight into which members of the family were present during those years, and how those adults sometimes entertained themselves after dinner. In 1804, 'Mrs Hornby' is recorded as the author of riddle no.35:

> 'My first is a thing often worn on the head
> My next was a substitute one year for Bread
> Of my whole lovely fair ones I pray you beware
> If you're govern'd by it I shall grieve and despair'.[20]

The most popular entertainer of the children was Edward Lear, whom Lord Stanley had met in 1832 and invited to Knowsley to paint the animals in the menagerie. Lear's first collection of limericks, *A Book of Nonsense* (published in 1846) was dedicated by him to 'the great-grandchildren, grand-nephews, and

grand-nieces of Edward, 13th Earl of Derby' but he notes, in parentheses, 'The greater part of which were originally made and composed for their parents'! Lear reputedly preferred making up rhymes to the onerous and exacting task of painting animals. It was during Lear's time at Knowsley that the 12th Earl died and his son succeeded to the title.

For the next seventeen years, a widower after 1817, the 13th Earl devoted himself to Knowsley, his natural history pursuits and the family.

Above The west front of Knowsley Hall in 1826, by J.P. Neale. Note the northern wing on the left (here partially obscured by trees), since demolished (LM).

[1]Toynbee 1903 vol.ix: letter 1541 to Sir Horace Mann, 8th June 1774. [2]Adam's Chandos House (1771); 20, St. James Square (1774) and 20, Portman Square survive, but the US Embassy now stands on the site of Derby House. [3]Letter from George Hornby to the 14th Earl, 7th February 1864 (K). [4]Foreman 1998: 63. [5]Ibid: 67. [6]Llanover 1862. Quoted in Cox 1974: 54. [7]Argyll 1910: 267. [8]LRO, DDK vol 1 25/5/1. [9]LRO, DDK vol 1 25/5/17 *Case for the opinion of Dr Bever* 22nd February 1783. [10]Lady Derby to her Mother, from Spa, 21st August 17[79?], in Argyll op.cit: 270. [11]Ibid: 282-3. [12]Toynbee op.cit vol.xv: 206; letter to Miss Mary Berry, 29th September 1793. [13]Hill, 1948: 58. [14]University of Cambridge statutes; 1785 edition: 514. [15]*Remarks on the Enormous Expence* [sic] *on the Education of Young Men in the University of Cambridge* (London, 1788). Quoted in Searby 1997: 62. [16]In a letter from Avignon, dated 9th December 1825, Samuel Long describes his wife's illness. Louisa died two days later. This and a letter, dated 3rd January 1826, are in (K). [17]Cox 1974: 99. [18]The Creevey Papers, edited by The Rt. Hon. Sir Herbert Maxwell (London, 1903) quoted in Cox 1974: 112. [19]Ibid: 114-5. [20]Answer: 'caprice' [cap/rice]. The mss. volume containing these riddles is at Knowsley.

THE 13TH EARL OF DERBY AS A LANDOWNER

ALAN G CROSBY

The importance of land to the upper classes in Victorian England cannot be overstated. It was fundamental to their place in the social structure, and the main source of the money which was essential for the maintenance of expensive lifestyles. Efficient estate management was crucial and most landowners employed a professional agent, who kept abreast of developments in surveying, land drainage and farm design, and knew about marketing, accountancy and leasing law. Landowners rarely participated actively in running their properties; their role was passive, approving strategies and checking accounts but not concerning themselves with routine and detail.[1] When we consider the Derby estates, we must recognise that the Earl himself played only a limited part, but it is clear that he took the keenest personal interest in what happened within the park walls of Knowsley.

At the end of his life the Earl of Derby's estates covered over 45,000 acres. He was by far the greatest landowner in the north-west and one of the richest in Britain. His estates were unusually concentrated geographically. Most were in Lancashire, where his dominance was unchallenged. There was a London house, and some properties in Ireland, North Wales, Westmorland, and Cheshire, but in south-west Lancashire it was possible to travel for many miles without leaving Derby lands. The estates were administered in 32 separate units, each supervised by a local steward responsible to the agent based at Knowsley. Separate accounts, lease books and rentals were kept for each unit, and thus a detailed supervision of the progress of each was maintained.

The properties included three large urban areas - Preston, Bury and Liverpool – from which an increasingly large income was generated by working-class housing and commercial properties. Urban land was less prestigious, but was important in estate management because returns per acre were generally higher. Like other Lancashire landowners, the Earls of Derby also owned important mineral resources, such as coal, stone and clay. In some of Derby's estates, notably at Bury and Pilkington, Bickerstaffe and Rainford, these made a substantial contribution to total income without any investment by the landowner, since the working of minerals was undertaken by lessees who bore the risk and guaranteed royalty payments.

The 'Black Boy' Sun and Moondial. The square bronze horizontal dial, which has 460mm sides, was made by Thomas Wynn of London in 1720. The gnomon bears the crest of the Stanley family and their motto 'Sans Changer' and the dial is embellished with Liver Birds and leaves, as well as the names of 20 foreign cities. The dial was originally supported by a statue of a boy, and the two have recently been re-united. They must have been very familiar to the 13th Earl (K).

Opposite Model, and key, to the Knowsley estate. This model reconstructs the layout and appearance of the estate at Knowsley as it was in 1851, the year of the 13th Earl's death. It reveals the major improvements to the area around the Hall, and the development of the areas for living animals, and the Home Farm and lodges, all key elements in the Earl's strategy for the enhancement of his property. The most notable feature, however, is the great expanse of parkland, lakes and woodland, much of which was planned by the 13th Earl. Model constructed by EDM Ltd (LM).

Key to the Knowsley Estate

1	Knowsley Hall	17	'The Nest'	32	Fountain Clump
2	Chapel	18	The Hermitage	33	Hercules Coppy
3	Conservatory	19	Home Farm	34	Statue of Hercules
4	wing now demolished	20	Kennels	35	Mole Earth Pit
5	Brewhouse Pond	21	Ormskirk Lodge and	36	Old Dairy
6	Mill Pits		northern part of wall	37	Old Quarries
7	Old Aviary	22	Kitchen Garden	38	Riding Hill
8	Walled Garden	23	Pigeon House	39	Turkey Lodge
9	Animal pens	24	Berry Hill	40	The Paddocks
10	New Stables	25	Dock Plantation	41	Huyton Lodge and
11	Apple Orchard Lodge	26	White Man's Dam		southern part of wall
12	New Aviary	27	Stand Wood	42	Oak Plantation
13	The Well	28	Dungeon Dam	43	Crow Pits
14	Boat House Lodge	29	The Octagon	44	Ash Plantation
15	Aviary Cottages	30	Octagon Pond	45	Jack's Brow
16	Laundry	31	New Dam (Home Pond)		

Old photograph of the 'Mushroom House' and the New Stables. The Mushroom House, so-called because of its shape, was the central part of the New Stables at Knowsley, built by the 13th Earl in 1846 to improve accommodation for his horses, grooms and their supplies (Huyton Library, Knowsley).

Only one wing survives today (NMGM, courtesy Knowsley).

Not long after the 13th Earl's death it was reported that 'the maintenance of his menagerie and aviary, which necessitated the occupation of upwards of one hundred acres of land within Knowsley Park … cost him upward of £15,000 a year'.[2] This sum (perhaps £650,000 today) emphasises that natural history was a costly business. To put this figure in perspective, in 1835 expenditure on plantations and woodlands at Knowsley amounted to £2,500, on the gardens £3,086, and on the home farm and park £9,700. Domestic wages amounted to about £2,000 and contributions to charitable causes about £650. Annuities to the family totalled approximately £14,000 in 1835, the major recipient being Lord Stanley (later the 14th Earl) with £5,000 per annum. However, the largest outgoing of all was the interest payments on borrowings, for the estate was heavily encumbered by a massive mortgage and by borrowings to cover deficits on the current account.[3]

How much money did the estates generate? Records for 1835 suggest that annual income then was about £75,000 (about £3.1 million today), including rents, mineral royalties, and sales of timber and cattle. Approximately 34% came from urban rents and 61% from agricultural rents. By far the most valuable property was Bury which, with neighbouring Pilkington, generated £21,930, 30% of the total revenue of the Derby estates. The next most lucrative area was Liverpool, Bootle and Kirkdale, collectively accounting for another £9,840. Thus, the agricultural acres provided status, and were the essence of the landed estate, but it was the tightly-packed housing along the Mersey, and the shops and collieries of Bury, which made the most money.

Most English landed estates were heavily in debt, with large mortgages and other forms of borrowed capital. Creditors were willing to lend because of the prestige of their clients, but also because there was a reliable security - the estate itself. Foreclosure was unlikely, but there were unwritten obligations, the most important being that repayments and interest payments should be reliable. Estate stewards sought to honour these requirements, but employers often failed to understand financial realities. Brought up to expect whatever they desired, they spent as though money came from an inexhaustible well. Most landowners found financial restraint unpalatable and insulting.

Stewards tried to maximise revenue from whatever source, combining careful accounting procedures with coercion and persuasion. They exploited the land market, enforced estate reorganisation and updating of leasing arrangements, encouraged agricultural improvement, developed mineral resources, and diversified into urban property. The stewards of the 13th Earl used all these devices with conspicuous success, boosting short-term income and long-term prospects. The estate bought contiguous properties and merged them with its holdings, undertaking agricultural improvements such as drainage works and reorganising individual farms. At Bickerstaffe and Rainford, for example, land was bought in the 1840s to consolidate the Derby estates and facilitate large-scale drainage of the mossland. This turned previously undervalued property into a lucrative asset. Comparable consolidation at Huyton and Roby became more intensive in the 1840s when, encouraged by rising land values after the opening of the railway, the estate bought most of the non-Derby property in the township.

Individual tenants were encouraged to invest in improvements. Rents for improved farmland were higher, but increased yields and efficiency savings meant that the growth in the tenant's income could be even greater. The 300-acre farm at Halewood, tenanted from 1838 by Robert Neilson, was described in 1849 as 'one of the most complete and perfect establishments in the country'. Neilson introduced steam power for a wide range of tasks, drained his entire farm so that it was suitable for intensive arable use, and constructed light railways for transporting manure and produce around the property. Other tenanted properties given special attention included Mossborough near Knowsley, which was reorganised into an efficient unit of almost 500 acres, and Fairhurst near Parbold, where the new farm buildings, paved yards and machine-threshing were exemplary.[4] The effect of changes such as these is seen in rent incomes. At Bickerstaffe the rental value increased by 139% between 1835 and 1849 and at Burscough by 116%, at a time when inflation was negligible.

In areas such as Bootle and Kirkdale it was recognised that urban growth would soon take place and that as the Liverpool docks extended downriver, Lord Derby's ownership of the foreshore would be of particular value. At Bury, Preston and Liverpool, policies of buying land for urban development meant that rent income increased steadily during the 13th Earl's time. Mining, too, offered potential, but the Earl was opposed to any possibility of collieries within the park at Knowsley. In 1838, when there was a suggestion that stone should be worked in the south-east corner for estate building schemes he told the steward that 'you know my horror of opening Quarries or sinking shafts' and refused permission.[5] But coal was exploited at Bickerstaffe, Rainford and Pilkington, and Knowsley Hall was supplied from the Earl's own colliery at Eccleston, close to the park but invisible from the house. Liverpool's water supply was provided by the Bootle Waterworks Company which tapped springs on the Earl's land. In 1842 he received £696 in royalties from the sale of water by the company, although its takeover by the town council in 1848 ended this arrangement.[6]

The determined work of the estate stewards thus maintained high-income growth throughout the Earl's time: from 1835 to 1849 the increase was 44% in real terms. The proportion derived from rural properties fell steadily, from 61% in 1835 to 56% in 1849, for although the reorganisation of agricultural estates produced genuine growth, income from urban and industrial properties grew even faster. Agricultural improvement also cost more, so the net return was substantially less, whereas urban development cost virtually nothing and was almost entirely profit.

The 13th Earl had little personal attachment to most of his estates, which lay in what was generally perceived as the uninteresting or ugly Lancashire plain and its industrial towns. He rarely visited these estates, and had little incentive to do so – but for Knowsley he felt the deepest love. Today the park is an oasis in an urban landscape, edged by housing and motorways. To the 13th Earl it was a haven where he could escape from a world where public duties were a nuisance. There he had his aviary, menagerie, glasshouses and gardens, and there he could be a scientist and natural historian. He was familiar with every inch of the park. His detailed knowledge is revealed in a letter of April 1835, concerning improvements to the shore of the White Man's Dam:

'It would be well if fresh cut willow boughs were driven into the soil by the Edge. They would probably soon strike out roots & assist in holding the Banks together, & if not ultimately allowed to grow could at any time be cut down to any height. In the sheltered Bays of the Island I wish Somerville to plant some of the Water Lilies; the Sweet Scented Reed; Yellow flag Iris; Bulrushes, & other Water Plants'.[7]

As soon as Edward Stanley succeeded to the title he began major alterations to the park.[8] The accounts for January 1835 include payments to 'Mr Gilpin, for Time & Travelling expences marking out the intended alteration in the Park &c at

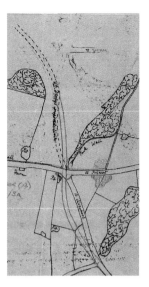

Plan showing proposed alterations to roads on the Knowsley estate sent from Robert Statter (steward 1834-1839) to William Brown (architect) in 1837. These were part of ambitious plans for the 13th Earl's improvements at Knowsley. He completely remodelled the road network within the park, using long sweeping curves, gentle bends and easy gradients (Liverpool Record Office, Liverpool City Libraries).

25

Huyton Lodge. This building was one of several designed by William Burn, the architect employed by the 13th Earl for many of the more important building projects within the estate during the period 1835-1851. The lodges controlled all access to the park (Clemency Fisher, courtesy Knowsley).

Right South front of Knowsley Hall. Painted by J. Harwood and engraved by J.B. Allen, in about 1835. Lord Derby was an enthusiastic breeder of greyhounds, and sent some to Syria in the hope of receiving exotic living animals in return (LM).

Knowsley'.[9] This design work formed the basis for improvements over the next fifteen years and was set out in a lengthy memorandum, with sketches, sent by William Gilpin to the Earl.[10] William Burn was commissioned to design a new boathouse[11] and Derby planned a perimeter wall for the park and replacement of the existing lodges, an ambitious scheme implemented in 1838-1844 and one in which he took the closest interest:

'I certainly never had any idea that such a plan for the Privies could be in contemplation … I remember speaking … about the drain that would be necessary to carry off the Soil from the Cesspool, & settled that it sh'd be taken into the Brook below the Back Stable Gate, so as to allow the people at the Lodge to use the Water for such purposes as might be wanted (I do not mean for drinking, of course) without danger of coming in contact with any of the impurities of such a place'.[12]

Lord Derby gave much attention to providing a water supply to the aviary and menagerie. Writing from London, he had a clear picture of the exact place for wells:

'… one place would be Eastward of Shaw's Lodge above the Low Ground which I have been talking of damming up above the old Hen house at the Dungeon Dam. There is a spot always wet on the slope of the Hill from Shawe's, not far from the new Plantation & between that & the Old Bath'.

Another project was a network of roads, on which gangs of Irish labourers were employed, to link the hall with the lodges and outer areas of the estate. The most remarkable was the four-mile private coach road to Barrow Nook, by which the Earl could travel to Bickerstaffe almost without setting carriage wheel upon public highway.

These schemes caused difficulties for his faithful stewards, Robert Statter (1834-1839), Richard Earle (1839-1848) and George Hall (1848-1851). Each struggled with the demands of managing a great estate and tried to balance the books. They urged financial restraint upon their master, but ultimately the decision-making power rested with the Earl. Richard Earle soon began to question the wisdom of

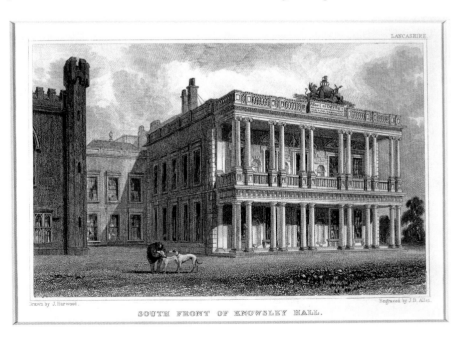

LANCASHIRE.

Drawn by J. Harwood.   Engraved by J.B. Allen.

SOUTH FRONT OF KNOWSLEY HALL.

certain proposals - particularly the grand schemes for the aviary and associated buildings. In February 1840 he commented that plans then being drawn up would cost £1,010 (over £50,000 today) and suggested that 'some middle course could be hit upon'.[13] The Earl, however, was not deflected from his purpose and during the next four years the cost of building work grew inexorably. Lodges, walls, replacement of insanitary dwellings in Knowsley village with model cottages, roads … all these Richard Earle could countenance, though with growing disquiet, but he regarded the natural history projects as unwarranted and unaffordable.

A crisis loomed in January 1845, when estimates of £6,500 (perhaps £350,000 today) were submitted for the construction of a magnificent new conservatory. Earle issued a warning to his employer:

> '[I] regret, that so very large an expenditure on such an object could not at all events for the present be avoided … The General Expences of effecting improvements on the Estate are larger than your Lordship is probably aware of: in the building department I certainly wanted more breathing time, & on that account, postponed suggesting to you the expediency of applying to Mr. Burns for a design & plans of New Stables &c - to do this & to spend any such sum as £6000 on a Conservatory will not be prudent, & therefore, if the Conservatory is to go on, the Stables must give way … It is true the Green-house Plants are ill-housed: some temporary plan for them might be hit upon. Your Horses are not over-well housed - Your Carriages are worse, while the dilapidated appearance of the intended Site of the New Stables is so unseemly as to counteract the effect of any improvements elsewhere'.[14]

Eventually Earle, realising that Lord Derby was determined to go ahead, urged that the most modest plan should be adopted as this would be 'ample … & so far as my knowledge extends surpassing most private Conservatories in the Country'. He reinforced his argument with some cogent facts about the state of the Earl's finances:

> 'I will venture to entreat your Lordship to have regard to the cost … For many years the annual outgoings on your fine Estate have exceeded the receipts by very large amounts; and had it not been for the improving nature of some parts of the property this annual excess of expenditure would have produced even [more] embarrassing results; as it is, large sums have been borrowed & the payment of interest on them lessens the net annual income to a very serious extent … my wish is to produce a surplus income, not by throwing obstacles in the way of carrying out projects in which, though of an expensive character, you feel a peculiar interest, but by reducing expenditure on every side. This, however, I cannot do, if money is to be poured forth on every side & a large expenditure to be crowded into a small period of time'.[15]

All was to no avail. In March 1845, when the 'orchidaceous house' was under way, Earle suggested that there must be severe reductions in expenditure elsewhere, but again the 13th Earl overruled his steward. He was in no sense unusual among his contemporaries and equals. Their simple belief was that the estate would always provide and that their will would always prevail.

Towards the end of his life Derby determined to build a new museum at Knowsley to house his splendid collections. In autumn 1848 preliminary plans were drawn up but the steward, George Hall, was aghast at the possible cost and, in words less suppliant than those of his predecessor, wrote:

> '… from the magnitude of the building and the costliness of the internal arrangements I think your Lordship cannot be aware of the Expense of such a work. From an

'Garden Memoranda'. This is an article, which gives very useful details of Knowsley Hall and the park, from the *Gardeners' Chronicle* of 11th August 1841. The author was particularly impressed by White Man's Dam and the Boathouse, the walled kitchen garden and the 13th Earl's orchids, but the highlights were 'the aviary and museum'.

Carriage road to Bickerstaffe. The estates at Bickerstaffe, north of Knowsley, had been part of the ancestral property of the 11th Earl of Derby. In the time of the 13th Earl, these estates were still of major importance, and he built a private road from Knowsley to Bickerstaffe, avoiding public roads completely. It allowed the Stanley family to travel between the two houses in privacy and safety (Clemency Fisher, courtesy Knowsley).

Yearly rental accounts for the town of Liverpool 1849. The Derby estates were run by stewards, who were the main channel of communication between the 13th Earl and his tenants. The estate papers include details of rent income, rent arrears and notes on tenancy arrangements. This example shows one page of the 1849 booklet for the town of Liverpool, one of the most lucrative of the Stanley properties (Lancashire Record Office, Preston).

estimate formed from the present unfinished state of the outline of the proposed building, it would appear that it cannot cost less than £11,000 and my own opinion is that it will much exceed that amount'.

Hall explained the reality of the finances:

'... there is an actual debt upon the Estate, for which security has been given, amounting to £305,000, and in addition to this there is a balance due to the Bank on the running account of £40,000 for which no Security has been given, and which must be paid off next year. It would appear also from the accounts that in 1847, the expenditure for the year exceeded the actual income by £39,000. Under these circumstances I have felt it my duty, however unwillingly, to bring this subject under your notice, and to submit for your Lordships serious consideration, whether or not it would be desirable to postpone ... the execution of an undertaking on so large a scale'.[16]

In modern values, the secure debt represented about £12.9 million; the unsecured deficit on the current account (to be paid by the end of 1849) amounted to £1.7 million; and the expenditure in 1847 had exceeded income by £1.5 million. Expenditure was out of control and there was a massive mortgage. The sterling work of the stewards had increased income by almost 50% since 1834, but efforts to control expenditure were unsuccessful. The grand projects ate up the income and contributed to huge borrowings.

The museum project was not even started when the 13th Earl died in 1851. Had the scheme been initiated a few years earlier the collection might have been permanently housed at Knowsley, Liverpool would never have benefited from the bequest, and the Derby finances would have been even more precarious. In many ways the 13th Earl was very typical of his peers, yet in his passion for natural history he was of course completely exceptional. His seventeen years' incumbency saw far-reaching changes at Knowsley. The 15th Earl wrote that his grandfather:

'... found this place a wilderness − it had been neglected for upwards of fifty years ... Justice has never been done in the family to [the 13th Earl] whose plans were excellent, though he was too hasty in their execution, and thus left everything unfinished ... all that we do now is to work upon, and complete his designs'.[17]

The thirty-five divisions of the Derby estates in the time of the 13th Earl

Diagrammatic map of the Derby estates in the time of the 13th Earl. The estates were arranged in 32 separate divisions, each with its own local steward, answerable to the head steward at Knowsley. This map shows the location of these divisions and demonstrates how significant the family were as landowners in Lancashire (NMGM).

Knowsley was the 13th Earl's private heaven. In March 1835 he travelled to London and three days later wrote to Robert Statter, telling him of the journey and the weather: 'it [is] more like June, or even July, than April, but I begin already to wish myself back again'.[18]

[1]The best general introduction to the aristocratic landowners and their estates in the early nineteenth century is Beckett, 1986. [2]Pollard 1871: 115. [3]These figures are derived from unpublished analysis of the estate ledgers and rentals: LRO DDK, nos. 1807-1826. [4]Garnett 1849: 12-14. [5]LRO DDK 1681, Stewards' letters 1835-1838; 8th May 1837; LRO DDK 197/6. [6]LRO DDK 1817/121 (loose letter from Secretary of Company, giving royalty calculations, 25th November 1842); LRO DDK 491/3. [7]LRO DDK 1681 (Stewards' letters 1835-1838), letter 10th April 1835. [8]A comprehensive historical account of the development of Knowsley park is given in Sholl (unpublished). [9]LRO DDK/1847 Journal 1832-1838. [10]LVRO 1/66/1. [11]Burn's proposals for improvements, including lodges and other buildings, are detailed in a letter to the Earl, 3rd July 1837 (LVRO 1/26/3; 1/26/8 for designs of lodges 1846. [12]Estate letters, 10th October 1843 (K). [13]Estate letters, 6th February 1840 (K). [14]Estate letters, 24th January 1845 (K). [15]Estate letters, 27th February 1845 (K). [16]Estate letters, 20th November 1848 (K). [17]Vincent (ed.) 1978: 234. [18]LRO DDK 1681 (Stewards' letters 1835-1838), letter 2nd April 1835.

The 13th Earl of Derby's Equestrian Interests

AMANDA ASKARI

AMANDA ASKARI

The Earl of Derby's Staghounds, engraving by R. Woodman (1823) after James Barenger. From left to right are depicted Lord Stanley (later 13th Earl of Derby); his son (the Hon. Edward Stanley); Jonathon Griffin, Huntsman (on Spanker); Jem Bullen, first Whipper-in (on Noodle) (K).

THE EARL OF DERBY'S STAG HOUNDS.

Whilst the Derby name is perhaps most famously associated with horse-racing, it would appear that Edward Smith Stanley did not inherit his father's great passion for the turf. The 12th Earl had given his name to the Derby (which was established in 1780), was an active member of the Jockey Club and excelled in providing frequent entertainment for fellow members at his sporting lodge 'The Oaks' in Epsom.[1]

Despite having grown up surrounded by the excitement of horse-racing society, the 13th Earl clearly preferred to spend his time and money elsewhere.[2] It is significant that nineteenth century diarist and racing enthusiast Charles Greville, who gives many interesting insights into the lives of his contemporaries caught up in the politics of the turf, makes no mention of the 13th Earl at any race meetings, remarking simply that 'he spent a million in kangaroos'. By contrast, Greville describes Lord Derby's eldest son, later the 14th Earl, as 'a lively rattling sportsman, apparently devoted to racing and rabbit-shooting' and it was as his guest that Greville stayed at Knowsley in 1837, whilst attending the Liverpool Races.[3]

The 13th Earl seems to have been quite happy to let his son pursue a genuine interest in horse-racing, leaving him free to concentrate his attentions on the welfare of more exotic species. It was therefore Edward Geoffrey Stanley who took up the subscription to the Racing Calendar when his grandfather died in 1834 and it was he who was responsible for the success of horses such as Canezou, who won the 1000 Guineas in 1848 and the Goodwood Cup in both 1849 and 1850.

What lack of interest the 13th Earl showed in horse-racing[4] was certainly

compensated by his enthusiastic participation in other equestrian sports such as stag-hunting. Whilst his father had been caricatured as possessing a somewhat rounded physique,[5] Edward Smith Stanley was a man of athletic stature[6] and it is not difficult to imagine him galloping across the Banstead downs in pursuit of one of the stags which had been purpose bred and brought down from Knowsley.[7] His hunting diary of 1824[8] often records the name of the horses he rode, such as 'Graham' and 'Blacker' and on Tuesday 9th March he noted that the hunt followed a deer called Moses. Success was varied and on one occasion he noted that the hunt 'did not run well, but sulkily took him [the deer] in about 50 minutes'. An engraving by R. Woodman after James Barenger, 'The Earl of Derby's Stag Hounds' (1823), depicts Edward Smith Stanley (far left) and his eldest son (second from left) at the start of a hunt on Banstead Downs.[9] On the engraving at Knowsley Hall the names of some of the hounds depicted (Jason, Graceful, Forager, Nelson) have been added in pencil by Lord Stanley himself.

Engraving, by G.F. Prosser (1828), of 'The Oaks', the Stanley's country home at Banstead, Surrey (Sutton Books). The famous horse-race is named after this house (London Borough of Sutton Local Studies Library).

[1]Cunningham 1993. [2]The anonymous author of an article, dated 1863 and bound into a Knowsley Hall copy of Moore's 1851 sales catalogue of the animals at Knowsley, noted that many might perceive the Knowsley aviary as 'the hobby of a man who spent an enormous rent-roll in this manner rather than on the turf or in electioneering'. [3]Greville famously remarked that Knowsley was 'immense, with no good room in it but the dining room'. Strachey & Fulford 1938, vol.3: 385. [4]It should not be overlooked that the 13th Earl was part of a syndicate which established the 'Grand National' at Aintree in 1839 (see page 36). [5]For example James Gillray's 'A Peep at Chrysties', see page 17. [6]List at Knowsley Hall headed 'The Following weights were copied from the register kept by Berry Brothers at the Coffee Mill, 3 St. James' St. SW' Lord Stanley is recorded as measuring '6 feet 1 inch' Feb. 7 1811, and weighing 12st.1^3/$_4$. [7]See the account of Old Billy on page 91. [8]LVRO, document in misc. boxes, between folders 6 & 7. [9]See Egerton 1978: 232-234.

THE 13TH EARL OF DERBY AS A SOCIAL AND CULTURAL FIGURE

ARLINE WILSON

A less flamboyant and colourful character than his father, the 13th Earl of Derby has nonetheless been described as one of 'nature's noblemen', who enjoyed 'universal esteem' and whose chief characteristics 'were hospitality and benevolence'.[1] Despite his exalted position, he was first and foremost a family man, and his letters reveal deep affection and concern for the well being of his family.

As Lord Stanley he fulfilled his public duties diligently and proved himself a conscientious MP. Increasingly, however, Knowsley was to become the beloved centre of his life, and once he had succeeded to the Earldom, he was more than willing to leave the traditional Stanley role in party politics to his more politically minded son, Edward Geoffrey.

On his succession, the 13th Earl was appointed Lord Lieutenant of the county of Lancaster, a post he held until his death in 1851. He also held the offices of vice-admiral of the coast of Lancashire, Custos Rotulorum (Keeper of the Rolls) of the County of Lancaster and he was a colonel of the Lancashire militia. He was patron of many church livings (for instance that of Macclesfield Forest), a Knight of the Garter and a member of the Privy Council, and as chief magistrate of the County he was reputed to have carried out his duties efficiently. Although he appears to have eschewed the limelight on a personal level, he seems to have harboured ambitions to add to the lustre of the family name. An entry in the diary of Queen Victoria suggests that he was 'desirous of being made a Duke' at the time of her coronation. Interestingly his son, the future 14th Earl, is said to have declined a dukedom 'not wishing to exchange his fifteenth century coronet for brand new strawberry leaves'.[2]

At social and public functions, although lacking the charisma of his father and the oratorical skills of his son, the 13th Earl's speeches have been described as:

> '… marked by great good sense and propriety, if not by originality or depth of thought. We recollect, some twenty years ago, of his electrifying the company of a public dinner at Manchester, by an unexpected sally which fairly set the table in a roar'.[3]

Regionally, prior to the nineteenth century, it was Preston rather than Liverpool which served as something of a local capital for the Stanley family. They had enjoyed a long relationship with the town, wielding considerable influence over its social and political life. Patten House (a fine building much admired by Daniel Defoe) appears to have been a popular family home – the natural centre of the Stanley interest in Preston. The long-standing, if occasional, feuds between successive Earls and the corporation of Preston do not appear to have extended to the general populace. Patronage allowed the Stanleys to exert considerable influence over the town's affairs. This could take the form of gifts to local charities, sponsorship of a sport or their presence at major events. Although at least some members of the corporation may have resented what they considered to be Stanley interference in their affairs, the 'Derby interest' obviously brought them direct and considerable financial benefits. The Stanleys's patronage of social events is perhaps best exemplified by the Preston Guilds, but included more modest affairs such as Lord Stanley's coming-of-age celebration in April 1796, or sporting events. Cock

Opposite St Mary's Church, Knowsley, endowed by the 13th Earl of Derby and where all Earls of Derby since the 13th have been buried (K).

Holy Trinity Church,
Bickerstaffe, endowed by
the 13th Earl of Derby
(Clemency Fisher).

fighting was a fashionable sport well into the 19th century and was organised in conjunction with the Preston horse races.[4]

However, the defeat of Edward Geoffrey Stanley by the radical Henry 'Orator' Hunt in the Preston election of 1830, shocked the Stanleys. This rejection by the Preston electorate was to estrange the Stanley family from Preston and Patten House was visited less and less frequently. After 1833, the horse races on Fulwood Moor (on the outskirts of the town), of which the Stanleys had been prominent patrons, were abandoned and the cockpit there also closed down in the 1830s. Gradually, the family 'withdrew from everything of a popular or prominent nature in or about the town, which, heretofore, they had willingly patronised'. The town was never forgiven and one of the first things that the 13th Earl did on his succession to the title was to sell Patten House.[5]

The relationship between the town of Liverpool and the Stanley family had a somewhat more contentious history than had been the case with Preston. Tensions between the House of Derby and the townsmen had made the family's position in Liverpool increasingly difficult after the Restoration in 1660. The increasingly prosperous merchants sought to throw off all landlord control, in particular resenting the state of affairs which saw Stanley after Stanley occupying the Mayoralty and dominating the parliamentary representation of the Borough. There was no mistaking the anti-aristocratic mood of many of the leading burgesses. It was they who wanted to become established as the aristocracy of the town.[6] Thus although a later commentator claimed: 'At no time have these families cordially fraternised, as if they shared our local corporate sympathies',[7] this owed more to the merchants' wish to wrest control than to antipathy on the part of the Derby family.

However, as the good relationship between the Derby family and the people of Preston waned, Knowsley Hall became an increasingly important venue for social events and gatherings under the auspices of the 12th Earl and his second wife, Elizabeth Farren. These functions were attended by many of the foremost political figures of the day (such as Charles James Fox and Henry Brougham) and it was here

that that the future 13th Earl mingled with the leading men of the period. The balls held at Knowsley were widely reported at national level. One notable occasion was attended by:

> '… about 200 guests consisting of the nobility of Lancashire and Cheshire in the vicinity of his noble mansion … one of the most magnificent entertainments that has been given in this neighbourhood for many years'.[8]

In the summer months local residents were offered the opportunity to glimpse life at Knowsley and tour the estate. Open days were held – generally on Thursdays – for a period of four weeks in late July and August.

Members of the family regularly attended social functions in Liverpool, notably during the triennial music festivals, which were important occasions in the social and cultural life of the town. Lord Stanley is listed as a steward for the 1830 festival, and members of the family attended the fancy dress balls at the end of the festival week. Considerable sums were raised for local charities at these events.

On occasion, members of the family played an active part in raising money for local Liverpool charities. One example in 1822 was 'Lady Derby's Benevolent Society or Annual Sale of Ornamental and Fancy Works':

> 'On this occasion, her Ladyship, with many other ladies of respectability, become shopkeepers for the day, and sell articles [made by themselves] to purchasers. The proceeds were divided amongst different charities, at the discretion of the committee of ladies'.[9]

After succeeding to the title, the 13th Earl continued this tradition of philanthropy and devoted a considerable amount of his income to charities. He built and endowed churches, erected parsonage houses, and contributed liberally to the various organisations attached to Church of England places of worship. It was reported that 'he did not make any parade of his gifts, but made them with a remarkable degree of modesty, if not of humility'. He erected Knowsley, Bickerstaffe, Westhead (in Lathom) and Newborough Parish Churches and he donated the land for St Paul's Church, Bury. Knowsley Parish Church, built

between 1841 and 1844, was dedicated to St Mary the Virgin and consecrated by
John Birch, Bishop of Chester on 6th June 1844. It was reputed to have cost its
patron £20,000. The total amount of the 13th Earl's contributions in connection
with churches and schools is estimated at £100,000.[10]

Although it was the estate at Knowsley, rather than the social scene, that
increasingly became the pivotal interest of the 13th Earl, he retained some of the
traditional family love of the turf. Towards the end of 1838, the 13th Earl joined a
syndicate consisting of such dignitaries as the Earls of Sefton, Eglinton and Wilton,
Lord George Bentinck, Lord Stanley and Lord Grosvenor and plans were
formulated for a Grand Liverpool Steeplechase to be run at Aintree in 1839. The
first 'Grand National' was held on 29th February 1839 and it was an immediate
success, with thousands of visitors flocking to the area. Parties were held at
Knowsley and Croxteth, hotels for miles around were fully booked and the town
was said to be overflowing with people. The size of the attendance was claimed to
be about 30,000.[11]

The 13th Earl also played a prominent role in several national learned societies.
In addition to these, his name appears on the membership roll of a number of
provincial societies. He became a corresponding member of the Liverpool Literary
and Philosophical Society in 1835 (the same year as Lord Brougham and the Earl
of Ellesmere), although there is no evidence of him playing an active role. His name
also appears as a member of the Historic Society of Lancashire and Cheshire
(founded in 1848). Again his involvement appears to have been more titular than
active. However, he did adopt a more proactive role on the occasion of the visit of
the British Association for the Advancement of Science to Liverpool in 1837. This
was an era in which interest in science was growing amongst the emerging middle
classes, and for the wealthy citizen science was to become not only a private
pleasure but also a civic duty. Science was a good leveller - it was non-sectarian and
on occasion (exemplified by the Liverpool meeting) could join aristocracy, gentry
and middle classes in a common cause.

Ormskirk Parish Church; the 13th Earl of Derby was buried here on 2nd July 1851, in the Derby Chapel within the main church (Clemency Fisher).

The British Association had been founded in 1831 with the aim of 'combining the Philosophical Societies, dispersed through the provinces of the empire, in a general co-operative union'. The provincial associations were quick to realise the potential of the week-long meetings as occasions for displaying local resources and local organisations to a nation-wide audience. When Liverpool was awarded the 1837 meeting, the town set out to mount an impressive display of its amenities. The festivities embraced visits to institutions, public and commercial buildings, churches, sculpture, gardens, shipyards, and manufacturing works.

Lord Derby's interest in the proposed visit led him to write personally to the secretary, offering any help he could give. Despite a somewhat ungracious response from the secretary,[12] the final itinerary included a visit to Knowsley Hall to view the 13th Earl's collection of animals. The Liverpool meeting was a great success – attendance was close to two thousand – and civic pride did much to ameliorate old divisions amongst the elite of the town.[13]

The latter years of the 13th Earl's life saw him devote himself almost entirely to his estate and tenants at Knowsley, and to his collections. He died at Knowsley Hall on 30th June 1851 and was buried in the family vault at Ormskirk Parish Church – the last Earl to be buried there, subsequent holders of the title being buried at St. Mary's Church, Knowsley. His coffin was made from a favourite oak tree on the Knowsley estate, and the funeral procession was reputed to have been more than a mile in length. It was fortunate for Liverpool that the son did not share his father's passion for natural history - the Derby collection becoming the core of the town's new museum and a lasting memorial to the 13th Earl.

Sterling silver trowel engraved with the Stanley family coat of arms and motto, 'Presented to the RT. HONORABLE LORD STANLEY July 17 1822 By the committee of the FEMALE PENITENTIARY Liverpool … For his kind assistance in laying the FOUNDATION STONE of that INSTITUTION'. The penitentiary, which it was hoped would restore women 'to a respectable station in society', was erected in the Hope Street area of Liverpool (K).

37

[1]Draper 1864: 282. [2]Cockayne 1916: 219. [3]Ross 1848: 42. [4]Hunt 1992: 135-137. [5]Hewitson 1883: 135-136. [6]Mullet 1972: 31. [7]Orchard 1893: 9. [8]*Gentleman's Magazine* for 16 October 1818. [9]Simey 1992: 28. [10]Aspden 1873: 34. [11]Farrer & Brownbill (eds.) 1907: 480. [12]'Lord Derby has written to offer all the help he can give, but this is not thought likely to amount to more than inspection of the aviary'. Morrell & Thackray (eds.) 1984: 248. [13]Wilson (unpublished): 146-150.

Londonderry

Stanhope

Newcastle

Aberdeen
+
Wharncliffe

Ellenborough

THE 13TH EARL OF DERBY AS A POLITICIAN

ALAN G CROSBY

Was the 13th Earl of Derby a professional politician? The answer is surely 'no', for although he was a member of the House of Commons for 36 years, and as Baron Stanley of Bickerstaffe and later as Earl of Derby occupied his place in the Lords for the remaining 19 years of his life, his interests lay elsewhere. Yet although the rough and tumble of parliamentary politics was uncongenial to him, his parliamentary career had its remarkable features, for during his election as MP for Preston in 1796 he played a central part in a celebrated political drama. Preston had a prominent place in the interests of the Derby family; they held extensive property there, and after 1768 they exercised patronage in borough politics. In Preston the right to vote was, from 1768, held by all adult males living in the town, the most extensive parliamentary franchise of any English constituency.[1] The Derby interest spent lavishly and unashamedly to elicit the votes of ordinary townsmen and from 1768 to 1796 Preston returned Whig MPs personally selected by the Earls of Derby. However, during the 1790s the town's rapid industrialisation made that control less certain. Population growth brought many new voters, who depended for their livelihood not on landed interests and aristocratic patronage but on cotton manufacturers, and any worker who voted against his employer's interests ran the risk of retribution.

In the dramatic election of 1796 the 21-year old Lord Stanley fought against John Horrocks, a cotton owner who, born in relatively modest circumstances near Bolton in 1768, had become the town's leading employer. Horrocks was a dyed-in-the-wool Tory, ambitious and brimming with the self-confidence of wealth, and decided to stand against Stanley in the general election. As the employer of so many working men among the voters, he was optimistic of success.[2] Both sides threw everything into the contest. The poll was held in public and spread over eleven days. For the first eight days Horrocks was in the lead, apparently heading for a dramatic victory. The Derby interest redoubled its efforts, persuading voters to its side and spending heavily on inducements. Lord Stanley wrote a hurried note to his father, in terms which his horse-racing parent would have readily appreciated: 'We are like well-bred racers that run upon bottom and keep their wind to make a general push at the end'. On the eleventh day Horrocks acknowledged defeat but the figures reveal how close-run a contest it was: Lord Stanley, 772 votes; Sir Henry Hoghton (the other Whig candidate), 756; John Horrocks, 742. Victory was achieved, but at prodigious cost. The Whigs spent £11,550 on electioneering, of which the 12th Earl and his son themselves provided £7,700. In present-day values these figures represent perhaps £1 million and £0.5 million.

Given his general reticence in parliamentary politics, we might wonder why Lord Stanley was standing in the first place. The answer lies in his birth - hereditary obligation gave him little choice in the matter. Among the heirs to the aristocracy there was a natural progression from Eton and Oxbridge to the House of Commons, a pattern exemplified by the 12th, 13th and 14th Earls of Derby. But the 1796 Preston election was more than an exciting political event, for it symbolised a fast-changing world. That the scion of a noble house, destined to inherit 45,000 acres, should be challenged by a man born in a cottage, without title, connections or standing except that which money could buy, was presumptuous. Ancient tradition was opposed by new wealth, the landed aristocracy by the self-made man, the rural by the urban, the agricultural by the industrial.

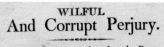

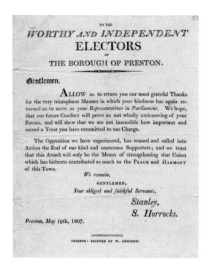

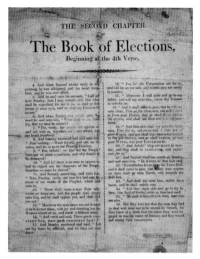

Political posters from the 1807 Preston election campaign. Lord Stanley and Samuel Horrocks won the contest by a handsome margin (Harris Library, Preston).

Huge sums had been spent, but next time both sides must surely have to spend even more. It was possible that Horrocks, with his fortune, might yet triumph and even that the second Preston seat might also go to a Tory. Derby control seemed threatened by financial exigencies and political realities, and the solution adopted seemed to contemporaries extraordinary and even now appears remarkable. The Derbys reached agreement with their opponents that at the next election they would share the political spoils, each side nominating one candidate. The two parties, so recently engaged in bitter rivalry, thereby 'fixed' the results, and in 1802 Lord Stanley and John Horrocks were duly returned unopposed. The 'coalition' quickly became a means of preserving the status quo. John Horrocks died in 1804 and was succeeded as MP by his elder brother, Samuel. At the 1806 general election Lord Stanley and Samuel Horrocks were returned unopposed, in accordance with the coalition strategy, but at the general election of 1807 they were challenged by an independent, Joseph Hanson, whose radical views were popular among Lancashire millworkers. The 'coalition' candidates united and ensured that virtually all their supporters used one of their two votes for Stanley and the other for Horrocks. Hanson finished more than 600 votes behind, but only three votes separated Stanley and Horrocks.

In 1812 Lord Stanley vacated the Preston seat and was elected as one of the two MPs for the county of Lancashire, a constituency which he represented for the next twenty years, but in the Commons, despite 36 years total service, he made remarkably little impact. Observers noted that he rarely spoke and when he did his speeches made only the lightest impression. In 1848 Ross commented that

> '... his lordship has never greatly distinguished himself as an orator ... but such of his speeches as we have had the fortune to listen to, were marked by great good sense and propriety, if not by originality or depth of thought'.[3]

For most of his Commons career Edward Stanley was a loyal Whig, dutifully voting with the party and supporting – because he was liberal in his views – such policies as the extension of the franchise and the repeal of the remaining anti-Catholic and anti-Dissenter legislation. He was personally tolerant and believed in freedom of conscience, though he was himself a devout Anglican.[4]

Nonetheless, by the mid-1820s the allegiance of the Derby family to the Whig

Independent Electors.

COLONEL HANSON, now upon the Hustings, has come forward and offered himself as a Candidate for this Borough. Before you give your Votes to him, consider whether you will be more Independent than you now are; or what Benefit you will reap from such an Act.

Are our late Respectable and Independent Members, LORD STANLEY and Mr. HORROCKS, unworthy of your Choice? Have not the Ancestors of the NOBLE LORD spent their Property, and spilt their Blood for the Sake of Independency and to secure our Rights as Englishmen?

Has not his worthy Colleague been (I had almost said) the sole Cause of raising *Preston* from Nothing, to a Town of considerable Repute? Has he not enriched all, or nearly all the Inhabitants by their Property, advancing in a treble Proportion, since he established his concern? And has not the trading Electors also been considerable gainers by him?

What wonderful Deed will HANSON perform? Will he cause our Manufactures to advance? Will he raise Wages, about the Depression of which such a Clamour has been raised? Will he be a more Independent Member in the House of Commons than either of our former ones? Will he cause a reduction of Taxes? Will he cause Peace? Will he be the Means of Trade flourishing?—*Not one of these Things will he effect for you.*

The Supporters of this *Independant Man,* no doubt, are *respectable,* their Characters I do not need to expose, are well known. I could not but mark J—s H—n, shoemaker, and G—dy, auctioneer, who were at the Head of the Band a few hours ago; they, no doubt, are honorable.

Have the present Members trampled on Independency? Will they do so? If they did not exert themselves in the Cause of Independency, and our Rights as Britons, who would vote for them?

Fellow Townsmen; exert yourselves in the good old Cause of Independency, which is a bye Word used by our Opponent, or his Friends, and vote for our late Worthy Members, who have, and will stand by us, in Protection of OUR LIBERTY, and OUR RIGHTS as ENGLISHMEN—*the Loss of which may we never survive!!!*

A BRITON.

MAY 7th, 1807.

PRESTON: PRINTED BY W. ADDISON.

41

cause was beginning to waver. Nothing exemplifies this better, perhaps, than the career of Lord Stanley's son, Edward Geoffrey, who was elected in 1820 at the age of 21 as a Whig, in 1827 joined the Tories, in 1828 returned to the Whig fold, in 1834 left them and sat for three years as a cross-bencher, and finally in 1837 became a Tory once more, eventually serving three times as Conservative prime minister. With such peripatetic allegiances among his immediate family, it is not surprising that Lord Stanley's own party views were challenged. The most public demonstration of this uncertainty was in 1824, when Joseph Hume promoted a bill to determine the value of real estate owned by the Church of Ireland. Hume's proposal was interpreted by Lord Stanley and his son Edward as a direct attack upon the Protestant Church. They voted with the Tories against the proposal, and the waspish Whig MP, Thomas Creevey, commented to a correspondent that 'you may well suppose this heresy was mightily extolled by the enemy … Lord Derby [the 12th Earl] has been made really ill by it'.[5]

Thus, when his specific personal interests and causes were threatened, Lord Stanley could show his political stripes. This is most apparent in his response to the infamous Peterloo massacre, which took place in Manchester in August 1819. The demonstration in St Peter's Fields had gathered to promote the cause of parliamentary reform, franchise extension and the granting of liberties to working people. Walmsley, in his detailed assessment of Peterloo, considers that had the demonstration not turned into a disaster, Lord Stanley's mild encouragement of the reformist agenda would probably have continued. But the Manchester Yeomanry charged into the crowd with sabres slashing, and the political consequences were momentous.

Lord Stanley played a direct role in the events after Peterloo in two ways. He joined in the heated parliamentary debates, and he served as foreman of the grand jury which heard the indictments relating to the massacre. In parliament, he emerged as a champion of reaction, giving firm support to the militia and to the magistrates who sent soldiers into the crowd. This deviation from the path of liberalism appalled the more radical Whigs, who were convinced that the authorities had been culpable. In 1822, while the arguments still raged, the Whig commentator in *The Elector's Remembrancer* (an annual guide to politics) noted that Stanley had consistently 'voted well' on reformist issues, but in the case of Peterloo had sided with the Tories: 'it is melancholy to see a man of his principles degrading himself into the defence of such conduct'.[6] Henry Hunt, the radical leader at Peterloo, was more forthright:

> 'This Whig, Lord Stanley, was also one of the most violent against a parliamentary inquiry into [the massacre] … The Lord deliver us from the tender mercies of the Whigs, I say'.[7]

The Whigs were at this time in opposition. Not only were Lord Stanley's views regarded as inappropriate, but by siding with the Tories on this issue he was marked down as disloyal. In December 1819, after he had spoken in the Commons justifying the militia and casting doubt upon the peaceful intentions of the demonstrators, *The Manchester Observer* opined that:

> '… the ministers it appears have got a new and powerful ally in Lord Stanley (the son of our own dignified Lord Lieutenant). In a speech of considerable length, he contrives to vilify the character of the meeting and vindicate the conduct of the Yeomanry. He deals roundly in assertions - did we not feel inclined to be courteous to high rank - we should have said lies'.[8]

Lord Stanley's role as foreman of the grand jury hearing the indictments brought him further opprobrium. The jury summarily rejected the bills of indictment brought against the Manchester Yeomanry for, as Ross later put it, 'their butchery of the people at the Peterloo massacre'. Partly as a result of Stanley's influence, the militia were exonerated from blame. *The Elector's Remembrancer* of 1822, while acknowledging that Lord Stanley was basically a man of principle, acutely observed that his liberal voting instincts were followed 'except when Lancashire magistrates, Lancashire yeomanry, or Lancashire gaolers are concerned'.[9]

This perceptive remark defines the other guiding principle of Stanley's political role. His role as 'crown prince' of Lancashire was undertaken with great seriousness. He was guardian of the interests of his fellow-magistrates, including their independence of action, and had a major responsibility for the militia and yeomanry. It was scarcely conceivable that he would support any move which threatened these key elements in county society. The magistrates and the militia officers were gentlemen, and in a world where social status determined the functioning of society itself, any challenge to them was impossible. If he had condemned the actions of those immediately beneath himself in the social hierarchy, Lord Stanley would have seriously undermined his own position. Solidarity of class and status made support for the magistrates and yeomanry essential. This consideration outweighed the wider party political allegiance which otherwise guided his actions.

Lord Stanley could have held high ministerial office, but did not wish to do so. A political role had been thrust upon him, but his obvious preference was for a more scholarly and studious existence. His career was, as the *Gentleman's Magazine* phrased it on his death in 1851, 'noiseless and unobtrusive', and when in 1832 he was elevated to the Lords as Baron Stanley of Bickerstaffe he welcomed the less public role. Two years later, on becoming 13th Earl of Derby, he retired from active politics altogether.

Detail from *Members of the House of Lords*, c.1835, attributed to Isaac Cruikshank, showing the caricature of the 13th Earl. See the illustration on page 38 (By courtesy of the National Portrait Gallery, London).

---

[1]For more details see Proctor 1959. [2]The election is described in detail in Dobson 1868; Pollard 1871; and Urbanski (unpublished). [3]Ross 1848: 44. [4]Walmsley 1969: xiii and 437. [5]Maxwell 1903: 76. [6]Walmsley 1969: 39. [7]Walmsley 1969: 400 (quoting Hunt 1820: 637). [8]Walmsley 1969: 342. [9]Walmsley 1969: 39.

Calœnas maculata, Lath.

THE 13TH EARL OF DERBY AS A SCIENTIST

CLEMENCY FISHER AND CHRISTINE E. JACKSON

'... and when I saw him on his knees, having spread my drawings on the floor, the better to compare them, I forgot he was Lord Stanley, I knew only that he too loved Nature' (John James Audubon's journal for 5th August 1826).[1]

Edward Stanley was interested in natural history as a young man;[2] he kept caterpillars and made extensive notes on their activities. He also copied out sections from the text of existing books such as Buffon's *Histoire naturelle des oiseaux* (1770-86) into a series of small notebooks.[3] No other member of his immediate family was interested in natural history – rather more in horses and game birds – but it is probable that the young Edward was influenced by his cousins, the Hornbys, who lived locally and were much more curious about nature. He corresponded with them throughout his life, married Charlotte Hornby, and his brother-in law Phipps and niece Elizabeth became two of his most enthusiastic collectors.

The first page of Lord Stanley's manuscript catalogue, which lists John Abbot's birds (LM).

Opposite Portrait by Joseph Smit of John Latham's 'Spotted Pigeon' *Caloenas maculata*, from the collections of the 13th Earl of Derby. The pigeon appears to be unique (from *Bulletin of the Liverpool Museums* 1898 vol. 1; opposite page 83).

Politics claimed much of his attention until 1832 but, despite this, he managed to acquire by self-education an extensive and impressive knowledge of zoology and botany. In 1814, he described several birds new to science. Over the next four decades he came to be regarded as a knowledgeable collector of birds, mammals and plants. He communicated widely, and on equal terms, with other natural scientists of his day. This metamorphosis can be traced through the vast amounts of correspondence and other documents which still exist,[4] and his magnificent collections. In the pursuit of his passion for natural history, the 13th Earl created - almost inadvertently - a resource of great significance for others, such as John Latham, John Gould and John Edward Gray. This resource remains hugely important in modern times and it is on this achievement that the 13th Earl's reputation as a natural historian rests.

Lord Stanley was first interested in British birds, which he kept alive in his father's aviary at Knowsley and also in the family's London house in Grosvenor Square. He simultaneously began to build a collection of museum specimens, and these increasingly were of foreign species. Birds were purchased from an early age, the first two apparently being acquired from Sir B. Harwood in 1794, while Lord Stanley was still at Trinity College, Cambridge. Fifteen years later, he began to catalogue his growing museum, including the important collection of birds he had purchased at the sale of the Leverian Museum in 1806. However, the first entries in his manuscript 'General Index of the Birds in my collection at Knowsley'[5] were of John Abbot's American birds, purchased from William Bullock in 1810.

One of the main attractions in London between 1775 and 1806 was the 'Leverian Museum', founded by Sir Ashton Lever and sited first in Leicester Square and later near Blackfriars Bridge. There Lord Stanley must have seen thousands of exotic birds, fish, mammals, insects, shells, weapons and costumes, including items brought back from the South Seas by Captain Cook after his second and third voyages of exploration (1772-1779). Lever's museum is known to have included some 2,300 birds, representing approximately 1,500 to 1,600 species, from all parts of the world.[6] In the early 1800s Lord Stanley became acquainted with John Latham, the foremost English ornithologist of his day.[7] Latham made extensive use of the specimens in the Leverian Museum while writing *A General Synopsis of Birds*

(1781-85); between 1821 and 1828 he updated this work with *A General History of Birds*. Lord Stanley clearly admired Latham's work and applied Latham's names to his own bird specimens and paintings. Many of his specimens were shown to Latham for an opinion and indeed some of Latham's own drawings were based on birds in Lord Stanley's collection.[8]

When at Knowsley, Lord Stanley must often have travelled the eight miles into the centre of Liverpool to visit William Bullock's museum (in Lord Street between 1800 and 1804, and from 1804 to 1809 on the corner of Church Street and Whitechapel). The Bullock Museum had a large collection, of '4000 curiosities',[9] and Bullock sold both living birds and skins to Lord Stanley from about 1805 until 1819.[10] In 1809, Bullock moved his collection to London; he sold it ten years later. At the Bullock Museum sale, Lord Stanley acquired some of the most important specimens in his collection (see White Swamp-hen, Catalogue entry 52).

Apart from Buffon and Latham's publications, few other bird books of the early eighteenth century included coloured illustrations of foreign species with which Lord Stanley could compare his specimens. Mark Catesby's book of North American birds included 113 figures; George Edwards illustrated about 300 species. George Shaw's *Naturalists' Miscellany*, Vieillot's publications and Levaillant's work on African birds were also used by Lord Stanley, but he only had access to published illustrations of about a tenth of the bird species presently known to science. He painstakingly copied many of these illustrations himself (for example, see Catalogue entries 12 & 13),[12] in order to be able to store them in taxonomic order for reference, but was anxious to buy original paintings of birds that might also give him clues to the identity of the many unknown specimens in his collection.

Although much has been written about the zoological specimens in the 13th Earl of Derby's museum, less has been published about his important collection of natural history art.[13] Both the Leverian and Bullock Museums attracted artists anxious to draw the rare specimens they displayed. Sarah Stone (c.1760-1844) was employed by Lever to record the zoological and ethnographical objects in his museum; it was there she met Lord Stanley, who later bought many examples of her work.[14] Other eighteenth century paintings he purchased were by Thomas Davies (c. 1739-1812), whose large collection of watercolours he obtained at 'Van Holde's Sale' in 1817; John Abbot (1751-1839); Samuel Howitt (1756-1822), George Edwards (1694-1773) and Sydenham Edwards (1768-1819). Sydenham Edwards was employed by Lord Stanley, as early as 1808, to seek out and paint unusual species in London museums and exhibitions of live birds by proprietors such as Gilbert Pidcock. William Bartram's album of American drawings (which was first in the collection of Peter Collinson, then that of Aylmer Lambert, see Catalogue entries 20 & 71) was purchased from Bohn of London in 1842. Originals by John Frederick Miller (1745 – post 1796) and Thomas Lewin (born 1774) were purchased from Bohn in 1846.

It was at the Zoological Society of London that Lord Stanley first met Edward Lear (1812-1888) and admired his lively and accurate bird portraits. As the various parts of Lear's book on parrots were being issued between 1830 and 1832, Lord Stanley decided to hire Lear to record the rare species in his own collections. He invited Lear to Knowsley and set him to work. The priceless result was the 108 natural history watercolours which are still housed at Knowsley Hall.

From the 1840s, the 13th Earl of Derby's purchases of watercolours tended to be either commissioned records of his own specimens, painted by Lear, Benjamin Waterhouse Hawkins (1807-1889) and Joseph Wolf (1820-1899), or selected

J.Smit del et lith.

Necropsar leguati, Forbes.

Mintern Bros. imp.

watercolours purchased from John Gould (1804-1881). Gould was a particularly close colleague, who often visited Knowsley, and his relationship with Lord Derby is the reason the 13th Earl's collections of Australian paintings and zoological specimens are of such outstanding importance. Some of the work by Lear and Hawkins was later published in *Gleanings from the menagerie and aviary at Knowsley Hall* (Gray 1846a, 1850).

Following his purchase of over a hundred mounted birds at the Leverian Museum sale in 1806[15] and of John Abbot's North American skin collection four years later, Lord Stanley began to acquire specimens in earnest. In 1814 he obtained the type of the Brown Kiwi *Apteryx australis* (the first Kiwi ever seen in Europe) at the sale of George Shaw's collections. In the same year he also purchased, from John Smith of Glasgow, 28 foreign and 14 British cases of birds belonging to Dr. McDougall. Forty-five specimens of British birds were acquired at the sale of Edward Donovan's collection in 1818. By the time a complete inventory of Lord Stanley's museum was made in the 1820s, the collection numbered over 1,600 specimens.[16]

Until he became Earl in 1834, Lord Stanley showed some restraint in his spending, but as Lord Derby he freely bought specimens, alive and dead, and commissioned his own collectors to travel overseas. They sent back packets, boxes and barrels of specimens (as well as living animals) from all quarters of the globe. In Britain, Lord Derby purchased specimens mainly from dealers in London[17] and Liverpool; overseas his main sources were the Verreaux Brothers in Paris and, indirectly, C.J. Temminck at the Rijksmuseum in Leiden. He also obtained a significant number of African specimens at the sale of Dr Andrew Smith's collection in 1838.

Portrait by Joseph Smit of one of Lord Derby's most interesting specimens, *Necropsar leguati*, long thought to be a unique starling from Madagascar, but which from recent DNA tests is actually a West Indian mockingbird (from *Bulletin of the Liverpool Museums* 1898 vol. 1; opposite page 29).

The Waterfowls' Lawn (at the Zoological Society of London) by Georg Scharf (1788-1860). Edward Stanley was President of the ZSL from 1831 until his death in 1851 (The Zoological Society of London, Regents Park).

By the time of Lord Derby's death, in 1851, his museum collections were truly international and covered every major group of birds and mammals.

Lord Derby's surviving papers give a clear impression of his astonishing international network of collectors and agents. These included John Bates, Thomas Bridges, Joseph Burke, Hugh Cuming, David Dyson, Phillip Gosse, Adolphe de Lattre and Stuart Thomson in the New World; Edward Blyth, George Windsor Earl, Robert Fortune, Brian Hodgson and Rajendra Mullick in the Far East; Joseph Burke, Louis Fraser, John Fry, Henry Salt and Thomas Whitfield in Africa; George Caley, John Gilbert, John Gould, John MacGillivray and Frederick Strange in Australasia.

Lord Derby was therefore in communication with some of the greatest natural historians of the day and had many distinguished guests at Knowsley. John James Audubon visited in 1826, Charles Lucien Bonaparte (Emperor Napoleon's nephew, the Prince of Canino and Musignano) in 1837 and again in 1849. The Reverend Edmund Dixon of Norfolk visited in 1849.[18] He and Lord Derby exchanged many long and delightful letters about breeds of domestic birds; some included very critical remarks about Charles Darwin's theories on the hybridization of poultry. Lord Derby certainly met Darwin, and indeed was one of the assessors of the value of Darwin's *Beagle* collection.[19] John Gould dropped in to Knowsley on his way to go fishing with Sir William Jardine in Scotland. Thomas Eyton, the Shropshire-based landowner who became the world expert on ducks, geese and swans, was much more likely to visit Lord Derby than to write to him,[18] so we unfortunately have little record of their long relationship.

As a scientist, Lord Derby was not a prolific writer. He published a few notes in various journals, including the *Proceedings of the Zoological Society of London*,[20] but his

A group of birds and mammals from Lord Derby's collection, the Australian material collected by John Gilbert between 1838 and 1845. Many are types, or of extinct species (LM).

most important scientific paper, written in 1814 when he was almost 40, involved the descriptions of 12 new species of birds obtained in Africa by Henry Salt.[21] However, Lord Derby obviously spent much time researching specimens both in his own collection and at the British Museum[22] and many of his manuscripts bear long and careful notes on anatomical matters and the identification of specimens.[23]

Lord Derby's museum took up a suite of rooms (including the 'Library', the 'Middle Room' and the 'Last Room') on the first floor of Knowsley Hall, overlooking the formal gardens to the east.[24] Most of his specimens were mounted and arranged in conventional glass cases according to their taxonomic groups[25] and were set off by linen backdrops. There were also cabinets with drawers of skins. In the early days Lord Derby does not seem to have employed a formal curator, but had a taxidermist, John Sherlock, from about 1813.[26] There are passing references to 'Thomas', who was setting up a toucan in 1838 and a lemur in 1839.[27] Clayton is recorded as the taxidermist in 1849-1851, but was probably there earlier. He was assisted by Wilson, who did jobs like cleaning display cases, writing labels, putting eyes in mounted birds and birds on stands. Louis Fraser became the first curator at Knowsley, transferring (probably in 1845) from the museum of the Zoological Society of London. Fraser's Museum Report for April and May 1849[18] gives us some idea of the duties of the museum staff at Knowsley: 'Dosing Wild Boar with Corrosive Sublimate', collecting camphor in blocks[28] and cutting it for the skin boxes, cleaning 'turpentine glasses'. Lord Derby appears also to have had a small

49

ethnographic collection, as Wilson was recorded as 'Dusting South Sea War Instruments' on December 29th 1849. Fraser, Clayton and Wilson were on duty on Saturdays, Christmas Eve and Boxing Day.

Louis Fraser, although apparently a difficult person, was a Jack of all trades. He had been naturalist to the Niger Expedition of 1841-42, before he went to the Zoological Society's museum as curator; in 1850 he left Lord Derby's service for a diplomatic post in West Africa. By that time Fraser had catalogued about a quarter of Lord Derby's bird collection (with full data and lists of synonyms) in six manuscript volumes, and had also listed 450 species of mammals in the same meticulous way. Thomas Moore finished cataloguing the birds after the collections were transferred to Liverpool Borough Council, but there was very little information with his entries. David Dyson took over as curator at Knowsley until Lord Derby's death in 1851. He seems to have spent most of his time identifying and arranging shells.

As a leader in the natural history world, Edward Stanley was pivotal. He was elected Vice-President of the Linnean Society (the premier society for discussing natural history classification) in 1817 and was President from 1828 to 1834. He was a founder member of the Zoological Society of London in 1826 and its President from 1831 until his death in 1851. The latter was a particularly close association, with much information and livestock exchanged between the Knowsley Menagerie and the zoo in Regent's Park.

Even in old age, the 13th Earl of Derby was very much at the centre of natural history matters in Britain and abroad.[29] However, towards the end of his life there is evidence that Lord Derby was turning increasingly towards botany and horticulture as his main interest, corresponding widely on botanical matters and receiving at Knowsley many seeds and tubers which he hoped to propagate. His greatest legacy, though, was his bird and mammal collections, that he had originally intended to bequeath to the British Museum. It was David Mitchell, Secretary of the Zoological Society of London, who in 1847 suggested the collections should be given instead to the people of Liverpool.[30]

When the 13th Earl died in 1851, his son described the collection as the 'labor of his life'. The 13th Earl recorded that he hoped his museum would be used for the 'benefit of the rising generation' of local people, and requested that the newly-housed collection be named after him.[31] 20,000 birds and mammals were bequeathed to the people of Liverpool. The 'large collection of eggs, fishes and reptiles'[32] went elsewhere.

Thomas Moore, the Deputy Superintendant of the living collections at Knowsley, remained with the museum collections (David Dyson having gone abroad) and the specimens went first to the Union Newsrooms on Duke Street in central Liverpool. The collection soon outgrew these premises and in the 1860s a new building was erected on Shaw's Brow (now William Brown Street). Moore became the first Director of the Derby Museum, later renamed the Liverpool Museum - an institution that continues to build on the excellence of the 13th Earl of Derby's original bequest.

[1]Audubon 1897 (1994 reprint, vol.1 : 109). [2]In his letter to Liverpool Borough Council, bequeathing his collections, Lord Derby hoped that his museum would become 'a memorial of the interest I have from boyhood felt in the study of Natural History' (K). [3]Lord Stanley not only translated Buffon but added many notes of his own, which showed that he was already familiar with the classification of species (six notebooks at K). He also transcribed long extracts from William Dampier's descriptions of his voyages

(LVRO misc folders). [4]See 'List of abbreviations' on page 5. [5]LM Zoology archives. [6]Jackson 1998: 148. [7]The earliest known letter between Lord Stanley and Latham is dated June 1811 (K), but they must have met before this date. They agreed entirely on the superiority of the Linnaean system of classification and thought badly of his main rival; in a letter to Derby in 1826 (K), Latham quoted Thomas Pennant as saying that Buffon 'not content with robbing ye Swede, had murdered him, to conceal the theft'. [8]Six bound volumes of Latham's drawings are in the NHM, and include several paintings which Latham annotated as being based on Lord Stanley's specimens. In a letter to Stanley dated 4th June 1815 (K) Latham asked to borrow several birds which he wanted to describe in his *General History*. [9]Alexander 1985: 120. [10]Birds from New Holland, Senegal and the John Abbot collection etc. were purchased for Lord Stanley by Bullock (LVRO misc. folder 4). [11]Lord Stanley purchased over 100 specimens from the Bullock Museum between 1819 and 1821 (Morgan & Brennan 1977: 21). [12]In 1805 Lord Stanley carefully listed those 'Birds whose pictures I had then finished' (K). Most were copied from the books by Catesby and Vieillot. [13]Fraser 1850, Morgan & Brennan 1977, Wagstaffe 1978, Largen & Fisher 1986, Largen 1987. See also Forbes & Robinson's multipart 'Catalogue [of birds] … in the Derby Museum', published in *Bull. Liv. Mus.* between 1897 and 1900. Povey (1954) gives a short account of the original artwork at Knowsley. [14]When Lord Stanley bought a large collection of Sarah Stone's watercolours from Matthew Gregson of Liverpool in 1830 (LVRO 2/4/68), he inscribed on one (K, watercolour no 8) the words: 'Abt this time [when she had painted it] I was in London & saw Miss Stone at Museum'. [15]Largen 1987. Lord Stanley acquired about 117 birds at the Leverian Museum sale, of which at least 25 still survive in the Liverpool Museum. Several of Lord Stanley's manuscripts list his purchases and the prices paid (e.g. LVRO misc. folder 4, no 7). [16]LVRO misc. folder 8. [17]Lord Derby acquired more material from the Leadbeaters (1047 specimens from 1811) than anyone else. John Gould was the next biggest source (543 specimens from 1830). Morgan & Brennan 1977: 22 & 24. [18]*Museum Report for 1849, daily entries by Louis Fraser*. Dixon visited on 29th May (also see Dixon to Derby, LVRO 1/46/16-18). Thomas Eyton visited on 7th August and 2nd November. His Royal Highness the Duke of Cambridge visited on 21st September. Charles Bonaparte visited on 25th September. *Museum Report for 1851, daily entries by David Dyson*. Eyton visited with Philip Lutley Sclater, the first editor of the ornithological journal *Ibis*, on 28th February. Thomas Nuttall visited on 7th April (Nuttall, although English, became a great expert on American birds, and the first American ornithological society was named after him. He died at his home near Liverpool in 1859). Charles Bonaparte visited again on 25th July, after the 13th Earl's death, presumably to see the living collections and museum at Knowsley before they were dispersed. NMGM Archives MM/2/1& 2. [19]Burkhardt *et al*, 1986: 17. Darwin is also recorded as having used information on Lord Derby's aviary and menagerie at Knowsley for his notes on breeding in his *Natural selection* and in *Variation* (Burkhardt *et al* 1987: 405). [20]A letter from Lord Derby, concerning his living collections at Knowsley, was for instance published in *Proc. Zool. Soc. London* in 1841. Lord Derby also wrote an account of the breeding of the Néné at Knowsley (see endnote 60 on page 95). [21]Stanley 1814; also see Largen 1988 and Catalogue entry for the Black-winged Lovebird (page 53). [22]John Gray to Derby, 3rd February 1843 (LVRO 1/69/14): 'Since you have been at the museum … ' Lord Derby also served as a Trustee of the British Museum. [23]For instance, a document in NMGM (MM/8/K/8: 3) is a very extensive and detailed set of corrections and comments to a manuscript on the duck family by Thomas Eyton. [24]Moore 1890: 10; also Reverend G. Hornby's letter to the 15th Earl of Derby from Naples, 8th March 1870 (K). [25]'Birds numbered and where placed' (LVRO misc. folder 8, part 2/6). [26]LVRO 1/148/1-2. [27]LVRO misc. folder 5/2. [28]Pests were obviously unwelcome. Fraser recorded that they received 20 lbs of camphor on 22nd April 1851 and another 20 lbs on 20th May. [29]The 13th Earl's copy-book for 1851, even in June, the month he died (K) shows an undiminished attention to his correspondence. [30]LVRO 1/118/23 & 26, & see *Introduction*. [31]See *Introduction* for a fuller extract of Lord Derby's memoranda and draft will, taken from a copy of the acceptance of the collections by Liverpool Borough Council on 16th July 1851 (K). The collection of eggs, fish and reptiles was not included. The 13th Earl specifically excluded his shells and bequeathed them to his daughter-in-law, Mrs Charles Stanley. [32]Pollard 1871: 115.

Length nearly 7½ Inches. Bill Blood-red, the feathers of the whole front from the base of the upper Mandible all round to about half way on the Crown are of a fine Scarlet which colour surrounds the Eyelids, passing round in almost a hair streak, of very minute feathers & ending in a point at a little distance behind the eyes giving the same effect to the Eye as if it were placed in a naked Skin like that of the Partridge; the general colour of the plumage of the body is green, paler beneath; this colour occupies the remaining part of the Head, the neck has a tinge of reddish mingled with the green & in some other parts the green, occasionally, according as the light falls upon it, assumes a bluish cast. the upper tail coverts which are so long as to reach within half an inch of the tip of the tail are of a yellowish, tipped with grass green. The tail itself is about 2 Inches & a quarter in length, & what I should term rounded at the end, (but Dr Latham calls it slightly cuneiform) the outer feathers being not half an Inch shorter than the middle; which last are rather more pointed than the others, their colour is a pale greyish green tipped with half an Inch with black, which forms a bar across all the others, approaching nearer to the end on the pair immediately adjoining, & receding on each till on the outer it is 3/8 of an inch from the end the exterior Web of the outer feather is light green the inner yellow which encreases on all the intermediate feathers, the extreme tips of all but the two middle are green, in some lights having a cast of blue. below the feathers are dusky yellow barred with black & tipped with green, but all dusky: The upper surface of the wing is divided longitudinally between green & black, the former colour occupying all the feathers nearest to the Body while the outer half of the wing being black, this colour however

1. BLACK-WINGED LOVEBIRD
Family Psittacidae (parrots)

Henry Salt (1780-1827) began his diplomatic career in 1809, when he was sent deep into the remote highlands of north east Africa carrying messages of goodwill from King George III to the Emperor of the country then known as Abyssinia. Salt had been encouraged by Sir Joseph Banks to obtain natural history specimens during the course of the expedition, and so was able to bring to England (in January 1811) the first zoological collection ever to emerge from this part of Africa. The collection included 78 bird skins, which were given to Lord Stanley the following year.[1] In his only significant taxonomic publication, Stanley later described and named (in an appendix to Salt's *Voyage to Abyssinia*) 12 species that he believed to be new to science.[2] Particularly noteworthy is the fact that Stanley's manuscript draft relating to the Black-winged Lovebird still survives in the archives of the Liverpool Museum.

Salt recorded how his expedition traversed the maritime plain and ascended the north eastern slopes of the Abyssinian plateau, via the precipitous track that provides a pass to the heights of Mt Taranta.[3] Large flocks of parrots were observed around the summits of this massif and it was one of these, collected on 3rd March 1810, that subsequently became the holotype of *Psittacus Taranta*. The species is a common forest endemic in the central highlands of Ethiopia and Eritrea, where it is found living in small flocks at altitudes of 1400-3200 m.

ML

[1]Largen 1988. [2]Stanley 1814. [3]Salt 1814.

Above Watercolour by Henry Constantine Richter (John Gould studio), inscribed on mount 'Gould/Malacoturnix superciliosus/Slate-coloured Partridge'. 356 x 534mm. Drawn from the Derby specimens now numbered D.259 and D.259a (Private Collection).

Right Watercolour signed 'Edward Lear. del. July 1836' and subsequently inscribed 'Rollulus superciliosus, Gray. India? Drawn from specimens in the Knowsley Museum (Mss. Cat. No 259). The original of the Plate in the 'Gleanings'.' 360 x 530mm. Lear's painting was also based on Lord Derby's specimens, now numbered D.259 and D.259a (K).

Below Two syntypes of *Ophrysia superciliosa* (J.E. Gray 1846), described as *Rollulus superciliosa*, the 'Eyebrowed Rollulus', in *Gleanings from the menagerie & aviary at Knowsley Hall*, 1: 8, pl.XVI. Cabinet skins from India ('Mussorie'), purchased by the 13th Earl of Derby from Tucker in 1836. Length about 200mm (LM D.259, male and D.259a, female).

What little is known about the Himalayan Mountain Quail is derived from a few observations made during the mid nineteenth century. These birds were seen close to Mussourie and Nainital in northern India, but are apparently no longer found in this area. The species could be extinct, but it is equally possible that populations still survive in remote wilderness areas of the Himalayas.

Only nine specimens are known and, apart from the two in the Liverpool Museum, all were collected during the period 1865 to 1876. The birds were encountered in groups of six to ten individuals, amongst tall grass and scrub on steep hillsides and were very reluctant to fly. When flushed they would rise into the air with a shrill whistle then, after a brief period of slow and heavy flight, return to the grass at the earliest opportunity. Virtually nothing more is known about the biology of this species.

EF

3. GOLDEN PARAKEET
Family Psittacidae (parrots)

Both Lear's paintings are inscribed '*Conurus luteus* Brazil'; one is dated 1831 and the other July 1836. The name *luteus*, which appears also in Louis Fraser's manuscript catalogue of birds in the Knowsley Museum, represents a misidentification of the species illustrated and derives from an error in the published works of John Latham.

Lord Derby owned at least four specimens of the Golden Parakeet. The earliest acquired, without locality and purchased at the sale of General Davies' collection on 6th June 1812, was one of the birds on which Latham[1] based his 'Brasilian Yellow Parrot'. This specimen has failed to survive and, since it was not included in Fraser's catalogue, must have been lost during Edward Stanley's lifetime. Two further Golden Parakeets were bought by Lord Stanley on 21st May 1819, at the sale of William Bullock's museum. These were the specimens to which Latham[2] later applied the name 'Yellow Maccaw Parrot'. Only one is still extant;[3] a young bird that is clearly not the specimen painted by Lear; though both are in fact excluded from consideration because they are labelled with the erroneous locality 'Cayenne' (French Guiana), where the species does not occur.

Only the specimen numbered D.735 has the correct provenance, 'Brazil', and all the evidence strongly suggests that it was this bird that Edward Lear painted, twice, prior to its death in the Knowsley Menagerie on 17th April 1838.

Confined to a limited area of tropical rainforest in north-eastern Brazil, this species is seriously endangered by massive and accelerating destruction of its habitat, exacerbated by hunting for both food and sport. As one of the world's most prized cage-birds, it is further threatened by the activities of smugglers operating on an international scale.

ML

Above Two watercolours by Edward Lear, dated 1831 and 1836 (top), both depicting *Guaruba guarouba* and almost certainly modelled on the same living bird (now specimen D.735). Both are 365 x 530mm (K).

Left Cabinet skin (foreground), formerly mounted for display, of the Golden Parakeet *Guaruba guarouba*, which died in the Knowsley Menagerie in April 1838. Length 370mm (LM D.735).

---

[1]Latham 1781: 226. [2]Latham 1822, 2: 144. [3]LM D.735a, which is also illustrated (entry a).

4. PARADISE PARROT
Family Psittacidae (parrots)

Above Plate 34 from volume five of Gould's *Birds of Australia*, depicting *Psephotus pulcherrimus* (K).

Right Crayon sketch by John Gould, depicting two male Paradise Parrots. 550 x 375mm. This painting, from a bound volume entitled 'Original drawings of Australian birds', provided the original for Plate 34 in the fifth volume of Gould's *Birds of Australia* (K).[2]

Below right Cabinet skin; adult male paratype of *Platycercus pulcherrimus* Gould 1845, now known as *Psephotus pulcherrimus*, collected by John Gilbert at the Condamine River, Darling Downs, Australia on 17th May 1844.[1] Length 295mm (LM D.789a).

In his letter from Darling Downs, in what is now southern Queensland, John Gilbert wrote excitedly to John Gould about his discovery of a 'totally new parrot … the most beautiful … in Australia' and sent several specimens to his employer in England. Gould named the new species in the following year, using an almost verbatim transcription of the description in Gilbert's letter[3] and in July 1845 sold one of the specimens to the Earl of Derby. Gilbert's original letter is lost, but Gould must have shown it to Lord Derby and he, very fortunately, made a copy.[4]

The Paradise Parrot once inhabited parts of eastern Australia, but has not been seen since 1927 and is thought to be extinct. The species fed on native grass seeds and usually nested in holes in termite mounds. Its extinction was probably caused by diminished food supply, due to drought, overgrazing and spread of the Prickly Pear cactus.[5]

CF

[1]Fisher (1986: 10-12) first recognised this specimen as a paratype of the species. The holotype (ANSP 22915) and another paratype (ANSP 22912) are in the Academy of Natural Sciences, Philadelphia. Only the Liverpool Museum specimen still has Gilbert's original field labels attached. [2]Gould 1840-1848. [3]Gould 1845a. [4]This copy is now in LVRO [5]Joseph 1988.

5. RED-BELLIED WOODPECKER
Family Picidae (woodpeckers, wrynecks and piculets)

Left Watercolour by John Abbot, depicting *Melanerpes carolinus*, purchased by Lord Stanley in 1817. 240 x 300mm (K).

Below Cabinet skin of bird formerly mounted for display; male Red-bellied Woodpecker *Melanerpes carolinus*, collected by John Abbot in Georgia, U.S.A. and purchased by Lord Stanley in 1810. Length 245mm (LM D.3920).

John Abbot (1751-1840), who was born in London, emigrated to North America at the age of 22 and eventually settled in Georgia. There he remained for the next 64 years, supporting his family by selling paintings of natural history subjects and collections of specimens. He was not a seeker after fame and fortune, but Abbot nevertheless achieved distinction through the quality of his work as a naturalist and artist in what was then a rather remote and little-known corner of the continent. William Swainson described Abbot's specimens as 'the finest ever transmitted as articles of commerce'.[1]

In October 1809, a consignment of Abbot's bird skins reached London. 64 of these were sold to Lord Stanley by the naturalist William Bullock in the spring of the following year.[2] Soon afterwards, Stanley began to compile the first comprehensive catalogue of his growing museum, entitled 'General Index of the Birds in my collection at Knowsley'. Though certainly not the earliest of his acquisitions, the Abbot collection has the distinction of comprising the first 64 entries in the 'General Index' (see illustration on page 45). Among the 40 species represented, a pair of 'Carolina Woodpeckers', purchased for seven shillings, appear as items 50-51.

In 1815, John Abbot completed a set of 221 annotated watercolours and these were sold to Lord Stanley two years later. Painting No.46 depicts a 'Carolina Woodpecker' and carries the legend 'Frequents the woods, is fond of mulberries'. The same reference to mulberries appears in Latham (1822, 3: 388) and, though unattributed, must surely have been derived from the note appended to Abbot's portrait. By such means was scientific information circulated in the early nineteenth century.

This woodpecker is a common bird in forests of eastern North America, extending from southern Canada to Florida.

ML

[1]Swainson 1840. [2]Largen & Rogers-Price 1985.

6. FIERY TOPAZ
Family Trochilidae (hummingbirds)

Above Plate 67 from volume two of *Monograph of the Trochilidae*, depicting the Fiery Topaz (K).

Right Watercolour by John Gould, depicting *Topaza pyra* (Gould 1846).[1] This painting is number 28 in a bound volume entitled 'Gould's original drawings' and provided the basis for Plate 67 in the second volume of Gould's *Monograph of the Trochilidae*.[2] 535 x 365mm (K).

John Gould's published plate of *Topaza pyra* differs greatly from his earlier drawing. The top bird in the original watercolour was omitted and the lower male bird seems to have been re-deployed to provide instead one of the males in his illustration of *Topaza pella*. The specimens of *T. pyra* depicted in *Monograph of the Trochilidae* are the types of the species and can be found in The Natural History Museum collections at Tring,[3] but of the nest and eggs, given to Gould by W.H. Edwards, there is no trace.

The Fiery Topaz inhabits open woodland, along the edges of streams in the central Amazon region of South America. Some naturalists believe that it is not specifically distinct from the Crimson Topaz *Topaza pella*.

CF

[1]The painting is composed on the back of an uncoloured Gould lithograph of the Australian Warbler *Xerophila leucopsis* Gould. [2]Gould 1849a-1861. [3]The holotype is BMNH 1888.7.25.158; see Warren 1966: 239.

7. WHITE-THROATED TOUCAN
Family Ramphastidae (toucans)

Watercolour by John Gould and Henry Constantine Richter, depicting the unique type specimen of *Ramphastos Inca* Gould 1846, *Proc. Zool. Soc. London*: 68, then in the possession of the 13th Earl of Derby. This name is no longer considered to represent a distinct species and is most probably a synonym of *Ramphastos tucanus*. 354 x 530mm (K).

This painting is conspicuously different from the illustration of a single example that is reproduced in *Monograph of the Ramphastidae,* though both are inscribed 'Gould & Richter del.'. It is well known that John Gould achieved his enormous productivity by employing artists such as Edward Lear, Joseph Wolf and Henry Constantine Richter (1821–1902) to turn his own preliminary, but brilliant, sketches into finished paintings and lithographs. It appears that two such sketches of *Ramphastos inca* were both completed by Richter, one then being acquired by Lord Derby, while the other was later used to illustrate Gould's monograph.

Thomas Bridges (1807-1865) collected extensively in the New World between 1827 and the time of his death, contributing numerous birds and mammals to the Knowsley museum, aviary and menagerie during the period 1842-1850.

John Gould[1] based his description of the Inca Toucan on what was clearly a unique bird 'brought to this country by Mr. Bridges, and now in the collection of the Earl of Derby'. The second edition of Gould's *Monograph of the Ramphastidae* (1854) includes a fine illustration of this bird (pl.7). The accompanying text records that: 'for knowledge of this species we are indebted to Mr. Bridges, who brought a single specimen from Bolivia', but the earlier reference to Lord Derby is omitted. Does this help to explain why the specimen is not present in the Derby collection today and why there is no reference to it in the surviving archives of the Knowsley Museum? Is it possible that Lord Derby gave the bird away, perhaps to John Gould himself?

The White-throated Toucan is a fairly common species in the canopy of humid forests, from the Guianas and Venezuela southwards to Bolivia and the Amazon region of Brazil.

ML

[1]Gould 1846.

8. 'WEEBONG SHRIKE' & 'AGILE HONEYEATER'

Family Pachycephalidae (whistlers or thickheads)?
Family Meliphagidae (honeyeaters)?

Above Watercolour, possibly by the 13th Earl of Derby, derived from original works in the second volume of 'Lambert Drawings' and bound into a further volume of paintings entitled 'The Zoology of New Holland'. One of the birds depicted is copied from plate 25, the other is copied from plate 72 and inscribed 'natural size. 1. Agile Honeyeater Certhia agilis. Ind. Orn. Sup. xxxviii B.2.72'. 360 x 490mm (K).

Right Watercolour, inscribed by the 13th Earl of Derby 'Lanius flavigaster'; plate 25 in the second bound zoological volume of 'Lambert Drawings'. 262 x 420mm (K).

The 'Lambert Drawings', which are bound into five volumes, are a series of natural history paintings by untutored artists (most probably convicts) who reached Australia with the 'First Fleet' in 1788. They are so named because they were acquired by the Earl of Derby at the sale of Aylmer Bourke Lambert's library in 1842.[1]

Scientific names, mostly derived from the publications of John Latham, have been added to many of the bird paintings in the Lambert volumes by Lord Derby himself, but the artwork is sometimes so minimalist that it is impossible to be certain about the identity of the species depicted. The name 'Lanius flavigaster' (inscribed on plate 25) derives from *Todus flavigaster* Latham 1790, a bird which Latham later called the 'Weebong Shrike'.[2] Most ornithologists have believed that this name might be a junior synonym of *Eopsaltria australis* (White 1790),[3] the Eastern Yellow Robin, but more recent opinion favours synonymy with *Pachycephala pectoralis* (Latham 1801), the Golden Whistler.[4] If so, the painter of the Lambert Drawing has omitted the black necklace, which is a distinctive feature of the Golden Whistler, although he has shown the claret eye.

The inscriptions attached to plate 72 of the second volume of the Lambert Drawings, and to the second bird in the painting attributed to Lord Derby, refer to the name *Certhia agilis* Latham 1801.[5] Latham later gave it the English name 'Agile Honey-eater'.[6] Again, it is difficult to match it with any known species. However, the two paintings are probably of *Melithreptus lunatus* (Vieillot 1802), the White-naped Honeyeater, but with the white nape omitted. That the bird is a honeyeater can be deduced from the slender bill and protruding brush-tipped tongue. The hint of orange in the mouth and around the eye, together with the black facial patch extending in a wedge-shape to the chin, all suggest *Melithreptus lunatus*.

CF

[1]Lambert was a personal friend of Lord Derby and fellow member of the Linnean Society of London. Two of the botanical paintings from his collection and one of the mammals are also included in the Catalogue (Catalogue nos. 14 & 84). [2]Latham 1801, *Gen. Syn. Suppl.* 2: 74. [3]See, for example, Mathews 1930: 684. [4]C.T. Fisher (unpublished); a view shared by R. Schodde (in litt. 2001). [5]Described in *Index Ornithologicus, Suppl.*: 38. [6]Latham 1822, 4: 204.

9. KOKAKO
Family Callaeidae (New Zealand wattlebirds)

Cinereous Wattle Bird.

The 13th Earl of Derby's first major acquisition of natural history material was the purchase of over 100 bird specimens at the sale of the Leverian Museum in 1806, including some which had been obtained on the voyages of Captain James Cook. The 'Cinereous Wattle Bird', Lot 2698, was bought for £1-16-0 on Friday 30th May, the 23rd day of the sale. It was most probably collected at Queen Charlotte Sound on Cook's second voyage (1773-1774) and passed to Sir Ashton Lever via Sir Joseph Banks.[1] While in the Leverian Museum, John Latham examined, painted and subsequently described the bird for the first time. The specimen was without doubt also the model for the account that appears in George Shaw's *Museum Leverianum* (1793, 1: 239-240), with an accompanying illustration by Charles Reuben Ryley.[2]

Latham's (1781: 365) notes on the biology of this species were derived from observations by Johann Reinhold Forster, official naturalist on Cook's second voyage: "The bird inhabits *New Zealand* throughout: it is often seen walking on the ground, and sometimes perched on trees, though less frequent: its food consists of various articles; berries of all kinds, and insects; and, according to the relation of some, small birds also. The flesh is good to eat, and was by some accounted even savoury. It has a kind of note not unlike whistling, and sometimes a kind of murmuring, though not an unpleasing one".

The typical form of this species is confined to forests in the southern islands of New Zealand, where it is endangered; the total population was estimated at about 1000 birds in 1989.[3] The North Island Kokako, *Callaeas cinerea wilsoni* is more common.

ML

[1]Medway 1976. [2]Largen 1987.
[3]Knox & Walters 1994: 270.

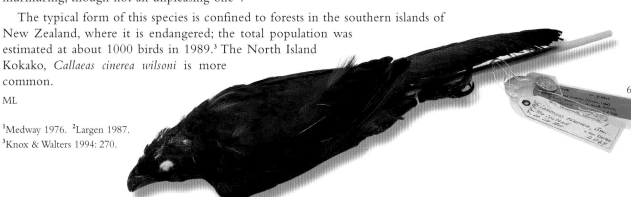

61

Original paintings from the third of a series of bound volumes entitled 'The natural history of Jamaica' by L.J. Robins, 1765, dismounted for exhibition (K).

Top left Untitled, '37'. Depicts a male and female Great Curassow *Crax rubra*. 397 x 278mm.

Top right 'Psittacus Aracanga. 13'. Apparently represents the Cuban Red Macaw *Ara tricolor*. 392 x 275mm.

The Cuban Red Macaw, which is known almost entirely from museum specimens, appears to have become extinct long before the close of the nineteenth century.[1] A spectacularly beautiful bird, about 500mm in length, it was reported to nest in holes in palm trees. Strangely, it has never been recorded from Jamaica, but then neither have any species of curassow. The existence of both *Ara tricolor* and *Crax rubra* (a native of Central and South America) among Robins' paintings seems to indicate either that the artist sometimes worked in locations other than Jamaica, or that he occasionally illustrated captive birds imported to that island.

Bottom left 'Picus. 26. April 30 1765'. Illustrates two male birds and seven chicks of the Jamaican Woodpecker *Melanerpes radiolatus*. 412 x 315mm.

Bottom right 'Certhia … 1. 2. 3. C. flaveola. Harapple (Chrysophyllum Gainito)'. Depicts at top: possibly a female Common Yellowthroat *Geothlypis trichas*; bird with chicks: Bananaquit *Coereba flaveola*; second from bottom: possibly a Cerulean Warbler *Dendroica cerulea* (a very rare migrant to Jamaica); at bottom: possibly a Black-and-white Warbler *Mniotilta varia*. 396 x 274mm.

Unfortunately, very little is known about Lieutenant Robins. His bird paintings, many of which appear to have been based on live specimens, display considerable artistic talent and enormous (if frustratingly vague) ornithological enthusiasm. This lack of precision means that some of his subjects are very difficult to identify with certainty. Other volumes of Robins' work housed at Knowsley Hall contain paintings of plants and invertebrates.

CF & EF

[1]Greenway 1967, Fuller 2001.

11. TWO PAINTINGS FROM THE COLLECTION OF LADY IMPEY
Families Cuculidae (cuckoos) and Anatidae (ducks, geese & swans)

Sir Elijah Impey was Chief Justice of the Supreme Court in Calcutta from 1774 to 1783. His wife Mary joined him there in 1777 and established on their estate a considerable aviary and menagerie, including many species of Asian birds and mammals which were at that time still unknown to western scientists. Lady Impey commissioned numerous watercolours of her living specimens, primarily employing three artists from Patna: Shaikh Zayn-al-Din and the brothers Bhawani and Ram Das. All were trained in the tradition of Mughal miniature painting.

Lady Impey brought these paintings to England in 1783 and they were sold at auction in May 1810, following her husband's death during the previous year. At the sale, or possibly subsequently, the 13th Earl of Derby acquired about 20 of the paintings and it was four of these that were purchased by the Liverpool Museum in 1998.[1]

The paintings are of scientific importance primarily because, while still in the possession of Lady Impey, many were examined by the distinguished ornithologist John Latham (1740-1837), who used them as a basis for his descriptions of several new species. Consequently, they effectively became type specimens (and pictures such as these are sometimes called 'iconotypes').

Latham's description of *Anas caryophyllacea*[4] may not have been based exclusively on the painting in Lady Impey's possession, but there can be little doubt that he must have seen and been influenced by Bhawani Das's drawing.[5] This species, apparently never very common, is now almost certainly extinct. It fell victim to the drainage of its former marshland habitat in northeast India, exacerbated by the merciless slaughter executed by pith-helmeted servants of the Britsh Raj, for whom this handsome bird held a peculiar attraction. The species seems to have disappeared as a wild bird during the 1930s, a date which corresponds very closely with the death of the last known captive specimen - at Foxwarren Park in Surrey. There is no evidence that the 13th Earl of Derby ever possessed live Pink-headed Ducks, but he did have three museum specimens. These are now in the Liverpool Museum.

CF, SG & JK

Above left Portrait in pencil and watercolour, heightened with white and gum arabic, executed in 1782 by Shaikh Zayn-al-Din and depicting the Lesser Cuckoo *Cuculus poliocephalus* Latham 1790. 527 x 663mm (LM 1999.36.2).

When Latham described *Cuculus poliocephalus*,[2] he observed that his account was derived 'from the drawings of Lady Impey'.[3] This is a relatively common forest species, widely distributed from Japan to eastern Africa and ranging in altitude from sea level to over 3600m in the Himalayas.

Above right Watercolour, heightened with white, painted during the period 1777-82 by Bhawani Das and depicting the Pink-headed Duck *Rhodonessa caryophyllacea* (Latham 1790). 340 x 473mm (LM 1999.36.4).

[1]See Christies' catalogues for the *Visions of India* sale, 17th June 1998: 134 (lots 170 & 171) and *Natural History* sale, 19th May 1998: 112 (lot 88) and 119 (lot 94). [2]Latham 1790: 214. [3]Latham 1822, 3: 269. [4]Latham 1790: 866. [5]Fisher & Kear (in press).

12. BLUE JAY
Family Corvidae (crows)

Above Plate 15 in Catesby's *Natural History of Carolina, Florida, and the Bahama Islands*; a hand-coloured lithograph of 'The Blew Jay', later copied in watercolour by Lord Stanley. 255 x 350mm (K).

Right Watercolour by Lord Stanley depicting a Blue Jay *Cyanocitta cristata*, copied from the illustration of 'The Blew Jay' in Catesby's *Natural History of Carolina, Florida, and the Bahama Islands*. 274 x 396mm (K).

Mark Catesby (1683-1749), a largely self-taught naturalist and artist, was born in England but spent 13 years of his life collecting and studying plants and animals in the New World. In 1826, he finally settled in London and began to prepare his monumental account of *The Natural History of Carolina, Florida, and the Bahama Islands*, issued in 11 parts of 20 plates each between 1729 and 1743, with an Appendix in 1747. Shortly after its completion, the Secretary of the Royal Society declared this publication to be "the most magnificent work I know since the art of printing has been discovered". Catesby's great work laid the foundations of American natural history and became the standard reference on this subject for many years, until eventually superseded by the contributions of Alexander Wilson and John James Audubon.

It is hardly surprising that Lord Stanley should have owned and treasured a copy of Catesby's outstandingly important publication, or that he should have chosen to make copies of many of the plates.

The Blue Jay is a frequent and familiar bird in many parts of North America, occupying woodland, suburban gardens and even towns, from southern Canada, through the eastern half of the United States to Florida.

ML

13. WESTERN STRIPE-HEADED TANAGER
Family Emberizidae (buntings, seedeaters & tanagers)

Above Plate 42 in Catesby's *Natural History of Carolina, Florida, and the Bahama Islands*; a hand-coloured lithograph of 'The Bahama Finch', later copied in watercolour by Lord Stanley. 263 x 356mm (K).

Left Watercolour by Lord Stanley depicting a Western Stripe-headed Tanager *Spindalis zena*, dated 24th December 1804 and copied from the illustration of 'The Bahama Finch' in Mark Catesby's *Natural History of Carolina, Florida, and the Bahama Islands*. 205 x 294mm (K).

In the early nineteenth century, when lithography was still in its infancy, the only way for Lord Stanley to obtain a set of illustrations, which he could then file in taxonomic order, was to make copies of the plates in the few published works then available. Two thick volumes of the copies he made of bird illustrations still survive at Knowsley; he must often have consulted these as a reference system for the birds of the world.

The Western Stripe-headed Tanager is a common resident, especially in woodland, of the Bahamas, Cuba, Grand Cayman and several smaller Caribbean islands.

ML

14. EASTERN QUOLL
Family Dasyuridae (quolls, devils, antechinuses)

Watercolour of two Eastern Quolls *Dasyurus viverrinus* with a slaughtered chicken. 'Pl. 5' from volume one (zoology) of bound original paintings (the 'Lambert Drawings', executed by settlers (probably convict artists) soon after the 1788 landing of the 'First Fleet' in Australia).[1] 220 x 160mm (K).

One of the first mammals encountered by the settlers of Australia's 'First Fleet' was the Eastern Quoll (or Eastern Native Cat), a carnivorous marsupial. At around a kilogram in weight, they are about half the size of a domestic cat, and are capable and fearless predators. This watercolour shows animals of two colours; they can be either black or fawn but always have white spots. Quolls were doubtless common around Sydney Harbour in the 1790s, where they would have fed on dead creatures washed up by the tide, and on smaller mammals and insects. They would have been very attracted to the hen-houses of the first fleeters and this painting is clearly the result of one such unfortunate encounter. Indeed the next two plates in this volume of the Lambert drawings, also of native cats, are ruefully inscribed " … very destructive to Poultry" and "… killed in a Fowl House where it had destroyed 20 Hens &c.". The infant settlement in Sydney Cove came perilously close to starvation in its early years, so the loss of any of the colony's chickens would have been counted as a catastrophe of the first order.

The Eastern Quoll once inhabited coastal regions from South Australia to New South Wales, but is now restricted to Tasmania. It seems likely that the introduction of foxes was responsible for their demise, although diseases and changed fire management may have played a role as well. They had disappeared from most of the mainland by the 1920s, but a relict population survived in inner Sydney (quite close to where this portrait was probably painted) until around 1970. Residents of the Vaucluse area would set out bowls of cat food for these last few quolls, but nothing was done officially to help them. Their ultimate demise may have come about as the result of a parks beautification program, during which a vast thicket of the aggressive weed Lantana was uprooted and burned, depriving them of cover.

TF

[1]See 'Weebong & Agile Honeycreeper' (Catalogue entry 8), and the two botanical plates illustrated in Catalogue entry 84, which are also from the Lambert volumes.

15. NUMBAT

Family Myrmecobiidae (the Numbat)[1]

Above Plate 4 from volume one of Gould's *Mammals of Australia*, a hand-coloured lithograph depicting the 'Banded Myrmecobius'. 395 x 510mm (K).

Left Lithographic proof entitled 'Myrmecobius fasciatus, Waterh[ouse] … Col[oure]d by J. Gould. Hab. Australia', from a bound volume of 'Original drawings of Australian animals' by John Gould & Henry Richter. This was the proof for the illustration of the 'Banded Myrmecobius' in Gould's *Mammals of Australia*. 395 x 510mm (K).

Below Cabinet skin and skull of adult Numbat *Myrmecobius fasciatus*, collected at Toodyay, Western Australia (probably in 1842) by John Gilbert.[2] Length of cabinet skin to end of tail 490mm (LM D.44a).

The Numbat, the emblem of the state of Western Australia, is a strikingly-banded marsupial which inhabits woodland and forest, where it excavates termites from their shallow runways. It was once widespread across much of southern Australia, but is now seriously endangered and confined to a small area of the extreme south-west.[3]

John Gilbert made extensive notes[4] on 'this beautiful little animal', which were used by his employer, John Gould, in his *Mammals of Australia*. Gilbert wrote that Numbats appeared much like squirrels when running and if pursued took to hollows in dead trees, where they could be heard making 'a sort of half-smothered grunt'. They were called 'Noom-bats' by the Aborigines of the York and Toodyay districts of Western Australia.

CF

[1]The Numbat is highly specialised for feeding on termites, which makes it so different from all other marsupials that it is classified in a separate family of its own. [2]Liverpool Museum did have two of Gilbert's specimens, although one was exchanged with Leeds City Museum in 1860 and cannot now be found. There are two in the BMNH, one of which was also collected at Toodyay and still has the original collecting date attached (6th September 1842). [3]Strahan 1995: 159-162. [4]These comments were entered into a manuscript notebook, based on a copy of G.R. Waterhouse's *Marsupialia*, which Gilbert had cut up and pasted with additonal notes of his own. This notebook is now in the Queensland Museum Library, Brisbane.

16. PIG-FOOTED BANDICOOT
Family Peramelidae (bandicoots & bilbies)

Above Sketch entitled 'Chestnut-eared Choeropus' and depicting three Pig-footed Bandicoots *Chaeropus ecaudatus* (Ogilby 1838).[1] This was the preliminary sketch for the illustration of the species in John Gould's *Mammals of Australia* and must have been executed either by Gould himself or by his assistant Henry Constantine Richter. 315 x 475mm (BMNH © The Natural History Museum, London).

Right Hand-coloured lithographic proof entitled 'Chaeropus castanotis. Lithographic Proof col[oure]d by J. Gould. Hab. Australia', from a bound volume entitled 'Original drawings of Australian animals'.[2] The drawing, although unsigned, is probably by H.C. Richter and was the proof for Plate 6 in the first volume of Gould's *Mammals of Australia*,[3] which depicts *Chaeropus ecaudatus*. 360 x 495mm (K).

John Gilbert collected at least two specimens of Pig-footed Bandicoot in Western Australia in 1843, but these were at first thought to be from an undescribed species because, unlike the mutilated type specimen of *Chaeropus ecaudatus*, they had tails.[4] John Gould recognized the error only after he had named them *Chaeropus occidentalis* in 1845. The preliminary sketch and lithographic proof both show three animals, which can be individually identified. The two browner animals on either side are those collected by Gilbert in Western Australia, while the greyer individual is probably the one obtained by George Grey in South Australia.

The Pig-footed bandicoot is one of the most bizarre and little known of Australian animals. It was once widespread in arid regions of the continent but only about twenty specimens were ever collected, the last in 1901, and the animal has not been seen for more than fifty years.[5] With only two functional toes on the forefoot, it is presumed these creatures probably behaved rather like small deer.
CF

---

[1] This species was first discovered in 1836 by Sir Thomas Mitchell, but the specimen he collected had lost its tail, hence the inappropriate scientific name *ecaudatus*, applied two years later by W. Ogilby. [2] Another proof lithograph of Pig-footed Bandicoots is bound into the same volume, but this version was never published by Gould. It is signed by H.C. Richter and inscribed 'Choeropus castanotis, young'. This picture shows two greyish animals, probably from South Australia, and was eventually published on the cover of *Australian Zoologist* (Fisher 1988). [3] Gould 1845b-1863. [4] See Fisher (1985) for details of a letter written by Gilbert to Gould in April 1843 (LVRO). The specimen mentioned in this letter was subsequently sold by Gould to Lord Derby, who was later given another specimen by Charles Sturt. Both were unfortunately destroyed when the Liverpool Museum was firebombed in 1941; most of the mammals were on display and only the cabinet skins were moved out of Liverpool to safety during the second world war. The second of Gilbert's specimens, obtained north-east of Northam in October 1843, survives at the BMNH (1844.7.9.22), as does George Grey's animal from South Australia. [5] Strahan 1995: 170-171.

17. GAMBIAN SUN SQUIRREL
Family Sciuridae (squirrels)

Virtually nothing is yet known about Thomas Whitfield before or after the nine-year period during which he worked for Lord Derby in West Africa. Between 1841 and 1849, he spent much time in the Gambia and Sierra Leone, his main objective being the collection of live mammals, birds and plants for the Earl's estate and he seems to have preserved only those animals which died after confinement. Once an adequate cargo of livestock had been assembled, Whitfield would accompany it back to London on the first available ship and then arrange for its conveyance to Liverpool by rail.[1] He was a highly accomplished collector who brought back to England the first examples of many species new to science, including several specimens of the Lord Derby's Eland (*Taurotragus derbianus*).

The Gambian Sun Squirrel is common in woodland and savanna habitats from Senegal to Ethiopia, southwards to Tanzania and Angola.

ML

[1]Largen & Fisher 1986.

Cabinet skin (with separate skull, shown enlarged below), derived from a formerly mounted specimen of *Heliosciurus gambianus*, brought alive from West Africa by Thomas Whitfield and housed in the Knowsley Menagerie until its death in December 1845. Length (of skin to end of tail) 440mm (LM D.43).

69

18. LONG-TAILED HOPPING MOUSE
Family Muridae (rats and mice)

Right Watercolour, entitled 'Hapalotis Gouldii', from a bound volume entitled 'Original drawings of Australian animals' by John Gould and Henry Constantine Richter. Unsigned, but probably drafted by Gould and finished by Richter. The painting depicts two *Notomys longicaudatus* and the models were probably the two Gilbert specimens now in The Natural History Museum (see endnote[1]). This painting is the original from which Gould derived his plate of the 'Long-tailed Hapalotis' in the first volume of *Mammals of Australia*. 505 x 310mm (K).

Below Cabinet skin of adult Long-tailed Hopping Mouse *Notomys longicaudatus*, collected by John Gilbert at the Moore River, Western Australia on 7th July 1843. A type specimen[1] from the series originally described by John Gould in 1844 as *Hapalotis longicaudata*. Length (with tail) 350mm (LM D.412a).

When he first described this species, John Gould seems to have had access only to museum specimens.[2] Later, field notes provided by John Gilbert allowed a more detailed account to be published in *Mammals of Australia*.[3] Gilbert observed that these rodents lived in mounds thrown up by other, larger, mammals and were pests of food stores, being 'extremely fond of raisins'.

The Long-tailed Hopping Mouse was once widespread in arid and semi-arid Australia, from the Western Australian coast to western parts of Queensland and New South Wales. The animal has not been seen alive since 1902 and, apart from Gilbert's hugely valuable field notes, very little is known about its biology.[4]

CF

[1]LM D.142 and D.142a are both paralectotypes, the former collected at Toodyay in September 1843. The lectotype (from the Moore River) is at the BMNH (1844.7.9.15), along with a further paralectotype (1844.2.15.28, collected at Victoria Plains on 20th August 1842). All were collected by John Gilbert. [2]Gould 1844b. [3]Gould 1845b-1863. [4]Strahan 1995: 577-578.

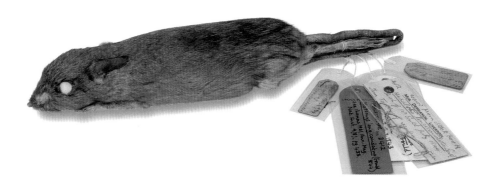

19. RED-FLANKED DUIKER
Family Bovidae (antelopes, cattle, sheep and goats)

Above Skull. Possible paratype of *Cephalophus rufilatus* Gray 1846, *Ann. Mag. Nat. Hist.* (1) 18: 166, collected in West Africa by Thomas Whitfield. Length of skull 150mm (LM D.53a?).

Left Watercolour, painted by Joseph Wolf in August 1850, depicting *Cephalophus rufilatus* and most probably based on mounted specimens in the Knowsley Museum, brought from West Africa by Thomas Whitfield. 370 x 545mm (K).

John Edward Gray[1] described *Cephalophus rufilatus* on the basis of specimens that included a female holotype[2] and a male. Both specimens at that time were 'in the museum of the Earl of Derby' (D.53 and 53a, respectively) and had been collected in West Africa by Thomas Whitfield. One at least reached England alive, since the female is recorded as having died in the Knowsley Menagerie during September 1843. Subsequently, Whitfield imported another live female (from the River Gambia), which must have been the mother of a young male that died in November 1847, shortly after its birth at Knowsley (D.53c and 53b).

On 16th August 1850, Joseph Wolf executed a painting at Knowsley that depicts two clearly different Red-flanked Duikers. Wolf must have based at least one of these animals on a type specimen. As Thomas Moore's (1851) catalogue of the mammals then alive on the estate makes no mention of *Cephalophus rufilatus*, the inference must be that all living examples of this antelope in Lord Derby's possession had died by 1850. Wolf therefore must have worked from mounted specimens preserved in the Knowsley Museum.

The only remnant of these animals that survives today is a single, inadequately labelled skull (the skin of the holotype is recorded as having been 'destroyed by order' on 20th June 1900). If one accepts as correct the symbol inscribed on this skull, then it is from the male paratype (D.53a), but further research is needed in order to establish this point beyond doubt.

Distributed from Senegal to northwestern Uganda, this antelope is still relatively common in riverine thickets and forest remnants within the savanna zone, though declining in areas heavily populated by humans.

ML

[1]Gray, J.E. 1846b. [2]Obtained at the village of Waterloo in Sierra Leone.

20. SNAPPING TURTLE
Family Chelydridae (snapping turtles)

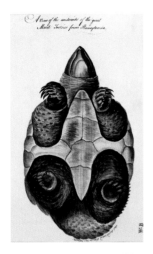

Two watercolours, painted by William Bartram (1739-1823), which depict a specimen of *Chelydra serpentina*. Side view 231 x 300mm: ventral view 211 x 325mm (K).

William Bartram was the first and certainly one of the most influential of the native-born American artist-naturalists. Based in Philadelphia, where his father established a world-renowned Botanic Garden,[1] Bartram achieved distinction as an enthusiastic and gifted observer and illustrator of plants, birds and other North American wildlife. He was clearly very familiar with the animal that he called 'The great Mud Tortoise from Pennsylvania', a species since discovered to have a much wider distribution and now more appropriately named the Snapping Turtle. It is common in all freshwater habitats from southern Canada through the eastern half of the United States to Ecuador.

This reptile, which can exceed 50 cm in length, is notorious for its aggressive disposition, an ability to strike repeatedly with great speed, and the possession of jaws that are quite capable of tearing human flesh. The typical offensive posture adopted by this animal when on land is to stand with hindquarters raised and mouth agape, before lunging forward at its victim. The accuracy with which this behaviour has been illustrated in one of Bartram's paintings leaves little doubt that the artist had personal experience of being threatened by a Snapping Turtle.

ML

[1]See Catalogue entry 71.

21. CANEBRAKE RATTLESNAKE
Family Viperidae (vipers, adders and rattlesnakes)

Two watercolours, painted in 1809 by Sydenham Edwards (1768-1819) and depicting a specimen of *Crotalus horridus atricaudatus*. 217 x 166mm; 219 x 167mm (K).

Notes appended to Edwards' paintings provide the information that this snake, six feet in length, was 'drawn from life' after having been 'brought to England by Mr. Fraser, Aug. 1809'. The animal is identified as a 'Black tailed Rattlesnake, La Crotale a queue noire. Latreille' – epithets that could easily lead to confusion with the species currently called the Black-tailed Rattlesnake (*Crotalus molossus*). In fact, Edwards' comments refer to a different reptile, the Canebrake Rattlesnake, to which Latreille in 1802 applied the name *atricaudatus* (from the Latin *ater* = black, *cauda* = tail).

All rattlesnakes are highly venomous and most give warning of their presence by rapidly vibrating the characteristic rattle at the tip of the tail. This consists of a series of loosely attached, hollow shells of keratin, to which a new segment is added each time the animal sheds its skin.

Crotalus horridus is widespread in eastern regions of the United States, with the subspecies *atricaudatus* occupying thickets and swamplands in the southern part of this range.

ML

22. ROYAL PYTHON
Family Pythonidae (pythons)

Little is known about Thomas Whitfield, although he collected for Lord Derby in West Africa between 1841 and 1849 (mostly in the Gambia and Sierra Leone). His main purpose was to obtain live mammals, birds and plants for the Earl's menagerie and he appears to have preserved only those animals which died during transportation. Lord Derby seems never to have been greatly interested in reptiles and those that he happened to acquire were generally passed to the British Museum, where his friend John Edward Gray was Keeper of Zoology.

The name of this snake was inspired by its splendid colour pattern and is not a reflection of the animal's size. Appreciably smaller than the more widespread and familiar African Python (*Python sebae*), it rarely exceeds 6 feet (1900mm) in length. Gentle, inoffensive and nocturnal, the Royal Python feeds mainly on small mammals and, when alarmed, has a tendency to coil its body into an almost perfect sphere. This explains why it is sometimes called the 'Ball Python'. It is distributed in savanna habitats from Senegal to southern Sudan and Uganda.

ML

23. RUTELID BEETLE

Two watercolours of the Rutelid Beetle *Chrysina macropus* by Sydenham Teast Edwards, undated. One version is inscribed 'Scarabus Kangurus'. 194 x 235mm and 210 x 286mm (K).

These colourful paintings are of a rather uncommon beetle, which is only found in the Potosi region of Mexico, where it is thinly distributed. The beetles are quite large (about 40mm long) and are highly valued by collectors.[1] Very little is known about their biology. The bright colours mimic those of distasteful insects and probably serve to confuse predators

Sydenham Edwards (1768-1819) was born in Usk, Monmouthshire and was trained by the botanist William Curtis, becoming the principal artist for the *Botanical Magazine*. He also composed zoological pictures and is known to have used Leverian Museum specimens as models for some of his bird paintings.[2] It is possible this beetle was in that collection.

It has not yet been possible to trace the source of the name 'Scarabus Kangurus', though 'Scarabus' probably represents a mis-spelling of 'Scarabaeus'.

IW

[1] Identification and information provided by Malcolm Kerley of the BMNH. [2] Jackson 1999: 232

a) Queen Conch, *Strombus gigas* (family Strombidae). Length 300mm (BMNH 1837.10.12.21).

b) Deer Antler Murex, *Chicoreus cornucervi* (family Muricidae). Originally labelled *Murex aranea*. Port Essington. Length 64mm (BMNH 1845.5.13.97).

c) Comb Pen Shell, *Atrina pectinata* (family Pinnidae). Originally labelled *Pinna strangei* form *assimilis*. Port Essington. Length 200mm (BMNH 1953.3.26.48. All three photographs by NMGM © The Natural History Museum).

(a) This shell is one of two from the West Indies given to the British Museum by Lord Derby in 1837.

Strombus gigas is found throughout the Caribbean, where it is widely used for food. The empty shells can be seen on sale to tourists throughout the region, although recently there has been a call for the species to be officially listed as endangered because it is threatened by over-fishing. The shell is also used to make buttons and inexpensive cameos and this species is also known to produce a pink pearl.

(b) This striking specimen was presented to the British Museum by the 13th Earl of Derby in 1845, part of a donation of 255 shells from Port Essington, at that time the only British settlement in northern Australia. Many of these had been collected by John MacGillivray, who was one of Lord Derby's sponsored collectors. MacGillivray was on board H.M.S. *Fly* during the British Navy's survey of the north coast of Australia, the Torres Straits and New Guinea between 1842 and 1846. The crew of the *Fly* dropped MacGillivray off at Port Essington to collect; he stayed there from September 1844 to January 1845. MacGillivray's original label is still kept with the specimen.

Chicoreus cornucervi is found only in northern Australia, where it is fairly common. Specimens from the Torres Straits (found at a depth of 20-40 metres) are smaller and more delicately formed than those collected on the northwest coast, where they live in shallow water under overhanging rock ledges.

(c) This is another of the Port Essington shells collected by John MacGillivray and donated to the British Museum by Lord Derby, probably in 1845, but it was not given a registration number until 1953.

Atrina pectinata is distributed in warm waters throughout southern and southeastern Asia, the East Indies, northern Australia and Melanesia. It is unusual to find a dried specimen still with the byssus, as it is in this case. The byssal threads anchor the shell to the substratum in life and are extremely strong; indeed they can be woven or knitted into a fine gold fabric, thought by some to be the origin of the legend of the Golden Fleece.

The 13th Earl of Derby was a friend and correspondent of many of the shell collectors and dealers of his day. Perhaps most notable was Hugh Cuming, an indefatigable traveller whose shell collection of over 60,000 lots was purchased by the British Museum in 1866. It was through the Earl's influence with the Spanish ambassador that Cuming obtained letters from Madrid guaranteeing him the assistance and protection of the authorities in the Philippine Islands, during his travels there in 1836-1840.

Between 1837 and 1851, Lord Derby himself presented almost 1000 shells and other invertebrates to the British Museum. The two earliest donations were bivalves from West Africa, registered in May 1837, then the specimens from Port Essington arrived in May 1845, followed by 636 more Australian shells in September 1846.

KW

Watercolour by Georg Ehret of three marine gastropod shells, from a bound volume of his paintings entitled 'Original drawings, botany & shells'. Top: West Indian Top Shell *Cittarium pica*, a common species sometimes used in the manufacture of pearl buttons. Centre: Atlantic Deer Cowry *Cypraea cervus*, the largest cowry, which is found from North Carolina southwards to the Caribbean and Cuba but is now endangered due to over-collecting and pollution. Lower figure: Bullmouth Helmet *Cypraecassis rufa*, from the tropical Indo-Pacific, which is the most widely-used shell for cameo-making. 313 x 451mm (K).

All three shells are listed as being among material from the collection of Ralph Willett of Merly, Dorset, sold at auction by Philipe in May, 1814.

The library at Knowsley contains other fine original shell plates by Georg Ehret (there are 14 in this volume). There are also ten mollusc plates painted by Lieutenant J. L. Robins, in one of the volumes of his 'Natural History of Jamaica', circa 1770. These plates show West Indian slugs, sea slugs, cephalopods, gastropods and bivalves. The library also holds some illustrations by Sarah Stone of shells from the Leverian Museum and from Gregson's sale of 1830.

KW

77

26. SARAH STONE

Watercolours from a bound volume of paintings by Sarah Stone (K).

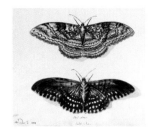

Above Top: dorsal view and below: ventral view, of the moth *Thysania* (probably *T. aggripina*), inscribed 'Sarah Stone Decr 4 1778 Phal[aena] Attae Habit. In Indies'. 270 x 360mm.

Right Male birdwing butterfly *Ornithoptera priamus*, from Java and Borneo. Top: ventral view; below: dorsal view. Inscribed 'Sarah Stone 1780'. 310 x 355mm.

Top: Five sea anemones. The four large specimens are of the Dahlia Anemone *Urticina felina*. The smallest is the Beadlet Anemone *Actinia equina*. 265 x 330mm.

Bottom: Five sea anemones. The two largest specimens are Dahlia Anemones and the three smaller ones are Beadlets. 265 x 330mm.

The birdwing has one of the largest wing-spans of any butterfly and the dull-coloured female is even bigger than the male. At the time this illustration was painted, it would have been the largest species of butterfly known to science.

The moth has the greatest wing-span of any insect. It is found in South and Central America, and the extreme south of the USA, where it is called a 'White Witch'. The underside can only be seen when the insect flies, and the sudden flash of black and white on the body and underwings is used to startle predators.

Both Dahlia and Beadlet Anemones are common on rocky British coasts. Since all her subjects appear to be attached at the base and several are fully expanded, Sarah Stone must have painted them from life to show the variety of forms these soft-bodied animals can adopt. One (c: top right) is depicted with the stomach everted – a behaviour commonly adopted for the ejection of undigested food. Red Beadlet Anemones are most common, brown and green forms rarer and, in nature, all the colours tend to be brighter than illustrated here.

Sarah Stone (Mrs John Smith, 1761/2-1844) was one of the most famous natural history painters of the late eighteenth and early nineteenth centuries. Many of her compositions were done at the Leverian Museum, where she was introduced to Edward Smith Stanley. Lord Stanley obviously admired her work and purchased many of her paintings, mostly at the sale of Sir Ashton Lever's possessions at Alkrington, near Manchester, following his death in 1788.

CEJ & IW

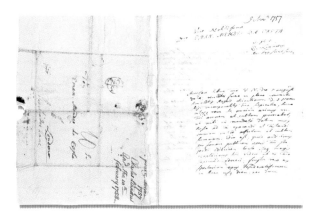

This letter was sent by Carl Linnaeus, the distinguished Swedish naturalist and Professor of Botany at the University of Uppsala, to Emanuel Mendes da Costa, Clerk of the Royal Society in London. On the reverse of Linnaeus's letter, da Costa noted that he answered on 10th February 1758.

Two sides of an autograph letter from Carl Linnaeus (Carl von Linné, 1707-1778) to Dr Emanuel Mendes da Costa (1717-1791), dated 9th November 1757. From a volume of autographed portraits and letters, dismounted for exhibition. 162 x 211mm, folded (K).

Carl Linnaeus is known as the founding father of the science of taxonomy, or biological classification; he devised the system of binomial naming of plants and animals which is still used today. His important collection of zoological and botanical specimens, books and manuscripts is now housed in the Linnean Society of London, off Piccadilly. Linnaeus must have been particularly revered by the 13th Earl of Derby, who was President of the Linnean Society between 1828 and 1834.

Emanuel Mendes da Costa was the London-based son of a Portuguese merchant,[1] whose main interests were in conchology and palaeontology. Linnaeus's letter demonstrates the scientific esteem in which da Costa was held. The Royal Society of Sciences in Sweden had read a recent letter from da Costa, and Linnaeus reported that "Your peerless wisdom and unique humane qualities inspired such love and sympathy for you that I was given the task to express these feelings and assure you of everybody's affection and high esteem".[2] The society were waiting with anxiety for a copy of a publication by da Costa, probably his *Natural History of Fossils*, as Linnaeus needed it for a work he was planning on 'singular stones'.

A translation of this letter was published by Sir James Edward Smith in 1821[3] and more recently another has been made by Johnny Strand of the Linnaean Letters Project.[4]

JE

[1]Goodwin 1887. [2]In 1768 da Costa was dismissed from his post at the Royal Society and later imprisoned for dishonesty. [3]Smith 1821: 488-489. [4]This translation is available from NMGM and from the Linnean Society.

Above Letter from Audubon to Mrs Rathbone of Greenbank Hall,[6] dated 10th September 1826, regarding the forwarding of letters from Audubon's family. From the same volume as below (K).

Right Engraving of John James Audubon, by Charles Wands after a portrait by John Syme, S.A. From a volume of autographed letters and portraits, temporarily dismounted for exhibition. 100 x 123mm (K).

Lord Stanley first met the American naturalist and artist John James Audubon (1795-1851) at the home of a Mr A. Hodgson near Liverpool in August 1826. He was so impressed by Audubon's knowledge of birds and his artistic talent, that he invited the self-declared 'American Woodsman' to call on him at his home in Grosvenor Street when Audubon was in London. Thus began a cordial and mutually beneficial relationship that would extend over a period of twenty years. Edward Stanley became a subscriber to Audubon's many publications, including his double elephant folio *The birds of America*. Audubon, in return, helped him obtain specimens of North American birds and mammals for the Knowsley aviary and menagerie, and for his museum collection. Audubon also named what he thought to be a new species of North American hawk *Falco stanleyi* ('Stanley Hawk') in his

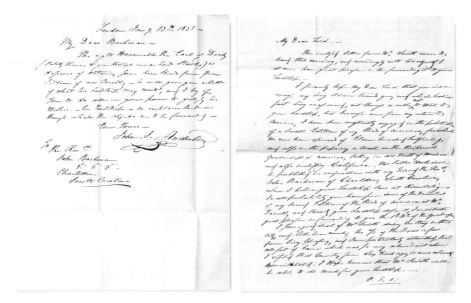

Far left Letter from Audubon in London to the Reverend John Bachman in Charleston, South Carolina, dated 13th January 1835. The letter is on behalf of Lord Derby and is a request for living American birds for Knowsley (K).

Left Letter from Audubon at 86, White Street, New York to Lord Derby at 'Knowseley', enclosing a letter from William Smith, dated 21st December 1841. Smith's letter, from Houston, Texas and dated 30th November 1841, describes the local fauna and flora and his attempts to procure living animals for Lord Derby; for this purpose Smith requests financial assistance. Audubon apologises for his 'long silence', for which he blames the production of *Viviparous quadrupeds*, and sends Lord Derby the first part of this publication. Audubon hoped Smith would be able to help the Earl and offers to personally collect for Lord Derby on a proposed expedition to the Rocky Mountains and the Yellowstone River[1] (K).

honour.[2] Unfortunately this bird had already been named *Falco cooperi* by Charles Lucien Bonaparte, in honour of the American ornithologist William Cooper, so Audubon's name for the hawk is now recognised only as a synonym.

There are no surviving documents to suggest that Lord Derby ever commissioned Audubon to paint the living specimens in his collection, as he did Edward Lear, Benjamin Waterhouse Hawkins and Joseph Wolf, but Audubon may have requested permission to do so on his own behalf when he was gathering information for his book *The viviparous quadrupeds of North America* in the late 1830s and early 1840s. Audubon's friend and co-author, the Reverend John Bachman (1790-1874), urged Audubon[3] to seek out and paint the American Moose [Elk][4] and other large North American mammals that were then living at Knowsley.

Such was his admiration for Audubon, that in November 1842 Lord Derby asked John Gould to obtain an engraving of Audubon on his behalf. Gould was happy to oblige, responding on 19th December 1842[5] that he had "purchased a plate of Audubon … with his own autograph written beneath". Gould may have been referring to this print, which is after a portrait by John Syme. In any case, Lord Derby's request for a visual memento to keep with an autographed letter from Audubon to Mrs Rathbone, of Greenbank Hall,[6] gives testament to the high regard in which he held the American naturalist.

RMP

[1]There is another letter from Audubon to Derby in the Knowsley collections, dated 9th January 1835. This concerns a live Snowy Owl and other birds from Nova Scotia. [2]Audubon 1831, pl. 36. [3]Letter from Bachman to Audubon, 5th July 1839, which refers to 'the moose [Elk] at Earl Derby's'. Bachman Papers at Charleston Museum. [4]Joseph Wolf was probably at Knowsley in October 1850 when he composed his delightful painting of Elk in snow. See Catalogue entry 50. [5]NHM General Library, Gould Collection. [6]Now part of the University of Liverpool campus, just off Sefton Park in south Liverpool. Audubon stayed with the Rathbones while he was in Liverpool, and did several drawings for the family. One, a watercolour of a European Robin, drawn for Miss Hannah Rathbone (with whom, from the inscription, Audubon had been unsuccessfully flirting), is now in the University of Liverpool's art collections.

Lithographs of the Ivory-billed Woopecker (opposite) and (left to right) the Passenger Pigeon, cut from John James Audubon's *The birds of America* (1827-1838) and the Great Auk and the Purple Heron by Edward Lear, from John Gould's *The birds of Europe*. 250 x 365mm approx (K).

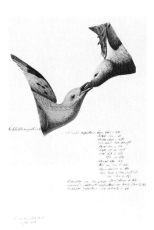

Among the most remarkable reference works in the library at Knowsley is a set of thirteen large box files, which contain visual representations of bird species from all over the world. The contents of these boxes were originally assembled by the English naturalist and publisher John Gould to use as a reference tool, "for a general history of Birds as well as to assist me in my duties as ornithologist to the Zool[ogical] Society [of London]".[1] Gould added that he no longer needed the box files and was, "most desirous of seeing them placed" in the hands of "one truly devoted to this branch of natural science".

The box files contain more than 1200 unbound sheets of paper. To these sheets have been affixed hand-coloured engravings and lithographs of birds, cut from some of the most important (and today the most valuable) scientific publications of the nineteenth century. In his letter to Lord Derby, Gould explained that the sheets, arranged in taxonomic order, "commence with the Raptores and terminate with the Natatores; and form the most complete illustration of the modern genera extant". The affixed prints include, among others, the works of John James Audubon, George Louis Leclerc (Comte de Buffon), William Jardine, Edward Lear, René Primevére Lesson, Eduard Rüppell, and Prideaux John Selby. There are also lithographs from two of John Gould's own books, *The birds of Europe* (1832-1837) and *A synopsis of the birds of Australia* (1837-1838).

In light of today's market value for any one of the plates in Gould's assemblage, it is incredible to think that he sold the entire set to Lord Derby for £12 per box. "I never, for a moment, expect to realize a little of the value of the books employed," wrote Gould in his letter to Derby, "as however valuable the collection may be the expense of its formation has been enormous". Lord Derby not only agreed to buy the box files as they had been assembled, but appears also to have taken up Gould's offer to, "continue them with other works not at present contained therein".

Although the four lithographs shown here were used by their respective owners purely as ornithological references, they are among the finest natural history illustrations ever composed - and by two of the most famous artists represented in the box file collection. Three are of extinct species.

RMP

[1]Letter from Gould to Derby, 26th August 1841 (LVRO 1/67/3).

Campephilus

~~Dryocopus~~ Principalis, ~~Bonap~~ G.R.Gray.

Picus Principalis, Linn. Syst. 1. 173
Gmel. Syst. 1. 425.
Lath. Ind. Orn. 1. 225
Bonap. Syn. p. 44
Wils. Am. Orn. 4. pl. 29.
Wagl. Syst. av. Picus sp. 1.
Jard. Brit. Wils. Am. Orn. 2. 8.
Aud. Birds of Am. 1. pl. 66.
"   Orn. Bio. 1. 341.
Picus niger Carolinensis, Briss. 4. 26. 9.
Id. 8vo. 2. 49.
Pic noir à bec blanc, Buff. 7. 46.   Pl. Enl. 690.
King of the Woodpeckers, Kalm 2. 85.
White billed Woodpecker Catesb. Car. 1. 6. 16.
Arct. Zool. 2. 156.
Lath. Syn. 2. 553.
Bart. p. 289.

Hab. N. America.
Pr. pr. Aud.

SALE OF THE KNOWSLEY MENAGERIE.

YAK.

BARA SINGHA DEER.—MALE AND FEMALE.

ELK.

GNU.

ZEBUS, BRED AT KNOWSLEY.—SEE NEXT PAGE

THE KNOWSLEY AVIARY & MENAGERIE

CLEMENCY FISHER

"There are herons hatched here — it is much better fun to watch these matters than to go to the H[ouse] of L[or]ds" (Earl Fitzwilliam to the 13th Earl of Derby).[1]

There are literally hundreds of manuscripts still in existence — letters, lists and bills — which concern the living collections at Knowsley.[2] At the sale in 1851 it was described as 'the most complete and important private zoological collection in the world'.[3] The Knowsley Aviary & Menagerie indeed has a deserved place in history, as the earliest collection where an enlightened policy of breeding species thought to be of future use to mankind was deliberately adopted as a priority. As Thomas Moore wrote: 'The object most earnestly pursued by the Thirteenth Earl of Derby was to introduce and, if possible, naturalize such Birds and Beasts as would be ornamental or useful'. Moore considered that Lord Derby was more successful in reaching these goals than the Zoological Society of London, or any similar establishment.[4] The 13th Earl was a thoughtful man, who had very modern ideas about animal husbandry and welfare. His animals were not shown off to a paying public avid for sensation, but primarily kept for his own scientific interest and love of animals,[5] and for his family's private enjoyment.

Several accounts concern the Knowsley collections. Lord Derby privately published two volumes of *Gleanings*, where the living animals were described by John Gray of the British Museum, with copious notes by Lord Derby and illustrated in colour by Edward Lear and Benjamin Waterhouse Hawkins.[6] The first volume included 17 species (mostly large birds and small mammals); volume two covered ungulates.[8] Thomas Moore, Deputy Superintendent of the living collections at Knowsley, compiled the sale catalogue. This is the only really detailed inventory of the occupants of the Aviary & Menagerie, although earlier partial lists also exist.[9] Many years later, Moore wrote a fond memoir of the animals at Knowsley.[10] A meticulous overview of the history of the Knowsley collections was written by Stephen Woolfall in 1990, with a list of those birds and mammals that had died at Knowsley and which are now preserved as cabinet skins in the collections of the Liverpool Museum.[11]

The living collections are otherwise immortalised in a wonderful collection of watercolours, most of which are still kept at Knowsley Hall. The annotations on these paintings indicate that many of the animals (such as the Anoa, a small and very rare Water Buffalo from Sulawesi, which had not been seen in Britain before) were painted on the day they died, indicating the desire Lord Derby had to record his animals properly, before they were sent to the taxidermist. Apart from originals by Lear and Hawkins, there are stunning portraits by Joseph Wolf, who some believe to be the greatest wildlife artist of the time. A few of the many paintings by John Gould and Henry Contantine Richter must also have been drawn from living animals at Knowsley, where Gould (the son of a gardener) was a much-welcomed visitor.

A complete account of the Knowsley Aviary & Menagerie would require a substantial book. This essay can be no more than a fleeting impression of the amazing zoological experience that visitors to Knowsley enjoyed between 1834 - when Lord Stanley became the 13th Earl of Derby and succeeded to the estate - and 1851, when he died. At his death the Knowsley collections totalled 318 species (1272 individuals) of birds and 94 species (345 individuals) of mammals,[12] in a

Opposite Page from the *Illustrated London News* for 11th October 1851, entitled 'Sale of the Knowsley Menagerie'. The Yak, Bara Singha Deer and Elk are by J.W. Archer, the Zebus by H.W. Weir. The latter had been hybridized at Knowsley with domestic cattle (LM).

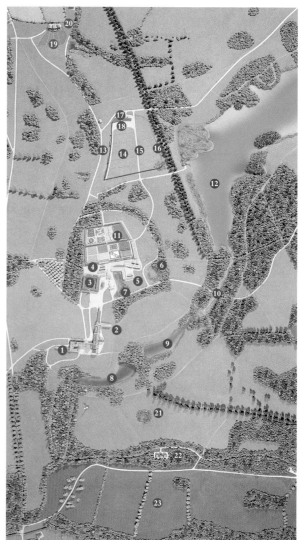

Diagram of the arrangement of the living collections at Knowsley (NMGM).

1	Knowsley Hall	13	Aviary Cottages
2	Conservatory	14	New Aviary
3	New Stables	15	The Well
4	Animal pens	16	raised wall embankment
5	Old Aviary	17	'The Nest' or Lake House
6	Mill Pits	18	Wire Aviary
7	Brewhouse Pond	19	Kennels' paddocks
8	Home Pond	20	Kennels
9	Octagon Pond	21	Mole Earth Pits
10	Dungeon Dam	22	Old Dairy
11	Walled Garden	23	The Paddocks
12	White Man's Dam		

Above Three views of the 'Old Aviary', improved in 1806 and the heart of Lord Derby's aviary and menagerie complex. The bottom photograph shows the heated part, or 'Stoves' (1 NMGM. courtesy of Knowsley. 2 & 3 Clemency Fisher, courtesy of Knowsley).

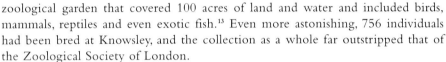

zoological garden that covered 100 acres of land and water and included birds, mammals, reptiles and even exotic fish.[13] Even more astonishing, 756 individuals had been bred at Knowsley, and the collection as a whole far outstripped that of the Zoological Society of London.

The 13th Earl's interest in keeping exotic species probably originated with the domestic animals more usually kept by aristocracy in the early nineteenth century. The 12th Earl and his second wife, Elizabeth Farren, kept ornamental pheasants and songbirds in what was later known as the 'Old Aviary', just north of the Hall.[14] The 13th Earl, throughout his years spent investigating new, foreign species, never lost his interest in game birds and indeed in breeding varieties of the humble chicken. He was also a respected breeder of Bloodhounds.[15]

During the early part of the nineteenth century Lord Stanley could not put into operation all the ideas he had for expanding the living collections at Knowsley. At least some of the live birds he owned at that time were kept in London, and he was greatly interested in the formation of the Zoological Society of London, of which he was a founder member in 1826. He was later on their Farm Committee, and was President from 1831 until his death in 1851, although he seldom attended meetings and was admonished for his 'want of exertion'.[16] However, a series of letters between Stanley and Richard Yarnall, the 12th Earl's gardener at Knowsley, concern extensive alterations to the area around the Old Aviary and Brew-House Pond at Knowsley in 1806.[17] The aviaries were walled in and covered by rat-proof wire, and the pond provided with islands and breeding boxes on poles for wildfowl.[18] Yarnall listed the 62 birds in residence at the time, mostly gamebirds, guans, parrots and song birds.

In the next few years the species kept in the aviary progressed from domestic stock, through cage birds such as parrots, to the more exotic and rare. A Gannet died there in 1811, and a Skua from the Orkneys in 1813.[19] At least 100 birds died between 1810 and 1812, including a Carolina Parakeet, a species now extinct. A few small mammals, mainly foreign squirrels, were also kept. However, in these early days most of the mammalian occupants of the aviary were of humble, local origin. Lord Derby himself played host to Field and Harvest Mice, but the Field Mouse was 'killed by the HouseMaid in mistake' while the Harvest Mouse, which had been brought home from Mossborough Fields in the Keeper's hat (while still on his head) eventually drowned 'in my washhand basin'.[20]

Left Black Polish Chickens, which were mentioned in several letters between the Reverend E.S. Dixon and Lord Derby. The Earl thought well of their topknots (K).

Above (Possibly) Sussex Chickens, by Edward Stanley. Behind the Sussex chickens, Edward Stanley has added a little figure threshing, a haystack and a group of foraging farmyard chickens (K).

Above 'A list of Birds in the Aviary at Knowsley', included at the end of a letter from Richard Yarnall to Lord Stanley, March 1806 (K).

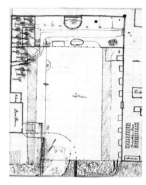

Top Sketch by Lord Stanley showing the alterations planned to the Brew-house Pond in 1806 (K), and *right* a view of the Brew-house pond today (NMGM, courtesy of Knowsley).

By 1830 the living collections had greatly expanded. Wildfowl were well established on the Brew House Pond; songbirds, pigeons and gamebirds lived in the Old Aviary, birds of prey, pheasants and a Raven in the Pheasantry. The Stoves, a heated part of the Old Aviary, housed foreign species such as macaws, curassows and orioles.[21]

In 1834, after his father's death, the new Earl could alter the Knowsley estate to his complete satisfaction. He hired 400 extra labourers and between 40 and 50 double-horse carts,[22] laid out a network of roads and paths, further upgraded the Old Aviary and built a series of 'New Aviaries' to the north of the Hall. Lord Derby expended an enormous resource on this area, building a wall and embankment around ten acres of woodland. Within this, he constructed a carriage drive and enclosed paddocks with hurdles. Each section had substantial buildings for ostriches, antelopes, zebras or extensive accommodation for waterfowl. Arched dens and terraces were built into the wall where it was higher on the eastern side. A huge wire aviary was built to the north of this area, completely masking the 'The Nest' (also known as 'Lake House'; home of the Superintendent, John Thompson, and later occupied also by Thompson's assistant and clerk, Thomas Moore). This massive cage had a series of glass-roofed houses at the rear, and was planted with dwarf shrubs and trees. Thomas Moore could lean out of his window in the morning and watch the Argus Pheasant shaking out his gorgeous train, the Himalayan Monal comporting himself in front of his mate and the mound-building Brush Turkey scraping leaves into heaps, looking at them with disgust (in the absence of a mate) and then rebuilding them all over again. Moore would also watch as the ostriches were let out of their house for daily exercise, in anticipation of enjoying the male bird's habit of sitting down, drawing in his neck and blushing until his neck looked like a huge but limp German sausage.[23]

Lord Derby increased the security of his animals by building a sandstone wall round the entire park, nearly ten miles long. Within this wall he could allow some of the deer to roam freely. Although Lord Derby almost always referred to his living collections as the 'Aviary' (the word 'Menagerie' being 'unmanageable and altogether foreign'),[24] he developed an extremely important collection not only of living birds but also of mammals, particularly those which might be useful sources

of meat or pelts. The Earl avoided keeping the larger cats (presumably for reasons of safety) and the higher primates; perhaps he agreed with his friend William Broderip, who said they always reminded him of poor relations.[25] Some of his mammals were kept in the 'Kennels' (north of the New Aviary), which Lord Derby adapted with radiating sandstone walls, giving the animals a pen and en-suite small paddock.

As a further investment, Lord Derby set up a network of natural history collectors overseas, many of whom were instructed to collect live animals. The Earl compiled lists of desiderata for them, often in great detail. These men included paid employees such as his own Superintendent, John Thompson, who often travelled abroad – to Germany for Bustards and to Norway and Sweden for Reindeer and Capercaillie.[26] Joseph Burke was sent to South Africa, and then later to North America; Thomas Whitfield to West Africa; John Bates (a Liverpool natural history dealer) and David Dyson to Honduras 'for Turkies'[27] (the rare Ocellated Turkey *Agriocharis ocellata*). Louis Fraser, Lord Derby's museum curator, was sent to Tunisia to collect in 1846. The draft agreement drawn up between Fraser and Derby[28] showed that it cost the Earl £420 a year, plus shipping charges, to keep Fraser in the field. Devereaux Fuller, engaged to collect in India and Singapore in 1846, cost the Earl even more but rewarded him with only 'a few birds' which arrived at Knowsley in 1847.[29]

Wild animals were difficult to capture and transport. John Bates' hummingbirds, collected by boys adept with blowpipes and fed on egg bread and 'spunge' cake, were carried by hand in a little cage, but despite this their feet swelled and they died. One of the deer which Bates had tethered in Government House grounds was eaten by an alligator,[30] although alligators could also come in useful.[31] George Windsor Earl's much loved Malayan Porcupine, which always punctually attended Mr and Mrs Earl's dinner hour, was friendly but not familiar and was almost as sagacious as an elephant, got stolen and eaten by locals and probably had its quills used for medicine.[32]

Page from the *Illustrated London News* for 4th October 1851, entitled 'Herd of Indian antelopes'. This was the Knowsley herd, six of which had been bred there. They were very nervous animals capable of jumping obstacles up to 13 feet high, so were represented ' … in a series of long and lofty springs, which they exhibit upon the least alarm' (LM).

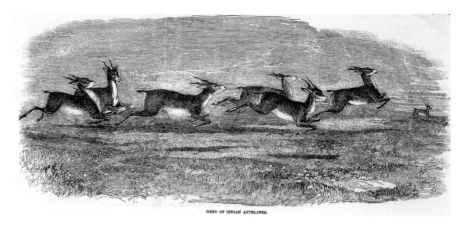

HERD OF INDIAN ANTELOPES.

If collecting was fraught with problems, then the voyage home was often a nightmare – steam ships only began to operate just before the 13th Earl's death. The Reverend John Fry had to load 20 goats, 8 sacks of barley, 4 sacks of gravel, 200 lb of bran, 3000 lb of hay and 'a number of caffir watermelons of which the ostriches are very fond' on board ship to feed living animals sent from South Africa to Knowsley.[33] Another letter to Lord Derby apologises for the crew of the *Cockatrice*, who had eaten the birds destined for Knowsley.[34] A Vicuña had to be forcibly restrained from eating tobacco and paint.[35] The Llamas sent on the Lucy refused to eat maize and starved themselves to death, although they did eat the straw used for packing wine.[36] Attempts to send 'passionate and easily irritated … Kèvès' (Kiwis) home from New Zealand, by shipping them with a supply of worms mixed with chicken entrails, unfortunately failed.[37] Knowsley itself seems to have had a narrow escape from a terrible disease. Three Gayals (a form of the Indian Bison) were supposed to be shipped from Calcutta on the *Duke of Argyll* in 1842 but were too big. All three had running 'saliva' from feet and mouth.[38] Even at the very end of his life, Lord Derby was still writing letters about acquiring living animals.[39]

Lord Derby's niece Elizabeth, daughter of Admiral Phipps Hornby, Commander-in-Chief of the Pacific Fleet, appears from her letters to have had a natural affinity with animals. Indeed the whole family, while stationed in Chile, seems to have collected for their relative and they helped Thomas Bridges to send home in the *Sampson* the first Black-necked Swans to reach Britain alive.[40] Elizabeth herself acquired two of these swans, both females, in 1850.[41] One was suffering from cramp, so spent some time recovering in her mother's bath, but afterwards lived quite happily in a tank in the garden. The swans were fussy feeders, but accepted soup made from oatmeal, bran and frogs. Another letter written by Elizabeth, from the *Asia* at sea,[42] revealed that she had embarked for the voyage home with seven swans and five cygnets, but had lost three at Cape Horn. The swans lived in a large tank in the pinnacle boat.

Lord Derby not only imported animals directly from the wild but also exchanged material with zoos in Britain and abroad; the Anoa, for instance, came from the Jardin des Plantes in Paris.[43] He exchanged many animals with Rajanda Mullick in Calcutta, who recycled a cage sent by Derby containing white and pure black Fallow Deer and returned it to the Earl inhabited by a Muntjak and a 'Munipore Buck'.[44] Closer to home, Lord Derby often exchanged animals with Thomas Atkins, who ran the Liverpool Zoological Gardens in Boaler Street between 1832 and 1863. The Earl helped set up the Manchester Zoo, which existed in Higher Broughton from 1838 to 1842[45] and many specimens were

returned to him when it closed. He also exchanged livestock with Earl Fitzwilliam and Sir Robert Heron. Lord Derby's most illustrious exchanges, however, took place between Knowsley and Queen Victoria's collections at Windsor Castle and Buckingham Palace. Her Angora goats, sent to Knowsley in 1844, were the subject of several letters to Lord Derby.[46]

The Aviary and Menagerie were renowned for the wellbeing of the inhabitants[47] but there were inevitably casualties. Hugh Neill, a surgeon from the Liverpool Ear and Eye Infirmary, was called to Knowsley to operate on the Indian antelope's cataracts. He did not think it 'infra dig to relieve the sufferings of the lowest animal' and examined another deer, which had rickets, while he was there.[48] Old Billy, a Red Deer stag, was born at Knowsley in 1819 and sent to the Oaks in Surrey in 1822 as hunters' quarry. After many years, still unscathed, he was sent back to Knowsley but was then wounded by a rival. As a result, he was allowed to frequent the yard of John Shaw, the Deer-keeper, where Billy learned how to open the acorn bin for himself. Lord Derby and his friends used to make special visits to pat him and Old Billy became such a favourite that the Earl commissioned his portrait to be painted by Richard Ansdell in 1842.[49] In his last few years Old Billy often entered the kitchen of the Deer-keeper's house and made himself comfortable in front of the fire. When he died in 1845, his remains were sent to the British Museum, along with an earlier and better set of his antlers.[50] Other animals that died at Knowsley were generally prepared by Lord Derby's taxidermists, either for his own museum or (particularly if they were large) for the collections at the Zoological Society of London or the British Museum.

Some of the Knowsley animals were awkward customers. The bull Bison escaped and swam White Man's Dam 'in search of Bovine Society'. The Elk chased the coachman up a tree and held him hostage all night; a Sambur Stag, a Wild Ass and a male Guanaco were considered quite capable of killing people. However, even these animals needed looking after. 'Field Days' were a fixture at Knowsley, when as many able-bodied staff as possible were directed to the business of animal management. A routine job was hoof paring, which involved Samson the Blacksmith in a battle of wills with the Zebras and Asses. The Wild Ass tried his best to seize his keeper with his teeth, his nostrils 'distended, like quart pots, with rage'.[51] Others, like the Alpacas, had to be individually washed and their wool clipped.[52]

Oil painting by Richard Ansdell, depicting Wild Asses, Zebras and their half-bred foals in Knowsley Park. This is the only one of Ansdell's paintings of the Knowsley animals, several of which were commissioned by Lord Derby, whose location is at present known. 990 x 1837mm (Private Collection, courtesy of Sotherby's Picture Library).

With which animals did Lord Derby have particular success? 'Deer and Antelopes, Zebras and Alpacas and Brahmin Cattle … Game Birds and Waterfowl, Cranes and the Ostrich' received his principal care.[53] The Earl successfully bred ten species of deer and all four species of Lamoids. He was responsible for first importing the Cape Eland into Britain. Lord Derby also did well with the kangaroos – as did Sir Robert Heron, with whom the Earl exchanged several individuals.[54] He even bred some of the smaller, rarer species; one of the keepers witnessed a Brush-tailed Bettong giving birth in October 1844.[55]

Lord Derby and his staff understood what made their living guests comfortable and in particular what encouraged them to breed. The Tree Pigeons 'like spoiled children' would not eat until the keepers realised these birds needed to be able to feed from tree boughs off the ground.[56] They also worked out that Passenger Pigeons would only breed if they were in large groups; knowledge unfortunately ignored at the sale of the collections in 1851, when they were split into small groups and sold separately.[57] There was much correspondence between Lord Derby and his colleagues about incubating eggs; they used various machines and still more various foster mothers.[58] The 13th Earl is credited with rearing several birds in captivity for the first time: Stanley Crane (1844),[59] Sandwich Island Goose, or Néné (1834)[60] and Crested Fireback Pheasant (1845). He probably was also the first to breed Ostrich, Quelea and Rhea in captivity. Lord Derby's wildfowl laid with enthusiasm and game birds also bred well.

As the living collections increased, so did the number of staff. Richard Yarnall was eventually replaced by John Thompson; he came to Knowsley from the Zoological Society of London in the early 1830s. Thomas Moore arrived in 1843. To these two men is owed much of the credit for the success of the Knowsley collections. According to Moore, thirty attendants were on the pay lists[61] and certainly thirteen men worked exclusively for the 'Aviary' in 1847; others could be called on for maintenance and building works.[62] No wonder Richard Earle, Derby's agent, complained that 'the expence of upholding the Aviary &c. is annually increasing by no moderate account'. According to Pollard,[63] the living collections cost about £15,000 p.a. to run.

The public were admitted, but they had to apply for permission by letter, and entrance was strictly limited to two parties daily, with a special guide and guard.[64] Some of the most prominent natural historians visited the estate – amongst them Charles-Lucien Bonaparte[65] (Napoleon's nephew, a distinguished ornithologist), the publisher and artist John Gould and the famous American explorer, naturalist and artist John James Audubon.

In the last few years of the 13th Earl's life the animals were at their peak. The living collections at Knowsley would probably have declined from 1850 onwards, even if Lord Derby had survived longer. In growing infirmity, and nagged about expenditure by his agent and by his son, Lord Derby increasingly turned to horticulture. After his death, at the end of June 1851, the living collections were sold by auction over several days from 6th October. There were 641 lots and the sale raised about £6,400; they were widely dispersed. As one observer commented: 'Of the experience he had so dearly bought, nearly all perished with him'.[66]

In his will the 13th Earl specified that Queen Victoria (who chose the five Himalayan Monals) and the Zoological Society of London (who chose the herd of five Cape Elands) should each make a selection before the rest were sold.[67] Annotated copies of the sale catalogue show that the London Zoo spent nearly £1,000 on 160 specimens of 62 species.[68] Other animals went to the zoos in Amsterdam and Paris, or were purchased by dealers.

The 13th Earl of Derby may well have been the greatest private animal keeper that England has ever seen.[69] A veritable din of animal sounds must have woken the overnight visitor at daybreak; numerous members of the cow family bellowing, a hundred members of the Parrot House limbering up, swans, geese and ducks of sixty species adding their contribution; all gathered within a radius of a mile of Knowsley Hall itself. What influence must this cacophony, which would have had contributions from animals with names like the Whiskered Yarke, the Jungli-bukra, the Aequitoon and the Ging-e-Jonga, have had on a visitor such as Edward Lear, who was already attracted to eccentric words?

Edward Lear cartoon showing the artist and Lord Derby's relation, Phipps Hornby. They are shown leaving Knowsley in 1841 for a holiday in Scotland, waved farewell by assorted peacocks, cranes and humans (Private Collection).

[1]MM/8/K/8 (1834). Earl Fitzwilliam had a collection of living forms at Wentworth; probably the second biggest private collection in Britain after Knowsley, although they were not cared for so well. Sir Robert Heron (who had the third in size, at Stubton in Lincolnshire) noted that the Fitzwilliams seemed to have no idea whether their animals were alive or dead (LVRO 1/80/unnumbered). [2]See page 2 for the location of the many extant letters written to, and by, Lord Derby. [3]*Illustrated London News* for 11th October 1851: 450. [4]Moore 1892: 1 & 1890: 10. [5]Lady Stanley to her husband: 'I have not been able today to make my visit to the Aviary or Pheasants … so I know nothing of your family' (K). [6]Hawkins suggested the project in 1843 (LVRO 1/76/1). [7]Gray 1846a, 1850. The first volume was illustrated by Lear, the second by Hawkins. They were issued from Knowsley by subscription. [8]Moore 1851. [9]For instance, documents entitled 'List of birds alive or dead procured in the year 1810-11'; 'Quadrupeds'; 'Birds'; 'Pheasantry' (LM ZDA). [10]Moore 1891, 1892. [11]Other accounts include Forbes 1898, Glover 1973, Keeling 1984, Bagley 1985, Keeling 2000. [12]Moore 1891: 5. [13]North American soft-shelled turtles were kept; a recently dead specimen was sent to the British Museum in 1843. A 'kettle of turtles' was sent to Derby by Fry from South Africa in 1839 (K). The first mud-fishes to be imported into Britain were brought back by Thomas Whitfield from the Gambia in 1843. They were placed in warm tanks in the greenhouses at Knowsley and successfully emerged from their hardened mud cocoons (Moore 1892: 9). [14]Richard Yarnall, senior gardener, wrote to Lady Derby in March 1807 to say her cock Golden Pheasant had died. He also mentions 'your Ladyships other birds' (K). [15]Lord Derby's Bloodhounds were discussed in letters from James Brierley dated 1848-1851 (LVRO 1/17/1-4). The Earl's hounds were called Caesar, Bran and Harmless. Two were sold at the auction in 1851. Other dogs performed as useful exchange material. Greyhounds sent to Syria by Lord Derby caused a sensation amongst the Turks, who the Earl hoped would collect animals for him (C.D. Hays to Captain Robert Low, LVRO 1/78/1). [16]Sir Robert Heron to Derby (K). Heron wished that Lord Derby would exert more authority at the London Zoo, so that animals could be moved without everything having to be referred to Council. [17]Letter from Yarnall to Stanley, 30th March 1806 (K). Other letters from Yarnall to Lord Stanley (K, MM/8/K/1 & 8, LVRO 1/196/1-2) give crucial information on the early days of the living collections at Knowsley. According to Yarnall, for instance, a bird he thought must be a Passenger Pigeon was resident in 1808 (MM/8/K/1) and there is much about the materials and costs involved in upgrading the Old Aviary to accommodate exotic species. [18]Moore 1891: 7. [19]Lord Stanley's manuscript 'General Index of the Birds in my Collection at Knowsley', LM ZDA entry 830; 'Skua Gull … died in a fit'. [20]Marginal remarks by Lord Stanley in his manuscript catalogue of the specimens in his museum, to numbers 1958 & 1959 (LM ZDA). [21]Woolfall 1990: 2. [22]*The Times*, 4th April 1836. [23]Moore 1891, 9-11. [24]Moore 1891: 3. [25]Broderip to Derby, 25th February 1850 (LVRO 1/19/1). [26]L. Lloyd (consul in Gothenberg) to Derby (LVRO 1/109/1-8). [27]The hunt for living specimens of Ocellated Turkey resembled a Hollywood disaster movie. Letters to Lord Derby, describing attempts to get specimens of this bird to Britain for him, were written by John Bates, George Skinner, Stuart Thompson and John Gray. Birds they managed to find died of eye disease, were killed by 'Tiger Cats' or were shipwrecked in rapids. If left with another bird, even another turkey, they did their best to kill it. Despite all this, at least one reached Knowsley alive (Stevens Sale 1851: Lot 505). [28]Fraser/Derby draft agreement, February 1846 (K). Fraser was allowed to supplement his wages by reselling lions and camels. [29]Fuller to Derby (LVRO 1/62/1-3). [30]Bates' diary of his trip to Belize, written in Liverpool, September 1843 (LVRO 1/9/4). [31]Reverend John Bachman to Derby, 7th

November 1838 (LVRO 1/7/1). Bachman (Audubon's great friend) swore by a mixture of rice flour and cheap meat (fish, rabbits or, best of all, boiled and finely chopped alligator) for raising ducklings. [32]G.W. Earl to Derby, 3rd February 1851 (LVRO 1/48/1). [33]The Reverend Fry to ?Derby, 25th April 1839 (K). [34]Elizabeth Hornby to Derby, 26th March 1849 (LVRO 1/85/9). [35]Elizabeth Hornby to Derby, 28th July 1849 (LVRO 1/85/11). [36]Edward Bennett to Derby, 23rd October 1833 (LVRO 1/11/5). [37]Thomas McDonnell to Derby, 1835 (LVRO 1/112/1). [38]John McClelland to Derby (LVRO 1/111/1-2). [39]Copy of a letter from Derby to Fry, 5th June 1851, written less than a month before the 13th Earl died. In this letter Derby remarks that 'my object is not so much the dead as living animals'. His writing is no worse than usual (K). [40]Bridges to Derby, September 1848 (LVRO 1/16/3) reported that he had shipped a Black-necked Swan. Elizabeth Hornby wrote confirming this, that Bridges had also sent a penguin, and warning her uncle that he should expect no more specimens, as Bridges had been seized by 'California Mania' (Gold Fever). She later remarked that the penguin looked like 'a sick Marine in his great Coat' (LVRO 1/85/5 & 9). [41]Elizabeth Hornby from Valparaiso, 22nd November 1850 (LVRO 1/85/13). [42]Elizabeth Hornby to Derby, 17th March 1851 (LVRO 1/85/18). She also wrote that her father, Admiral Hornby, was anxious that some of the Black-necked Swans and their cygnets should be sent to Queen Victoria. [43]G. Bibron (of Paris) to Derby, 31st October 1845 (LVRO 1/12/1). The Anoa arrived at Knowsley in January 1846. [44]Mullick to Derby, from Calcutta 3rd July 1850 (K). [45]Henry Sandbach to Derby, undated (LVRO 1/144/1). [46]Sir Charles Murray, on behalf of Queen Victoria and Prince Albert, to Derby, 1843 & 1844 (MM/8/K/3). The latter mentions a very soft and fine dress the Queen possessed, made from wool from her Angoras. [47]William Dawson to Derby, 1841 (LCL 1/44/1), on behalf of himself and General O'Brien: 'We were very much gratified at the healthy appearance of the animals'. Dawson was particularly surprised at the good condition of the Alpacas and asked Lord Derby if he could take them to an agricultural show (see Catalogue entry 47). [48]Neill to Derby, 1851 (LCL 1/26/1 & K). [49] This painting was sold in 1954, along with other paintings by Ansdell of the animals at Knowsley (such as one of the Addax, a rare antelope; see Gray to Derby (LVRO 1/69/11). Only the painting shown has since been located. [50]A letter from Shaw to Derby (LVRO 1/147/1) reported Old Billy's death in 1845, aged 25. [51]Moore 1892: 2-6. Perhaps to general relief, the Wild Ass, 'the most dreaded and dangerous beast of all', froze to death one night and was found with all his hair turned the wrong way, so that it was impossible to stuff him. [52]See Catalogue entry for Guanacos and Alpacas (no. 47). [53]Moore 1892: 1. [54]Heron to Derby, 28th August (LVRO 1/80/undated). Heron asked Lord Derby if he had a spare male Great [Grey] Kangaroo, as he had only 'a disconsolate widow & one hopeless virgin'. [55]See Catalogue entry for Brush-tailed Bettongs (no.42). [56]Moore 1891: 10. [57]See Catalogue entry for Passenger Pigeon (no. 37). [58]Sir Robert Heron sent a kangaroo and two female curassows to Lord Derby. The two birds travelled with 'their Mother in Law, a common hen' (LCL 1/80/unnumbered, 8th September [1835]). Heron also commented sadly that two years' experience had convinced him that 'Turkies cannot rear Rheas' (1/80/unnumbered, 24th August). John Thompson also experimented with foster mothers, trying Emu eggs under both turkeys and geese in 1835 (K). [59]See Catalogue entry for the Stanley Crane (no. 53). [60]In October 1834 Lord Stanley published extensive notes on this first ever breeding of the Néné in Britain. The Knowsley staff had first to overcome an unfortunate fixation the male bird had with one of the workmen. Stanley sent a young bird which had hatched at Knowsley in April 1834 to be exhibited at a meeting of the Zoological Society of London. Another from that same clutch, which was discovered dead and 'perfectly flat', is in the collections of the Liverpool Museum but is now rather nicely rounded. In 1850 Edmund Dixon made some prophetic observations on the future of the Néné in the wild; in a letter to his friend Lord Derby (to whom he dedicated his book *The Dovecote and the Aviary*) Dixon wrote: 'it will probably before long become extinct, now that the Sandwich islands are likely to become a sort of watering place to California, unless it be propagated in a domestic state' (LVRO 1/46/15). [61]Moore 1891: 3. [62]Richard Earle to Derby, 29th April 1847 (K). Earle pointed out that the 13th Earl had 245 people working on the estate, excluding the house servants. [63]Pollard 1871: 111. [64]Moore 1891: 8. [65]Stroud 2000: 136. [66]Comment (p. 158) of an article dated 1863 (pages 152-174), entitled *Acclimatization and preservation of animals in relation to the late Earl of Derby's extensive & magnificent collection*. A copy of this is at Knowsley Hall, bound together with Moore's 1851 sale catalogue. [67]Queen Victoria probably attended the sale. According to the *Illustrated London News* of 4th October 1851, she was scheduled to stay at Croxteth Hall, two miles from Knowsley, on 7th October. [68]Scherren 1905: 111. His information probably came from the annotated copy of the Knowsley sale catalogue in the Zoological Society Library. Among the lots the Society purchased were four Black-necked Swans, total cost £160, of which two females were given to Queen Victoria. The two remaining swans hatched four cygnets in 1857, the first successfully reared in Europe (Scherren 1905: 111). [69]Quotation from Janet Kear, Trustee of NMGM, at the Memorial Service to mark the 150th year since the 13th Earl of Derby's death, at Ormskirk Parish Church on 2nd July 2001.

April 8th 6

Stanley

30. BLACK SWAN
Family Anatidae (ducks, geese and swans)

Among the treasures at Knowsley are two bound volumes of work by various artists, which include a number of watercolours executed by Lord Stanley himself during the first decade of the nineteenth century. Inscriptions on several of these drawings indicate that they were 'copied' and the same is almost certainly true of his Black Swan, although the original source of this illustration has yet to be identified.

Black Swans were a conspicuous feature on the waters of the Knowsley estate for at least twenty years during the lifetime of Lord Derby. The museum specimen from his collection (D.519) died there on 10th September 1832, the species bred 'famously' during the years 1845 and 1846[1] and nine birds were present at the time of the Earl's death in 1851.[2] Indeed, Black Swans are still present at Knowsley today, though these are the result of a recent introduction and not descendants of the nineteenth century flock.

This Australian species is generally common, particularly in the western and eastern regions of the continent, wherever there is permanent water. Introduced to New Zealand in the 1860s, the Black Swan is now well established as a wild bird in that country.

ML

[1]Gray 1846a. [2]Moore 1851.

Opposite Watercolour by Lord Stanley, depicting *Cygnus atratus* and dated 8th April 1806. 290 x 325mm (K).

Below Cabinet skin of a bird formerly mounted for display. Female Black Swan *Cygnus atratus*, which died at Knowsley in 1832. Length 1300mm (LM D.519).

31. ORINOCO GOOSE
Family Anatidae (ducks, geese and swans)

Right Watercolour inscribed "Chenalopex jubata (Spix). Tropical America. The original of the Plate in the 'Gleanings'. Edward Lear. del July. 1836". The model for the single male goose in the foreground was probably the specimen now numbered D.198d. 363 x 530mm (K).

Below Male Orinoco Goose *Neochen jubata*, died in the Knowsley aviaries on 13th February 1837. Length 550mm (LM D.198d).

Below right Half-grown gosling Orinoco Goose, died in the aviaries July 1847. Length 280mm (LM D.198f).

Orinoco Geese are confined to tropical South America, extending from the Orinoco and Amazon Rivers and their tributaries south to Argentina. They are found in riverine forest, wet open grassland and on open, rocky river beaches. Generally seen in pairs or family groups, they frequently perch in trees and only rarely swim. Their food is primarily vegetation but they also eat worms, small molluscs and insects. They are noted to be quite tame and vulnerable, with a total population that has now declined to less than 100,000 birds.[1]

Edward Lear has captured typical Orinoco Goose behaviour in his watercolour. In the wild, males engage in fierce battles during the breeding season, uttering constant guttural honking and using bill and wings (which have sharp knobs) to attack opponents. In courtship display, both birds hold their bodies erect, with the head back as far as possible and wings extended, and give a wheezy *wi-chuff* with each forward movement of the chest, interrupting an otherwise constant whistling. In *Gleanings*[2], Lord Derby wrote of the Orinoco Goose: "You will find it figured in Lear's drawing, who was much amused by its manner of swelling out the breast like a Pouter Pigeon, which he represented". Lear was indeed amused; he used a little figure of an Orinoco Goose in full display and uttering 'goodbye - puff' to the departing Derby family in one of his cartoons (see page 20).

The Orinoco Goose was first introduced to Britain by Lord Derby, and they were bred successfully at Knowsley from 1844 onwards. Three were included in the sale of the Knowsley collection in 1851, and were bought for £14. Because of their tropical origins, Orinoco Geese are sensitive to cold and generally do not do well in zoos in Europe, so Lord Derby's achievement in breeding them - not only for the first time in captivity, but repeatedly - is all the more remarkable.

JK

[1]Brewer & Kreise; Orinoco Goose. *In* Kear (in press). [2]Gray 1846a: text to plate xv.

32. YELLOW-BILLED DUCK
Family Anatidae (ducks, geese and swans)

Watercolour by Joseph Wolf, from a bound volume of paintings by Wolf and Waterhouse Hawkins, of two pairs of Yellow-billed Ducks *Anas undulata*. A manuscript list attached to the volume, written by T.J. Moore in 1871, recorded the following details for this picture: 'Yellow-billed Duck or 'Guil-bec". Wolf composed this picture from living birds at Knowsley. 350 x 510mm (K).

The Yellow-billed Duck is found in Africa, where there are two subspecies. One extends from Kenya to Angola and South Africa, the other is confined to NE Africa.

Yellowbills use a variety of wetland habitats where there is plenty of marginal vegetation. They quickly find flooded grassland and flocks of up to 5000 may gather at times, feeding principally by dabbling in shallow water - although occasionally coming ashore to forage at night. Food consists mostly of seeds of aquatic plants and grains gleaned after harvest. There may be a population of about 200,000 in the wild.[1]

At the sale of Lord Derby's living collections, a number of Yellow-billed Ducks that had been bred at Knowsley were included; two were sold for £3 5s and three for £6 10s. Through this sale, the Zoological Society of London, of which Lord Derby was a founder, acquired its first specimens. The birds bred at the London Zoo in 1859 and 1860, and surplus offspring were supplied to other zoological gardens on the continent of Europe.[2]

JK

[1]Young, G. In Kear (in press). [2]Sclater 1880: 495-536.

Above Watercolour, executed on 21st November 1843 by Benjamin Waterhouse Hawkins. The two birds he painted later became syntypes of *Penelope niger*. The female (now D.484a) was already a museum specimen; the male was painted by Hawkins from a living bird in the Knowsley Menagerie (now D.484). 375 x 552mm (K).

Right Watercolour by Joseph Wolf, dated 10th August 1850, depicting two specimens (later syntypes) of Penelope niger. The male (D.484b) had died five days previously in the Knowsley Menagerie; the female was modelled on the same museum specimen that Hawkins had painted seven years earlier. 360 x 522mm (K).

Below Cabinet skin of a specimen once mounted for display, following its death in the Knowsley Menagerie on 5th August 1850; male. Syntype of *Penelope niger* Fraser 1852, *Proc. Zool. Soc. London* (for 1850): 246; the species is now known as *Penelopina nigra*. Length 580mm (LM D.484b).

The original description of *Penelope niger* was based on two males and a female in the Knowsley Museum[1] and all three syntypes still survive today in the Liverpool Museum collections (numbered D.484-484b). Two of these specimens were purchased in September 1843 from the firm of Leadbeater & Son, at that time one of the leading natural history agencies in London. Two months later these two birds were used as models for the watercolour by Benjamin Waterhouse Hawkins. The exact circumstances are made clear by notes inscribed on Hawkins' painting by Lord Derby, which record that the male was "drawn from the living bird at Knowsley, November 21 1843 by B. Waterhouse Hawkins … female dried skin. Obtained this specimen of the male still living thro' Leadbeater and the female I think by him from Paris".

At a later date, it is evident that a second living male of this species arrived in the Knowsley Menagerie, though all that is recorded of its history is that it died on 5th August 1850 and was painted five days later by Joseph Wolf. It was this second watercolour (in which the female specimen again features) that was the basis for Plate XXIX, which accompanied Fraser's type description.

Found in mountain forests of Central America, this species extends from southern Mexico to northern Nicaragua, sharing part of its range and habitat with the much rarer Horned Guan (*Oreophasis derbianus*).[2] Though still locally common, the species is declining in many areas due to alteration of natural environments.

ML

[1]Fraser 1852. [2]See Catalogue entry 51.

34. HIMALAYAN MONAL
Family Phasianidae (pheasants and partridges)

The first Himalayan Monals (or Impeyan Pheasants, as they were once known) to arrive at Knowsley were a pair purchased by Lord Derby in 1846. He was surprised to find them breeding in the following year, and the two females reared from this first clutch of eggs survived until 1848. The original pair bred again in 1849 and 1851.[1] At the time of the 13th Earl's death, five of these birds were alive on the estate, including three which had been bred there,[2] and it was evidently from amongst this group that Joseph Wolf selected the models for his painting. In accordance with the provisions of Lord Derby's will, all five birds were given to Queen Victoria for the royal aviary and menagerie.

This bird extends through the Himalayas from eastern Afghanistan to north-western India, inhabiting coniferous, rhododendron and bamboo forest at altitudes of 2100-4500 m. Although threatened by habitat destruction and over-exploitation for food, Himalayan Monals are at present common throughout their range.

ML

[1]Woolfall 1990. [2]Moore 1851.

Above Painting of Himalayan Monals by Joseph Wolf, showing adults and chicks, which was published in Elliot's *Monograph of the Pheasants* (1872, vol.1, Plate 19). 475 x 595mm (K).

Above top Mounted specimen of Himalayan Monal. Length 700mm; approx. 450mm high (LM 1994. 71.294).

Above left Watercolour depicting Himalayan Monals, painted by Joseph Wolf in October 1851 from male and female birds at Knowsley. 355 x 510mm (K).

Below Cabinet skin of a bird formerly mounted for display. Juvenile Himalayan Monal *Lophophorus impejanus*, which both hatched and died at Knowsley during the year of 1849. Length 305mm (LM D.1501).

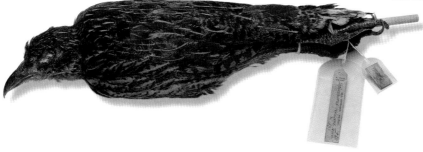

101

Family Phasianidae (patridges, quails & pheasants)

Watercolour by Joseph Wolf, dated 1851 and illustrating cross-bred pheasants, Ring-necked *Phasianus colchicus* x Green Pheasant *Phasianus versicolor*. The painting also features House Sparrows *Passer domesticus*. 350 x 510mm (K).

This warm-hearted painting serves well to illustrate both Lord Derby's fondness for game birds and his interest in developing potentially useful hybrids. The picture was probably drafted at Knowsley and may have been finished, as were many others by Wolf, after the death of the 13th Earl and at the request of his son.

In 1841 the Earl had a single Green (or 'Japanese') Pheasant, a male, which might have been the one mentioned in a letter to him from Edward Blyth.[1] Blyth was very surprised to hear that Lord Derby had a living bird and hoped the cross between a Ring-necked and this Green Pheasant, which the Earl was proposing, would be successful. Lord Derby again contemplated crossing these two species of pheasants in 1846, as a female *Phasianus versicolor* he had been sent from Amsterdam to provide a mate for his male had died on the voyage, and he was anxious not to lose the genetic diversity of the Green Pheasant entirely.[2] A letter of 1850, from Rajandra Mullick in Calcutta to Lord Derby,[3] indicates that the Earl had indeed been successful with hybridising these pheasants. Lord Derby offered some of the offspring to the poultry expert, the Reverend E.S. Dixon, who requested hybrids of both sexes and wondered whether future generations would eventually revert to the appearance of the ancestral species. Dixon eventually received a basket from Knowsley containing 3 three-quarter bred Green Pheasants, and announced his intention to write about them in the *Quarterly Review*. Dixon concluded with the remark that, "the ... cock and his two hens are grown into the most beautiful birds".[4]

CF

[1]Blyth to Derby, 1841 (K). [2]*Gleanings,* Gray 1846a: text to Plate XVI. [3]Mullick to Derby (K). [4]Dixon to Derby 1850, 1851 (LVRO 1/46/21, 23-24, 27-30).

36. CROWNED CRANE
Family Gruidae (Cranes)

Balearica regulorum.   South Africa.   The Original of the Plate in the 'Gleanings'.

Left Watercolour by Edward Lear, dated September 1835. Both specimen and painting represent the southern subspecies of Crowned Crane *Balearica pavonina regulorum.* 363 x 530mm (K).

Below Cabinet skin of Crowned Crane *Balearica pavonina*, which died in the aviaries at Knowsley on 16th March 1838. When alive, it may have been the model for Lear's watercolour. Length 1140mm (LM D.250).

Crowned Cranes must have been a very conspicuous feature of the aviaries at Knowsley. A bird was there as early as January 1814,[1] while by 1851 there were no less than six examples of the typical subspecies from West Africa, and five specimens of *B. p. regulorum*.[2] Despite the size of this flock, Lord Derby observed in July 1846 that, "the Crowned … Cranes have never bred here, or even paired, I believe".[3]

One of these living birds was undoubtedly painted by Edward Lear in September 1835 and this may have been the specimen which, following its death on 16th March 1838, was then prepared for display in the Knowsley Museum. Lear's illustration was later published as Plate XIII in the first volume of *Gleanings from … Knowsley Hall*.[4]

The Crowned Crane is a common species of savanna wetlands throughout much of sub-Saharan Africa, from Senegal to the Rift Valley lakes of Ethiopia and to South Africa.

ML

103

[1]Woolfall 1990. [2]Moore 1851. [3]Gray 1846a. [4]Ibid.

37. PASSENGER PIGEON
Family Columbidae (pigeons and doves)

Now extinct, this species was formerly widespread in the great deciduous forests of eastern North America, extending from southern Canada to Florida and sometimes even Mexico and the Caribbean. It bred in the northern part of this range and wintered in the south.

The Passenger Pigeon, once one of the most abundant birds on earth, regularly darkened North American skies with migrating flocks numbering millions of individuals. In the 1830s, Audubon described how, "the air was literally filled with pigeons; the light of noonday was obscured as by an eclipse". Naturally, the species soon came to be regarded as a pest and competitions were organised in which a hunter needed a bag of at least 30,000 birds in order to qualify for a prize.

The consequences of such carnage were almost inevitable. Huge populations which existed in 1870 had drastically declined by the end of that decade. The last wild specimen was shot in March 1900 and the species became extinct when 'Martha' died in the Cincinnati Zoological Gardens, on 1st September 1914.[1]

John James Audubon (1785-1851), the French-American explorer, collector and artist, was both illustrator and author of the largest and most expensive bird book ever produced. His four volume work *The Birds of America* was published in Edinburgh between 1827 and 1838. Audubon's first visit to Britain was undertaken in search of an engraver capable of producing this masterwork and he landed at Liverpool on 21st July 1826. Within the next few days, his paintings were exhibited at the Liverpool Royal Institution to great acclaim and he was received at Knowsley by Lord Stanley, who agreed to subscribe to the forthcoming publication. The two became mutual admirers.

Audubon later showed his gratitude for Stanley's generous patronage by donating live American birds and mammals to the Knowsley aviary and menagerie. These included a number of Passenger Pigeons, which very soon began to breed and fledged their first chicks in 1832. In fact, the birds thrived to such an extent that, as in their homeland, they eventually became a nuisance and so were allowed to fly free from the aviary, though it seems they were never recorded beyond the limits of the estate.[2] Presumably, they all had to be recaptured in 1851, when no less than 70 Passenger Pigeons were sold at the auction of the 13th Earl's living collections.[3]

It seems that no artist ever painted Lord Derby's Passenger Pigeons; neither do the few rather poorly documented specimens from the Knowsley Museum collection definitely include former inhabitants of the menagerie. Probably such attention was not merited by a bird so extraordinarily common! Fortunately, the three examples in the Yorkshire Museum include an adult male labelled, "one of several specimens from the Knowsley menagerie of Lord Derby. Purchased live by J.J. Audubon at New York in 1830".[4]

ML

Cabinet skin of a male Passenger Pigeon *Ectopistes migratoria*, that once lived at Knowsley after being sent to England by John James Audubon. Length approx. 400mm (YORYM: 1994.1344).

[1]Fuller 2000. Martha is now in the Smithsonian Institution, Washington. [2]Woolfall 1990. [3]Moore 1851. The annotated copies of this catalogue reveal that the birds were divided into five lots. [4]Denton 1995.

38. BUDGERIGAR
Family Psittacidae (parrots)

Above Part of a letter to John Gould from the 13th Earl of Derby, dated February 11th 1848 (© The Natural History Museum, London).

Left Formerly mounted chick ('very young')[1] of Budgerigar *Melopsittacus undulatus*, which died in the Knowsley Aviary in February 1848. Length to tip of beak 115mm (LM D.505g).

Although the Budgerigar is now the most common cage-bird in Britain, the species did not breed in captivity in this country until 1848. The 13th Earl of Derby is credited with having achieved this first record and the specimen now numbered D.505g was one of the first chicks to hatch.[2]

John Gould, the London-based ornithologist, had obtained living Budgerigars from his brother-in-law in Queensland, Charles Coxen, and passed those he could spare to the 13th Earl of Derby. One of these birds died in the Knowsley aviaries in July 1845 and is now preserved in the Liverpool Museum.[3] Lord Derby must have had several birds by 1848, because in this letter to Gould in February of that year, he announced:

> "I have the pleasure to tell you we have been most pleased here by the fact of a Pair of the Melopsittacus undulatus breeding. It was first observed by Thompson noticing that the Hen never left the hole she had taken to, but was regularly fed there by the male … we do not yet know anything more than that she certainly has hatched, for he can hear the young. But how many one can not even guess. This is curious & is I believe the 1st instance".

Budgerigars inhabit the drier regions of mainland Australia and are highly nomadic, usually travelling in flocks. They nest, often colonially, in tree-holes or cavities in fence posts. Although cage birds can be obtained in many different colour varieties, artificially produced by selective breeding, in the wild the plumage of both sexes is green and yellow.

CF

[1]Comment by Louis Fraser in Derby Stockbook, entry for both D.505g & h. [2]Another, D.505h, also died in February 1848 but unfortunately is now missing from the collections of the Liverpool Museum. A female which died in the Aviary in 1849 (now D.505j) may have been one of the parents. [3]D.505b, which must have been one of the birds that a neighbour of Lord Derby's, Joseph Garside, arranged to see. Garside also kept living budgerigars (LVRO 1/64/1).

39. CAPPED SEEDEATER
Family Emberizidae (buntings, seedeaters, tanagers etc.)

Right Watercolour by Sydenham Edwards, dated 1810 and depicting male and female specimens of *Sporophila bouvreuil* (for which the bird now numbered D.4272 might possibly have provided one of the models). 390 x 545mm (K).

Below Cabinet skin of a bird once mounted for display (carrying a label with data 'copied from stand'); male. Specimen of Capped Seedeater *Sporophila bouvreuil*, which once lived in the Knowsley Aviary. Length 100mm (LM D.4272).

Sydenham Edwards' painting, executed in 1810, is of particular interest because of Lord Stanley's pencilled annotation: "drawn last year from the living birds still in my possession". Though it is known that an aviary and menagerie was maintained at Knowsley by his father, the 12th Earl of Derby, this note provides some of the earliest evidence of the great collector's interest in keeping captive animals, as well as obtaining museum specimens.

The bird now numbered D.4272 is a specimen of considerable antiquity, with a label on which appears the single word 'aviary', so it is just possible that it might have provided one of the models for Sydenham Edwards' painting.

The many species of the genus *Sporophila*, which is common and widespread in Central and South America, are essentially ground-living birds associated with grassland and other open habitats. The Capped Seedeater extends from Suriname, through eastern Brazil and Paraguay to northern Argentina.

ML

40. RED-BILLED QUELEA & RED BISHOP
Family Ploceidae (sparrows and weaverbirds)

Left Watercolour by Benjamin Waterhouse Hawkins, dated 1st December 1843 and depicting Red-billed Queleas and Red Bishops *Euplectes orix* at Knowsley, from a bound volume entitled 'Original drawings of birds'.[1] 372 x 547mm (K).

Below Cabinet skin (background) of a male Red-billed Quelea *Quelea quelea*, which died in the Knowsley Aviary in June 1844. Length 130mm (LM D.4220a).

Until Lord Stanley became Earl of Derby in 1834, species kept in the aviaries at Knowsley were mostly game birds, waterfowl and songbirds. The latter included Weaverbirds, such as Queleas and Bishops, which would have been fairly readily available at this time through the trade out of Dakar (in Senegal) and, being seed-eaters, they are easily kept in captivity. Plumage details in Hawkins' painting suggest that his subjects were West African birds. The picture also seems to reflect Lord Derby's early realisation that such highly social species will not breed successfully unless they can do so colonially. There must have been many Queleas and Bishops that lived at Knowsley between 1834 and 1851, but no Red Bishops and only two Red-billed Queleas are extant in the Liverpool Museum collections.[2]

Queleas and Bishops are found throughout savanna regions of sub-Saharan Africa, where they feed mostly on grass seeds. Like other Weaverbirds, they build intricate, globular nests from strips of grass, as shown in Hawkins' painting. Male Weaverbirds have bright plumage only during the breeding season, but Queleas are conspicuous at all times of year because of their extraordinary abundance. Flying in flocks numbering tens of thousands and forming breeding colonies of millions of individuals, they provide one of the wildlife spectacles of Africa. Their vast numbers and seed-eating habits make them a major pest of cereal crops.

CF & PJ

[1]This painting is annotated by Lord Derby: 'Drawn by Waterhouse Hawkins from the living birds building these nests in the aviary at Knowsley Hall. Dec. 1st 1843. Tho' many nests and several eggs we did not rear any'. [2]The other is also a male, which died in the Knowsley Aviary in 1834 (LM D.4220), see foreground of the illustration to the right.

41. EASTERN QUOLL
Family Dasyuridae (carnivorous marsupials)

Above Letter from Edward Lear to Lord Derby, dated 17th December 1834 and concerning his painting of the Eastern Quoll. 91 x 222mm, folded (K).

Right Watercolour and watercolour mixed with gum, of an Eastern Quoll by Edward Lear, dated November 1834 and inscribed, 'Dasyurus Maugei Mas'. The animal in the picture is probably the individual now numbered D.257. 363 x 533mm (K).

Below Cabinet skin (length with tail 570mm) and relatively enlarged skull (length 65mm) of adult female Eastern Quoll *Dasyurus viverrinus*, which died at Knowsley on 8th July 1836. (LM D.257).

Edward Lear's expressive painting of the Eastern Quoll was undoubtedly done from a living animal, almost certainly the female now in the collections of Liverpool Museum (D.257). Dasyurus maugei is a synonym of *Dasyurus viverrinus*, credited to the explorer René Maugé.

Lear's letter reported that he had sent the 'drawing of the Mauges Opossum' to Knowsley with the hope that it would give Lord Derby pleasure. Lear had tried 'to imitate the fur most nearly'.

Eastern Quolls, otherwise known as the Eastern Native Cats, once ranged over much of south-eastern Australia but are now almost certainly confined to Tasmania. They feed mainly on insects, but also on fruit, ground-nesting birds and small mammals, and as scavengers on the carcasses of larger animals.[1]

CF

[1]See Catalogue entry 14 for another, earlier, painting of Eastern Quolls.

42. BRUSH-TAILED BETTONGS
Family Potoroidae (rat-kangaroos, potoroos and bettongs)

John Gould was a frequent correspondent of the 13th Earl of Derby, and many of his zoological specimens and original watercolours were sold to the Earl.[2] Indeed, there is evidence that Gould, with a view to the future sale of pictures to Lord Derby, took particular care to continue to produce paintings of kangaroos long after it became possible to produce printed lithographic plates from sketches drawn directly onto stone.

Gould's account of *Bettongia penicillata* in the *Monograph of the Macropodidae* relates how common he found the animal in south-eastern Australia, when he visited the continent in 1838-1839. He described how they lived in thick grassy nests, which they constructed in hollows in the ground so they were perfectly camouflaged. They dragged grass over the entrance with their tails to complete the deception. Gould also recorded how the Bettongs at Knowsley continued this curious behaviour in captivity, loading their tails with grass and moving it about the cage. Gould and Richter clearly showed this behaviour in their drawing.[3]

A letter from Lord Derby's Superintendent of the Aviary and Menagerie, John Thompson, to his employer gives an account of the death of two Brush-tailed Bettongs during the year 1846. At that time, a male and three females were alive, at least one of which had been born at Knowsley.[4] In their extensive correspondence Lord Derby and Sir Robert Heron frequently referred to Bettongs and how best to keep them in captivity; they exchanged several animals.[5]

Brush-tailed Bettongs (or Woylies, as they are sometimes called) have drastically declined in number. The subspecies which once inhabited south-eastern Australian is already extinct, and the only other forms remaining (in Queensland and in the south-west) are endangered. These little kangaroos feed mostly on fungi, which are digested by specialist bacteria in the animal's stomach.

CF

Above left Watercolour by Henry Constantine Richter, annotated, "Bettongia penicillata Gould. Mong. of Kang. No.1, tab 14 … H.C. Richter", from a bound volume entitled 'Original Drawings, Australian animals'. The published plate of the Brush-tailed Bettong in Gould's *Monograph of the Macropodidae*[1] was based on this painting. 355 x 510mm (K).

Above right The printed plate (no 25) for 'Bettongia penicillata' from Gould's *Monograph of the Macropodidae or family of Kangaroos*, 1841-44.

Below Skull of female Brush-tailed Bettong *Bettongia penicillata*, died in the Knowsley Aviary 11th January 1851. Length of skull 75mm (LM D.30a).

Bottom Skull of unsexed animal, died at Knowsley on an unknown date. Length of skull 65mm (LM D.31).

[1]Gould 1841-1844a. [2]See also Catalogue entries for Tammar Wallaby (59), Numbat (15), Pig-footed Bandicoot (16), Long-tailed Hopping Mouse (18), Paradise Parrot (4) and Tawny Frogmouth (55). [3]A surviving manuscript note by Richter further recorded the behaviour of both *Bettongia penicillata* and *B. gaimardi*, the Tasmanian Bettong, in captivity. He added several charming little sketches. One of these shows an animal asleep as in the published plate: "they invariably go to sleep in the following position". Richter also commented that they were, "very partial to bread & milk sweetened with sugar," (BMNH, Gould Collection). [4]Letter from Thompson to Lord Derby (LVRO 1/169/1). One specimen which had been bred at Knowsley was included in the sale of the Earl's living collections (Moore 1851). [5]LVRO 1/80.

43. MONGOOSE LEMUR
Family Lemuridae (lemurs)

Top Mounted specimen of a male Mongoose Lemur *Eulemur mongoz*, formerly in the collections of the Zoological Society of London and now in the Natural History Museum. Possibly one of the models for Wolf's paintings. Length to end of tail approx. 820mm (Clemency Fisher © The Natural History Museum, London).

Above and right Two watercolours by Joseph Wolf, both dated November 1851 and depicting *Eulemur mongoz* (Linnaeus 1766). Though these watercolours are in the Knowsley collection, they were completed after the death of the 13th Earl of Derby and were probably at least partly based on animals in the Zoological Society of London. 355 x 510; 345 x 505mm (see cover) (K).

One of Joseph Wolf's paintings illustrates a single female Mongoose Lemur, the other two males (or possibly the same animal in two different poses). They are dated 21st and 26th November 1851, but there is no evidence that Mongoose Lemurs ever lived in Lord Derby's menagerie. Indeed, it appears that the only example he ever owned was a museum specimen (D.468) of a female, which lacks data but is presumably the animal catalogued by Fraser[1] under the name *Lemur nigrifrons*.

These charming and very life-like paintings by Wolf demonstrate his great attention to aspects of the living animal such as the depth, lustre and texture of fur. They also illustrate Wolf's exceptional ability to convey the fine details and character of an animal's foot.

Confined to forest habitats in northwestern Madagascar and the adjacent Comoro Islands, the Mongoose Lemur, like most other Madagascan primates, is seriously endangered by widespread and indiscriminate destruction of the natural environment.

ML

[1]Fraser 1850: 19.

44. BLACK GIANT SQUIRREL
Family Sciuridae (squirrels)

Sciurus Javensis, Schreb. India.
The Original of the figure in the 'Gleanings.'

Left Watercolour by Edward Lear, completed at Knowsley in July 1836 and inscribed, '*Sciurus Javensis*. India'. It depicts *Ratufa bicolor* and was most probably based on the animal that died in June 1837 (now LM D.41c). 363 x 533mm (K).

Below Cabinet skin with separate (relatively enlarged) skull, derived from a formerly mounted specimen of *Ratufa bicolor* that died at Knowsley in June 1837 and was later catalogued under the synonymous name *Sciurus Javensis*. Length to end of tail 760mm. Skull 70mm in length (LM D.41c).

Edward Lear undoubtedly based his painting of this species on a living animal, but at least three examples are known to have been present in the Knowsley Menagerie during the relevant period and it is not entirely certain which of these provided a model. The female now numbered D.41c, which died on 30th June 1837, seems to be the most likely candidate.

Lear's painting was later published as Plate VI in the first volume of *Gleanings from the menagerie and aviary at Knowsley Hall*, edited by John Edward Gray.[1]

This large squirrel is a comparatively common, though secretive, denizen of the canopy layer in tall forest from Nepal and southern China to Malaysia, Sumatra and Java.
ML

[1]Gray, J.E. 1846a.

111

45. WOODCHUCK
Family Sciuridae (squirrels)

Right Watercolour by Edward Lear, completed at Knowsley in August 1836 and inscribed, 'Arctomys Empetra (Pallas). Canada'. It depicts *Marmota monax* and was almost certainly based on the specimen later registered as D.42a. 363 x 533mm (K).

Below Cabinet skin derived from a formerly mounted specimen of the Woodchuck (or Groundhog) *Marmota monax*, received at Knowsley in March 1835 and later catalogued under the synonymous name *Arctomys Empetra*. Length to end of tail 460mm (LM D.42a).

There is no evidence that this specimen, catalogued as having been received from a Mr. McCullock on 3rd March 1835, ever lived in Lord Derby's menagerie. It appears most likely that Lear based his painting on a dead animal that was on display in the Knowsley Museum. There was once a live Woodchuck (now D.42) in the Knowsley Menagerie, but it died in December 1841, so could not have been the example drawn by Lear in August 1836 (the species is known to have a life span of only 4-5 years in captivity).

Lear's painting was later published as Plate VII in the first volume of *Gleanings from the menagerie and aviary at Knowsley Hall*, edited by John Edward Gray.[1]

This burrowing rodent is common from Alaska, through southern Canada and the eastern United States to Alabama, wherever there is dry soil in fields, woodland clearings or on rocky slopes.

ML

[1]Gray, J.E. 1846a.

112

46. QUAGGA
Family Equidae (horses, zebras and asses)

Left Plate LIV in the second volume of Gray's *Gleanings from the menagerie and aviary at Knowsley Hall*, derived from a watercolour by Benjamin Waterhouse Hawkins, dated 1847 and depicting two clearly different specimens of *Equus quagga quagga*, then alive at Knowsley. 383 x 565mm (K).

Below Mounted Quagga, reputed to be the female from the Knowsley Menagerie that was sold in 1851 (On display in the Rothschild Museum, Tring. © The National History Museum, London).

This zebra formerly had a restricted range in the dry savanna habitats of Cape Province, South Africa, where herds of up to 50 animals were once reported. By the 1850s, numbers were declining, due to relentless hunting for meat and hides and competition from introduced domestic sheep for a limited food supply. Wild populations became extinct by the late 1870s and the last surviving captive specimen died in Amsterdam in 1883.

Taxonomists are currently unable to agree whether the now extinct Quagga was a distinct species, or just the most southerly race of the Plains Zebra, which remains widespread in eastern Africa and extends as far north as the Sudan. It seems to have differed from more northern zebra populations only in being browner and having a less pronounced pattern of stripes, though there was considerable variation in these features.

Benjamin Waterhouse Hawkins' painting of 1847 provides the earliest indication of Quagga being present in the Knowsley Menagerie, where there were also several examples of the more northern (and now similarly extinct) form *Equus quagga burchellii*. At least one of the animals illustrated appears not to have survived for very long, because when the living collections were auctioned in 1851, following the death of the 13th Earl of Derby, only one female Quagga was offered for sale.[1] It was bought by the Amsterdam Zoo and died there in 1853.[2] It is reputed that in 1889 this same Quagga was purchased as a mounted specimen by Walter Rothschild, for his museum at Tring in Hertfordshire. This is the animal illustrated, but the evidence linking it to the Knowsley Menagerie seems very tenuous.

ML

[1]Moore 1851. [2]Barnaby 1996.

113

Watercolour of two Guanacos *Lama guanicoe* by Benjamin Waterhouse Hawkins, inscribed by the artist: 'Drawn from the living Animals at Knowsley October 1844 ...' Inscribed on the back by the 13th Earl of Derby: 'Guanaco Auchenia Huanacus or the wild kind of Llama of which I have a pair but as the female showed no signs of breeding with her proper male,[1] she was put to a male Llama & produced a young one also a female'. From a volume of watercolours by Benjamin Waterhouse Hawkins and Joseph Wolf. This painting was the original for Plate 50 in *Gleanings*.[2] 570 x 370mm (K).

The taxonomic relationships between the four species of camelids from the Andes of South America are uncertain; all interbreed producing fertile offspring. The Llama and Alpaca are probably domesticated forms of wild Vicuñas and Guanacos.

The *Illustrated London News* engraving is accompanied by the remark: "In this group the Artist has represented the Curious and somewhat uncouth manner in which the animals stand and gaze at the appearance of a Stranger". However, Lord Derby's Alpacas and their wool were much in demand.[3] The Earl already had 14 animals by 1841; William Dawson admired them so much that he wanted to exhibit them at the Royal English Agricultural Show.[4]

Over a hundred more Alpacas arrived at Knowsley from South America in 1843; they had scab, which they gave to the other lamoids. All had to be clipped (after which the Alpacas resembled hares on stilts) and then individually washed with soft soap in big tubs in the Brew House. They showed their appreciation by, "violently regurgitating their champagne bottle dozes of physic, to the disgust of all concerned".[5] Some of these animals and their offspring were purchased from Lord Derby by Sir Titus Salt, as part of his unsuccessful scheme to naturalize them in the Pennines.[6]

The 13th Earl of Derby kept and successfully hybridised all four lamoids at Knowsley. The skull of a Vicuña which once lived in the menagerie at Knowsley[7] is in the collections of the Liverpool Museum, and there are lamoids from Knowsley in the Natural History Museum in London (for instance, the Black Llama mount illustrated on page 93).

CF

114

ALPACAS, IN THE KNOWSLEY MENAGERIE.

Left Watercolour by Hawkins, inscribed on front by the artist: 'Alpaca. Drawn from the living animals at Knowsley, July 23rd 1844 …' From the same bound volume as the Guanacos watercolour. This painting was the original for Plate 52 in *Gleanings*. 565 x 375mm (K).

Below left Engraving from the *Illustrated London News* for September 27th 1851, showing the Knowsley Alpaca herd of six male, four females and one fawn. 125 x 280mm (LM).

[1]It was probably the male Guanaco referred to in this quotation which was considered to be one of the most dangerous animals at Knowsley, and was always kept chained (Moore 1892: 2). According to Lord Derby, his Guanacos were, "vicious, active, watchful and restless … constantly trying to seize any person … springing against him with all its force, and then bites viciously … the female, though milder and of more quiet habits, is of a fiery disposition and ready to avenge any affront" (Gray 1850: 53). [2]Gray 1850. [3]Knowsley Alpacas and their wool were requested by Queen Victoria and by Prince Albert (LVRO 1/124/5, 7 & 9). Archduke John of Austria asked if Lord Derby had any surplus animals (NMGM MM/8/K/5: 54-55). Lord Derby also exchanged lamoids with Sir Robert Heron (LVRO 1/80) and corresponded with William Walton about breeding these animals in Britain (NMGM MM/K/8/5: 34-35). [4]Dawson to Derby (LVRO 1/44/1). [5]Moore 1892: 3-4. [6]Woolfall 1990. [7]LM D.(Ost.)17, probably from the animal which died in 1844, see Gray 1850: 53.

115

Family Bovidae (antelopes, cattle, sheep and goats)

Above Skull and horns on plinth, of a male Cape Eland *Taurotragus oryx*, collected by Joseph Burke from the Cape of Good Hope, given to the British Museum by Lord Derby in 1842 (Clemency Fisher © The Natural History Museum, London).

Right Watercolour by Benjamin Waterhouse Hawkins, painted at Knowsley on 3rd April 1845 and depicting three living specimens of Cape Eland (a female adult, half-grown male and a calf). 355 x 540mm (K).

Opposite One of the herd of five Cape Eland chosen by the Zoological Society of London at the dispersal of the Knowsley collections in 1851, photographed by the Count of Montizon at Regent's Park in about 1852 (Courtesy George Eastman House, Rochester, N.Y. © Barbara Morgan).

Joseph Burke, initially employed at Knowsley as an under-gardener, was sent to South Africa in 1839 to obtain specimens for Lord Derby's museum and menagerie. Included amongst the valuable collections which he brought back to Liverpool in November 1842 were living specimens (two males and a female) of Cape Eland, along with the preserved remains of three further individuals of this species that he had shot. Two of the latter were almost immediately donated by Lord Derby to the British Museum in London, where their skulls and horns still survive[1] but the third specimen, which was retained in the Knowsley Museum and later numbered D.161a, cannot now be traced and was presumably destroyed when the Liverpool Museum was bombed in 1941.

The live animals, two of which were painted by Benjamin Waterhouse Hawkins on 30th December 1843, soon became the progenitors of a small but actively breeding herd at Knowsley and some of their offspring were depicted in a later watercolour by the same artist, dated 3rd April 1845 (see b). Both illustrations were later published in the second volume of *Gleanings from the menagerie and aviary at Knowsley Hall*.[2] In December 1845, a male animal (probably one of Burke's original imports), was sent from Knowsley to the Jardin des Plantes in Paris, in exchange for an individual of the Indonesian dwarf buffalo known as the Anoa (*Bubalus depressicornis*). The Eland died in Paris on 13th April 1849.[3]

After the death of the 13th Earl of Derby in 1851, and in accordance with the provisions of his will, the five Cape Eland then at Knowsley were bequeathed to the Zoological Society of London and became the first individuals of this species ever to be exhibited at the Regent's Park Zoo. These animals, one of which was photograped by the Count of Montizon in about 1852, established a breeding stock that produced calves on an almost yearly basis from 1853 until well into the twentieth century. They bred so well that surplus stock was passed to Viscount Hill at Hawkstone, in Shropshire and he even took his animals to cattle shows.[4]

This very large, gregarious antelope was once widespread throughout most of south eastern Africa from the Cape of Good Hope to the Sudan, occupying both open savannah and relatively dense woodland over a wide altitudinal range. Though the species remains locally common, it has been eliminated from many areas of human habitation due to over-hunting. Easily tamed, Cape Eland have become semi-domesticated in parts of southern Africa, where they are ranched for their excellent milk and meat.

ML

[1]BMHM 1842.12.6.14 & 15. See illustration on page 116. [2]As plates XXVI & XXVII, in Gray, 1850.
[3]Glover's claim (1975) that this animal was a specimen of Lord Derby's Eland *Taurotragus derbianus* is now believed to be erroneous. [4]Pollard 1871: 119.

Above Invoice from Dr Stanger in Cape Town to Lord Derby, dated 30th December 1850, for a shipment of living animals. This included £23 10 shillings for, '3 Elands & Carriage', and a compensatory £1 for, 'Damages done to room in which animals were kept in P.M.B. [Pietermaritzburg, Natal]'. Two of these animals arrived at Knowsley in June 1851 and were part of the herd that went to the zoo in London. 420 x 320mm (unfolded) (Liverpool Record Office, Liverpool City Libraries).

49. BLESBOK
Family Bovidae (antelopes, cattle, sheep and goats)

Confined to South Africa, the typical form of this antelope (*Damaliscus d. dorcas*, known as the Bontebok) occupies a small area near the Cape of Good Hope, while a another subspecies (the Blesbok, *D. dorcas phillipsi*) is more widespread on higher ground inland. Both forms are now effectively extinct as wild animals, the survivors being commercially ranched or otherwise semi-domesticated.

Immediately after the death of the 13th Earl of Derby and just prior to the auction of his menagerie, Thomas Moore[1] catalogued all the livestock then present at Knowsley. He listed four Bontebok (of which at least two had been born on the estate) but only a single female 'Bless-bok'.

Among several distinguished painters employed by Lord Derby for the artistic documentation of his collections was Joseph Wolf (1820-1899), whose work is included in two bound volumes housed at Knowsley. One of these volumes includes a note by Thomas Moore, dated 28th April 1871, which records that nearly all the species illustrated, "were living at Knowsley at the breaking up of the Collection in 1851, and these sketches were doubtless made from those specimens either before or after their removal."[2] Consequently, it seems likely that Wolf's finished painting, although dated 17th April 1852, may be a composite derived from drawings of a single animal that were prepared during the previous year.

Bontebok and Blesbok are grazers inhabiting open grassland, usually in small groups of up to about 30 animals, though in the past these sometimes joined with others to form huge herds at times of seasonal migration. Joseph Wolf clearly (and very appropriately) used artistic licence to place his subject within the context of just such a large herd.

ML

[1]Moore 1851. [2]Woolfall 1990.

50. ELK

Family Cervidae (deer)

The history of Elk in the Knowsley Menagerie is not well documented. Although Woolfall[1] discovered that Lord Derby purchased a specimen in Liverpool on 13th December 1832, this transaction was apparently on behalf of the Zoological Society of London, to which the animal was later forwarded.

It seems likely that Joseph Wolf's painting of four Elk was based at least partly on animals then alive at Knowsley, although only one male was recorded as being present on the estate a year later – when the entire live collection was auctioned following the death of the 13th Earl.[2]

Though they may assemble into small herds during winter, Elk (which in North America are called Moose) are essentially solitary animals. Associated with woodlands and marshes that are subject to seasonal snow cover, the species occupies an enormous range from Norway to eastern Siberia, Alaska, most of Canada and adjacent parts of the northern United States. In some areas it remains abundant, though it has been much reduced elsewhere due to excessive hunting, a decline which began in Europe as early as the thirteenth century.

ML

[1]Woolfall 1990. [2]Moore 1851.

Above Engraving of Elk and keeper at Knowsley, from the *Illustrated London News* report of the sale of the Knowsley Menagerie, October 11th 1851. 90 x 112mm (LM).

Left Watercolour depicting Elk *Alces alces*, executed by Joseph Wolf on 14th October 1850 and assumed to be based on at least one animal then alive in the Knowsley Menagerie. 345 x 505mm (K).

THE PELICAN CHORUS.

Yes, they came; and among the rest,
The King of the Cranes all grandly dressed.
Such a lovely tail! Its feathers float
Between the ends of his blue dress-coat;
With pea-green trowsers all so neat,
And a delicate frill to hide his feet,—
(For though no one speaks of it, every one knows,
He has got no webs between his toes!)

As soon as he saw our Daughter Dell,
In violent love that Crane King fell,—
On seeing her waddling form so fair,
With a wreath of shrimps in her short white hair,
And before the end of the next long day,
Our Dell had given her heart away;
For the King of the Cranes had won that heart,
With a Crocodile's egg and a large fish-tart.
She vowed to marry the King of the Cranes,
Leaving the Nile for stranger plains;
And away they flew in a gathering crowd
Of endless birds in a lengthening cloud.

Species Named in Honour of Edward Stanley, 13th Earl of Derby

Clemency Fisher, Malcolm Largen and Ian Wallace

This section of the catalogue demonstrates the high regard in which Edward Stanley was held by the contemporary scientific community, as illustrated by the numerous species named in his honour. Until he became 13th Earl of Derby in 1834, these names tended to reflect his earlier title, Lord Stanley. Then, as now, it was accepted practice to compliment distinguished personalities in this way, even long after their death. Many plant species were also named in honour of Edward Stanley, such as Stanley's Wittmacanthus (page 135), but the following list includes only animals with names that are known or suspected to have been devised for this purpose. Those in bold-face have individual Catalogue entries and illustrations. All specific names are in lower case.

Opposite 'The Pelican Chorus'. Lear must have had a particular affection for the Stanley Crane, which was named after Edward Stanley in 1826 (see pages 124-125). The vignette at the top of Lear's *Nonsense Rhyme* shows a pelican, and a composite bird with upper half Blue Heron and lower half Stanley Crane. The crane is unscientifically embellished with frilly spats (words abridged and condensed from the original).

MAMMALS
Moschus stanleyanus **J.E. Gray 1836** = *Tragulus napu* **(Cuvier 1822), Greater Malay Mouse-deer**
Halmaturus derbianus **J.E. Gray 1837** = *Macropus eugenii* **(Desmarest 1817), Tammar Wallaby**
Paradoxurus derbyanus J.E. Gray 1837 = *Hemigalus derbyanus*, Banded Palm Civet
Didelphys derbianus **Waterhouse 1841** = *Caluromys derbianus*, **Lord Derby's Woolly Opossum**
Pteromys derbianus J.E. Gray 1842 = *Anomalurus derbianus*, Lord Derby's Flying Squirrel
Boselaphus derbianus **J.E. Gray 1847** = *Taurotragus derbianus*, **Lord Derby's Eland**

BIRDS
Anthropoides stanleyanus **Vigors 1826** = *Anthropoides paradisea* **(Lichtenstein 1793), Stanley Crane**
Podargus stanleyanus **Vigors & Horsfield 1827** = *Podargus strigoides* **(Latham 1801), Tawny Frogmouth**
Falco stanleyi Audubon 1831 = *Accipiter cooperii* (Bonaparte 1828), Cooper's Hawk
Otis stanleyi J.E. Gray 1831 = *Neotis denhami stanleyi*, Denham's Bustard
Gallus stanleyi J.E. Gray 1832 = *Gallus lafayetii* Lesson 1831, Sri Lankan Junglefowl
Aulacorhynchus derbianus **Gould 1835, Chestnut-tipped Toucanet**
Lyrurus derbianus Gould 1838 = *Tetrao tetrix Linnaeus* 1758, Eurasian Black Grouse
Nyctidromus derbyanus Gould 1838 = *Nyctidromus albicollis derbyanus*, Pauraque
Carduelis stanleyi Audubon 1839 = *Carduelis barbata* (Molina 1782), Black-chinned Siskin
Trochilus derbianus Fraser 1840 = *Ensifera ensifera* (Boissoneau 1839), Sword-billed Hummingbird
Oreophasis derbianus **G.R. Gray 1844, Horned Guan**
Chauna derbiana G.R. Gray 1846 = *Chauna chavaria* (Linnaeus 1766), Northern Screamer
Trochilus derbyi **DeLattre & Bourcier 1846** = *Eriocnemis derbyi*, **Black-thighed Puffleg**
Trochilus stanleyi Bourcier 1851 = *Chalcostigma stanleyi*, Blue-mantled Thornbill
Palaeornis derbianus **Fraser 1852** = *Psittacula derbiana*, **Lord Derby's Parakeet**
Platycercus stanleyi Vigors 1830 = *Platycercus icterotis* (Temminck 1819), Western Rosella
Saurophagus derbianus Kaup 1852 = *Pitangus sulphuratus* (Linnaeus 1766), Great Kiskadee
Orthotomus derbianus Moore 1854, Luzon Tailor-bird
Derbyomia G.R. Gray 1855 (valid as a subgenus, type species *Trochilus derbyi* DeLattre & Bourcier)
Porphyrio stanleyi **Rowley 1875** = *Porphyrio albus* **White 1790, White Swamp-hen**

REPTILES
Sternothurus derbianus J.E. Gray 1844 = *Pelusios castaneus* (Schweigger 1812), West African Mud Turtle
Zonurus derbianus **J.E. Gray 1845** = *Cordylus giganteus* **Smith 1844, Giant Girdled Lizard**
Zootoca derbiana J.E. Gray 1845, *Cat. Lizards Brit. Mus.*: 29 = ?
Eublepharis derbianus J.E. Gray 1845, *Cat. Lizards Brit. Mus.*: 274 = ?

INSECTS
? *Anoplophora stanleyana* Hope 1839, *Proc. Linn. Soc. London* 5: 43
? *Omma stanleyi* Newman 1839, *Ann. Mag. Nat. Hist.* 3: 304
Cetonia derbyana **Westwood 1843** = *Dicronorhina derbyana*, **Flower Chafer**

121

51. HORNED GUAN
Family Cracidae (guans and curassows)

Above Plate CXXI from vol.3 of G.R. Gray's *Genera of Birds*, an illustration of *Oreophasis Derbianus* based on a painting by David William Mitchell (1813-1859), also modelled on the single Knowsley Museum specimen. 285 x 380mm (K).

Right Watercolour, painted in 1843 by Benjamin Waterhouse Hawkins (1807-1889), based on a single specimen that had recently arrived in the Knowsley Museum (which would later become the holotype of *Oreophasis Derbianus*). 370 x 540mm (K).

Below Cabinet skin of formerly mounted specimen; male. Holotype of *Oreophasis Derbianus* G.R. Gray 1844, *Genera of Birds* 3: 485, pls 121 and CXXI. Length 850mm (LM D.210).

The early history of this specimen is exceptionally well documented[1]. Among the many collectors employed or sponsored by Lord Derby for work overseas was the 'Liverpool natural curiosity dealer' John Bates, who was despatched to Central America in June 1842. He returned to England in September 1843, bearing trophies that included the skin of a remarkable bird, given to him eight months earlier after it had been shot on the Volcan de Fuego in Guatemala.

Almost immediately after its arrival at Knowsley in 1843, this specimen inspired Benjamin Waterhouse Hawkins to compose a watercolour. His painting depicts two birds, although only the single example was available for use as a model. In the following year, this specimen became the holotype of a new species described by George Robert Gray[2]; the description being accompanied by a portrait by David William Mitchell, a talented artist who later became secretary to the Zoological Society of London. Gray, at that time head of the bird section at the Natural History Museum in London, simultaneously erected a new genus, *Oreophasis* – which, to this day, contains only the single species, *Oreophasis derbianus*.

Known only from subtropical forest on the higher volcanoes and mountains of Guatemala and adjacent regions of southeastern Mexico, this bird has become increasingly rare in recent times, due to habitat destruction and hunting.

ML

[1]Salvin 1860. [2]Gray, G.R. 1844.

52. WHITE SWAMP-HEN
Family Rallidae (rails, coots and gallinules)

Mounted specimen on stand; almost complete albino, except for some bluish-purple feathers in wings and tail. Holotype of *Porphyrio stanleyi* Rowley 1875; *Ornithological Miscellany* 1: 37 & Plate IX. This name is now synonymised with *Porphyrio albus* White 1790, the White Swamp-hen. Total length approximately 464mm (LM D.3213).

Very little is known about the White Swamp-hen, but it was probably confined to Lord Howe Island, off the eastern coast of Australia (the Liverpool bird is listed as being from New Zealand, but this is almost certainly incorrect). It is now extinct. There are contemporary accounts of White Swamp-hens on Lord Howe Island[1] and drawings of these birds by Thomas Watling and George Raper, composed in 1788 and 1790, respectively.[2] A sketch of three of these birds was also included in the 1788 journal of Surgeon Arthur Bowes Smyth of the *Lady Penrhyn*.[3]

The White Swamp-hen now in Liverpool was purchased by Lord Stanley for three guineas on the seventeenth day of the London sale of William Bullock's Museum (27th May 1819; Lot 60 – 'White Gallinule, F. Alba; New Zealand, rare';[4] Bullock's Catalogue number 1645). It is very similar to the holotype of *Porphyrio albus*, a pure white bird in the Naturhistorisches Museum, Vienna, which was acquired in 1806 at the sale of the Leverian Museum.

Both the Liverpool and Vienna birds differ from the Purple Swamphen *Porphrio porphyrio melanotus* of Australia and New Zealand in having shorter wings and toes.[5] Possibly they represent a species more closely related to the endangered Takahe of New Zealand, *Porphyrio mantelli*.[6] It is believed that albinism predominated in the species on Lord Howe Island and that these birds were exterminated by sailors in the early nineteenth century.

CF

123

[1]Phillip 1789: 273, pl. 44. Phillip suggested the birds with blue in their wings were males. [2]These are in various public collections, including the British Museum and the Natural History Museum. [3]Hutton 1990: 11. [4]Bullock 1819, 3: 103. [5]Greenway 1967: 251. [6]Ripley 1977: 304-305.

53. STANLEY CRANE
Family Gruidae (cranes)

Watercolour, painted by Benjamin Waterhouse Hawkins on 5th September 1845, depicting two chicks of *Anthropoides paradisea* recently hatched at Knowsley. 376 x 552mm (K).

Watercolour, painted by Benjamin Waterhouse Hawkins in December 1845, showing two half-grown chicks of *Anthropoides paradisea*. 376 x 552mm (K).

In 1826, a description of *Anthropoides Stanleyanus* was published by Nicholas Aylward Vigors,[1] along with an illustration of the species by James de Carle Sowerby, both based on a bird then living at the Tower of London. It was very soon realised that Vigors' scientific name was invalid, representing a species described over 30 years previously (*Anthropoides paradisea*), but the vernacular epithet 'Stanley Crane' has remained in use ever since. Vigors did not explain exactly why his species was dedicated to Lord Stanley, but it may have been because it was he who first drew attention to the existence of the bird in the Tower menagerie. Lord Derby's personal observations on Stanley Cranes, published by J.E. Gray,[2] record that: 'I possessed for some years several individuals of that species of the genus *Anthropoides* which my late friend Dr. Latham had done me the honour to distinguish by my name, in consequence of my having had the good fortune to draw his attention to the bird, which I had seen in the Tower of London'. Strangely, Derby seems to have forgotten who had named the species in his honour twenty years earlier, and perhaps also the individual to whom he had conveyed the original information!

Stanley Cranes lived on Lord Derby's estate for over 15 years and no fewer than 13 specimens, mostly juveniles, are listed in Louis Fraser's catalogue of the museum. In September 1835, Edward Lear painted an adult bird at Knowsley, an illustration later published in John Gray's *Gleanings*.[3] Four birds, including one bred at Knowsley, were living on the estate at the time of the Earl's death.[4] The cranes showed no inclination to breed until 1844–1845, when a total of 12 eggs were laid and three chicks hatched. Unfortunately, these failed to survive for more then a few weeks, but two were painted from life by Benjamin Waterhouse Hawkins in September 1845. Though subsequently prepared as museum specimens and included in Fraser's catalogue, these juveniles are not present in the Liverpool Museum today, neither is there good evidence that the adult bird painted by Lear still exists.

Lear must have had a particular affection for the Stanley Crane (as he did for the Orinoco Goose). The vignette at the top of the 'Pelican Chorus', from his *Nonsense Rhymes*, shows a pelican, and a composite bird with upper half Blue Heron and lower half Stanley Crane (see page 120).

Variously known as the Blue Crane, Paradise Crane or Stanley Crane, this bird occupies upland pastures and sometimes wetlands in South Africa, Botswana and Namibia. It is still relatively common in some parts of this range and occasionally seen in large flocks, but other populations have suffered serious depletion in recent years, mainly due to habitat loss, and the species is currently considered vulnerable to further decline.

ML

[1]Vigors 1826. [2]Gray, J.E. 1846a. [3]Vol. 1, pl. XIV. [4]Moore 1851.

Stanley Crane *Scops Paradisea* (Licht.) South Africa ~ The Original of the Plate in the Gleanings.

Left Watercolour, executed by Edward Lear in September 1835, depicting an adult specimen of Stanley Crane *Anthropoides paradisea* (Lichtenstein 1793) painted from life at Knowsley. 363 x 530mm (K).

Above Plate XIV from the first (1846) volume of Gray's *Gleanings from the menagerie and aviary at Knowsley Hall*, derived from the portrait of *Anthropoides paradisea* painted by Edward Lear in 1835. 383 x 565mm (K).

54. LORD DERBY'S PARAKEET
Family Psittacidae (parrots)

Right Watercolour by Edward Lear, dated 1831 and undoubtedly based on the bird which would later become the holotype of *Palaeornis Derbianus*. 363 x 530mm (K).

Far right Gould's *The birds of Asia*, Vol. 6, Pl. 9 (first issued in June 1858); the illustration being derived from John Gould's original painting of the holotype of *Palaeornis Derbianus*. 385 x 555mm (K).

Below Cabinet skin of formerly mounted specimen. Holotype of *Palaeornis Derbianus Fraser 1852*, *Proc. Zool. Soc. London* (for 1850): 245; the species is now known as *Psittacula derbiana*. Length 530mm to tip of bill (LM D.793).

The origins and early history of this specimen are obscure, but Gould (1858) recorded that 'it lived for some time in the Earl of Derby's menagerie at Knowsley'. It is not known whether the bird was still alive in 1831 when it was twice painted by Edward Lear. Neither of these works was reproduced in Lear's (1830-1832) *Illustrations of the family of Psittacidae*, presumably because the species was still unidentified at that time.

The same uncertainty surrounds the illustration by Joseph Wolf which accompanies Fraser's description of the species[1] - though, like the earlier drawings by Lear, Wolf's painting was undoubtedly executed at Knowsley.

Louis Fraser entered the 13th Earl of Derby's service, following employment as museum curator at the Zoological Society of London, and began to compile a comprehensive catalogue of the Knowsley Museum collection between 1848 and 1850. This enterprise was abruptly terminated when, through the patronage of Lord Derby, Fraser obtained appointment as Vice Consul at Whydah, on the coast of Benin in West Africa. Indeed, Fraser's description of several new bird species (including *Palaeornis Derbianus*), submitted to the Secretary of the Zoological Society in November 1850, was prompted by the fact that 'my stay in England is necessarily drawing to a close'.

In 1849, John Gould issued the first 17 plates of *The birds of Asia*, a monumental work which eventually appeared in 35 parts and was only completed two years after the author's death in 1881. Part 10 was issued in June 1858 and included an account of Lord Derby's Parakeet, accompanied by yet another illustration based on 'the original and [still] unique specimen now in the Derby Museum at Liverpool'. When the work was later bound in seven volumes, the picture of *Palaeornis Derbianus* became Plate 9 in Vol. 6.

This little-known parrot appears to be confined to the mountains of western China and southeastern Tibet, where flocks of up to fifty birds have been observed in coniferous and rhododendron forest, even as as high as 4000 m.

ML

[1]Fraser 1852.

126

55. TAWNY FROGMOUTH
Family Podargidae (frogmouths)

Above The published plate for *Podargus cuvieri* Vigors & Horsfield, in Gould's *Birds of Australia* (vol.2, plate 4). Note that this entry is for the Tasmanian form of the Tawny Frogmouth, *P. strigoides cuvieri*; *P. Stanleyanus* is considered to be a synonym of the south-east Australian form *P. s. strigoides*. Gould must have realised his mistake after he had labelled the original painting (left) and sold it to Lord Derby. 385 x 560mm (K).

Left Crayon sketch entitled 'Podargus Stanleyanus. [by] Gould' (possibly in John Gould's writing) from volume one of a series of bound volumes entitled 'Original drawings of birds' by Gould and others. This is the original (in reverse) of the printed plate above. 332 x 510mm (K).

Below Cabinet skin, unsexed. Holotype of *Podargus Stanleyanus* Vigors & Horsfield, now considered to be a synonym of the Tawny Frogmouth *Podargus strigoides* (Latham 1801). 'New Holland' [= New South Wales]. Length 460mm (LM D.1602).

Frogmouths are related to owls and have the same soft plumage and nocturnal habits. The Tawny Frogmouth is beautifully camouflaged and, at the slightest disturbance, will freeze into a posture that closely resembles a broken branch. It is found throughout Australia and feeds mainly on insects and spiders.

In the text accompanying his plate in Birds of Australia, John Gould commented that the native name for the bird, 'More-pork', came from its 'hoarse, unearthly cry'; it was also one of the most sluggish and confiding birds he had ever met, able in captivity to spend the entire day asleep on the back of a chair or other convenient perch.

CF

[1]D.1602 was the specimen 'in the collection of Lord Stanley' on which John Latham (1822, 7: 368) based the description of his 'Wedge-tailed Goatsucker'. It therefore became the holotype of *Podargus Stanleyanus* Vigors & Horsfield 1827 (*Trans. Linn. Soc. London* 15: 199), since these authors derived their description directly from Latham's account. It was also Latham who requested that they honour Lord Stanley in their choice of a specific name for this bird. Clearly, Warren (1966: 281) was wrong to suggest that the holotype of *Podargus Stanleyanus* is housed in the Natural History Museum, London.

Right Plate 279 from Gould's *Monograph of the Trochilidae*, depicting two males and a female of 'Eriocnemis derbianus, Derby's Puff-leg', painted and lithographed by John Gould and Henry Constantine Richter.[1] 395 x 555mm (K).

Below Formerly a fully mounted bird, displayed in a flying position, now partially reduced for cabinet storage; female. Specimen of *Eriocnemis derbyi* from the collection of the 13th Earl of Derby. Wing span about 120mm (LM D.1105a).

De Lattre & Bourcier's dedication, which accompanied their description of this species,[2] provides a clear indication of the international reputation enjoyed by both the Earl and his collections: 'Dédié à lord Derby, de Knowsley près Liverpool, possédant l'une des plus belles collections connues en ornithologie, le plus zélé et le plus généreux protecteur envers les hommes qui s'occupent des sciences naturelles.' Their description, however, was not based on a specimen in Lord Derby's possession.

The Black-thighed Puffleg is a bird of forest margins and similar rather open habitats at elevations of 2500-3600 m, in the Andes of Columbia and northwestern Ecuador. The 14 species of 'puffleg' hummingbirds derive their name from the conspicuous cluster of downy feathers carried on the upper part of each leg. These leg-puffs are black only in *Eriocnemis derbyi*, but white in all its relatives; their function remains unknown.

ML

[1]Gould 1849a-1861. [2]De Lattre & Bourcier 1846: 306.

57. CHESTNUT-TIPPED TOUCANET
Family Ramphastidae (toucans)

Even in the early nineteenth century, the spread of scientific knowledge could sometimes occur with remarkable speed. On 25th February 1835, Lord Derby purchased from a Mr. Tucker the skin of a bird collected in the 'Cordillerian Andes' of South America. By July of the same year the specimen had been shown to John Gould (1804-1881), had been recognised as a new species of toucan and had its description published in the *Proceedings of the Zoological Society of London*.[1] In December 1835, the third and final part of Gould's *Monograph of the Ramphastidae*[2] was issued and included a magnificent plate depicting *Aulacorhynchus derbianus* – drawn, painted, lithographed, printed and published in considerably less than a year!

Gould's illustration shows two birds, though it is clear from his own evidence that he had only a single specimen for use as a model. Considering that this was also a dead specimen, possibly still in the form of an unmounted skin, the artist's ability to animate his drawings is truly impressive.

The notes written by Gould to accompany this painting are also illuminating: 'For the loan of the only example of this fine species which has come under my notice I am indebted to the kindness of the Earl of Derby … In naming this bird after so distinguished and honourable an individual, I am influenced partly by the interest which His Lordship takes in the promulgation of science, especially ornithology, and partly by the desire I feel to testify my respect and gratitude'.

This toucan inhabits mountain forest, extending from Surinam through Venezuela, Colombia, Ecuador and Peru to northern Bolivia.

ML

[1]Gould, J. 1835b. [2]Gould, J. 1833-1835a.

58. LORD DERBY'S WOOLLY OPOSSUM
Family Didelphidae (American opossums)

Right Watercolour by Edward Lear, dated 18th March 1834 and painted at Knowsley from the specimen that would later become the holotype of *Didelphys Derbianus*. 363 x 533mm (K)

Above Plate 2★ from Waterhouse (1841), depicting the holotype of *Didelphys Derbianus* in a chromolithograph by William Dickes. 125 x 180mm (LM).

Below Cabinet skin, reduced from a mounted specimen in August 1897. Holotype of *Didelphys Derbianus* Waterhouse 1841, *Jardine's Naturalist's Library* 11: 97; the species is now known as *Caluromys derbianus*. Length to end of tail approx. 685mm (tail curled) (LM D.194).

There is no record of when, or from where, this specimen came into the possession of Lord Derby, but it cannot have arrived later than 1834 (when Lear drew it). There is no evidence that the animal was ever alive in the Knowsley Menagerie. In 1841, Lord Derby's specimen was the model for the type description of *Didelphys Derbianus*, written by the then museum curator at the Zoological Society of London, George Waterhouse. Waterhouse stated that he had 'taken the liberty of naming it' after the 13th Earl.[1] Waterhouse's little book, one of the series entitled *Jardine's Naturalist's Library*, includes chromolithographs of 36 species of marsupial, drawn by William Dickes (1815-1892).

Only in 1999 was it realised that there exists a much better picture of this animal, painted seven years earlier. This is by Edward Lear, but had been completely overlooked because the subject was identified only as a 'Tree Rat'. The model for Lear's watercolour can only have been the future holotype of *Caluromys derbianus*, because no other example of this species existed at Knowsley until much later (another arrived in September 1843 and was painted by Benjamin Waterhouse Hawkins during the following month). Another clue is that the tail on the animal in Lear's painting is coiled in an unlifelike spiral, identical to the way the tail had been badly set on the specimen, before it was extensively repaired in 2001.

Sometimes called the Central American Opossum, this nocturnal and arboreal marsupial is locally common in lowland forest from Mexico to Ecuador and Colombia.

ML

[1]Waterhouse 1841.

59. TAMMAR WALLABY
Family Macropodidae (kangaroos and wallabies)

Two watercolours of Derby's Wallaby *Halmaturus derbianus* Gray, 1837 by John Gould (probably assisted by Henry Constantine Richter). No. 23 and no. 24 from a bound volume entitled '*Original Drawings of Australian animals*'. The name *H. derbianus* is now considered to be a synonym of *Macropus eugenii*, the Tammar Wallaby. 345 x 515mm & 350 x 525mm (K).

John Edward Gray, Keeper of Zoology at the British Museum, named this species in honour of Lord Derby[1] because he had donated to the Zoological Society of London the living animal that later became the type specimen.[2] This gift seems to suggest that, even in the 1830s, this kangaroo was well represented in the Knowsley Menagerie and two individuals were included in the sale of the 13th Earl's living collections in 1851.[3]

John Gould sold Lord Derby two versions of paintings of the animal he called 'Derby's Wallaby'. The first version, where the more hunched animal is facing to the right, is unpublished, but the other version was the basis of Gould's published plate in *The Monograph of the Macropodidae*,[4] which was then re-used in his *Mammals of Australia*.[5]

The Tammar Wallaby is one of the smallest of the many species of the genus *Macropus* and was once widespread in Australia, but has now become extinct in many parts of its former range. The dark, grizzled little kangaroo is still found on several off-shore islands (such as Kangaroo Island and the Houtman Abrolhos) but on the Australian mainland is found only in south-west Western Australia and a small area of South Australia.[6]

CF

[1]Gray, J.E. 1837: 583. [2]BMNH 1855.12.24.64 from Swan River, Western Australia. [3]Moore 1851. [4]Gould 1841-1844a, Plate 10. [5]Gould 1845b-1863, volume 2, Plate 30. Note that the annotations on the paintings themselves, which record the first version as being the original of Gould's plate, are incorrect. [6]Strahan 1995: 330.

60. LORD DERBY'S ELAND
Family Bovidae (antelopes, cattle, sheep and goats)

Thomas Whitfield, towards the end of the nine-year period during which he collected for Lord Derby in West Africa, brought back from the Gambia in 1846 the horns of two huge male antelopes. He returned to England in the following year with headless skins, representing both male and female specimens of the same species. This was the material from which J.E. Gray prepared his original description of *Boselaphus Derbianus*, and on which Benjamin Waterhouse Hawkins based the painting of this species that Gray (1850) later published in *Gleanings from the menagerie and aviary at Knowsley Hall*.

The hunter's skins still survive at the Natural History Museum in London, but the original pairs of horns, though included in Louis Fraser's catalogue of the Knowsley Museum (D.376 and 376a), cannot now be traced and were almost certainly destroyed when the Liverpool Museum was bombed in 1941.

Also known as the Giant Eland, this huge antelope was once widespread in the relatively narrow belt of savanna woodland that extends from Senegal in western Africa to the River Nile in the east. The species has now been eliminated from most of this former range, by a combination of over-hunting and its exceptional susceptibility to rinderpest, a disease introduced into Africa with domestic cattle.

ML

[1]Gray, J.E. 1847. [2]Recent research indicates that Glover (1975) was wrong to suggest that the first specimen of Lord Derby's Eland reached England in 1842, after having been 'picked up at some West African port of call' by Joseph Burke on his way home from South Africa. Glover's belief that Hawkins' painting of this species was based on a living animal in the Knowsley Menagerie seems equally erroneous.

61. GREATER MALAY MOUSE-DEER
Family Tragulidae (mouse-deer and chevrotains)

Above Plate XXXV from the second volume of Gray's (1850) *Gleanings from the menagerie and aviary at Knowsley Hall*, depicting *Moschus Stanleyanus* and based on the painting executed by Waterhouse Hawkins in 1844. 383 x 565mm (K).

Left Watercolour by Benjamin Waterhouse Hawkins (1807-1889), painted at Knowsley in 1844 from a living specimen of *Moschus Stanleyanus* Gray 1836, *Proc. Zool. Soc. London*: 65; a name now considered a junior synonym of *Tragulus napu*. 370 x 560mm (K).

Moschus Stanleyanus was described by J.E. Gray from 'four living specimens in the magnificent collection of the Earl of Derby at Knowsley; and two others … It is not known from what exact locality any of them were obtained'.[1] None of these Knowsley syntypes seem to have survived as museum specimens, though two at least (a male and female numbered D.184a and 184b) are recorded as having been preserved after their deaths in the menagerie on 21st September 1836 and 4th October 1836, respectively.

Over eight years after *Moschus Stanleyanus* was described by Gray, Benjamin Waterhouse Hawkins completed a watercolour of the species, inscribed 'drawn fom the living animal at Knowsley, Dec. 31st 1844 … female'. This painting was later published as Plate XXXV in the second volume of *Gleanings*. There seems to be no good reason for assuming that the animal painted by Waterhouse Hawkins in 1844 was necessarily one of the type specimens, although it could well have been the one that Lord Derby donated, four years later, to the Natural History Museum in London.[2]

This solitary and nocturnal animal occupies forest habitats from southern Vietnam and Thailand to Malaysia and the islands of Sumatra and Borneo.

ML

[1]Gray, J.E. 1836. [2]It follows that the material at the BMNH, which consists of a skin (BMNH 1848.10.11.6) and separate skull (BMNH 1848.12.12.1), is of equally dubious type significance.

62. GIANT GIRDLED LIZARD
Family Cordylidae (girdled lizards)

Joseph Burke, initially employed as a gardener on the Knowsley Estate, was sent by the Earl of Derby in 1839 to collect for his museum and menagerie in South Africa. Burke returned to Britain in 1842 with a fine series of the mammals and birds which were of greatest interest to Lord Derby. Any reptiles, amphibians and fish the Earl happened to acquire were usually given to the British Museum in London. Among those obtained by Burke were several specimens of a large, spiny lizard which John Edward Gray described and named *Zonurus derbianus,* unaware that Andrew Smith (the former Director of the South African Museum) had already published an account of this species during the previous year.

Giant Girdled Lizards are colonial and live in burrows, which they dig for themselves in fine soil. They feed mostly on insects and spiders and are often seen on the surface during the day, each tending to bask near the entrance to its tunnel with the head held characteristically high and facing the sun. Such behaviour led early Dutch settlers to give the animal its alternative name 'Sonkyker' ('Sungazer'). The species is confined to South Africa and is declining in numbers, due to alteration of its grassland habitat by farming and the collection of animals for the pet trade.

Following exploits in South Africa that had much impressed his superiors, Joseph Burke was promptly dispatched by Sir William Hooker, Director of the Royal Botanic Garden at Kew, for further collecting in North America. This mission began in 1843 and lasted nearly five years, during which the Knowsley Museum benefited from several sizeable consignments of mammal and bird skins, but Burke returned only very briefly to London before settling permanently in America.[1]

ML

[1]Largen & Fisher 1986.

Above Spirit-preserved syntype of *Zonurus derbianus* Gray 1845, *Catalogue of Lizards in the British Museum*: 48; a name now known to be synonymous with *Cordylus giganteus* Smith 1844. This specimen was collected by Joseph Burke in South Africa and, in June 1843, donated by Lord Derby to the British Museum in London. Length about 382mm (Clemency Fisher © The Natural History Museum, London. BMNH 1843.6.15.11).

Below Mounted specimen of an African Flower Chafer Beetle *Cetonia derbyana* (now *Dicronorhina derbyana*). Length 45mm (LM 1957.108).

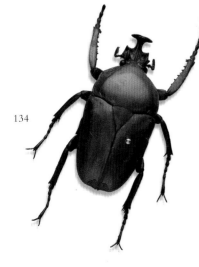

63. AFRICAN FLOWER CHAFER BEETLE
Family Scarabaeidae (scarab beetles)

Various forms of this attractive beetle occur in southern and eastern Africa. It is bred in captivity by enthusiasts around the world, being such a striking insect. The larvae are fed on decaying wood and leaves; adults on rotting fruit and flowers.

The beetle was first described by J. O. Westwood in 1843. The original specimens were collected by a Mr Burton in the Transvaal and passed to the Geneva businessman and amateur coleopterist Andre Melly,[1] who later settled in Liverpool. Melly became a leading figure of the Liverpool Royal Institution. Melly passed some specimens to Westwood (who was probably the leading British entomologist of his time) and it was Melly who suggested that the species be named in honour of Lord Derby. Melly and Derby were obviously acquainted; the 13th Earl of Derby was a supporter of the Royal Institution and donated several specimens.

This seems to be the only insect named after the 13th Earl of Derby.

IW

[1]Andre Melly was an ancestor of the jazz musician George Melly, himself a great supporter of NMGM.

64. STANLEY'S WITTMACANTHUS
(and other botanical species named after the 13th Earl of Derby)
Family Rubiaceae (madder family)

CALYCOPHYLLUM STANLEYANUM.

DEDICATED
TO THE RIGHT HONORABLE
LORD STANLEY
SECRETARY OF STATE FOR THE COLONIES &c &c
BY HIS MOST OBEDIENT
AND HUMBLE SERVANT
Robert H. Schomburgk.

Hand-coloured engraving by Henry Sowerby of Stanley's Wittmacanthus *Calycophyllum stanleyanum* R.H. Schomburgk (now *Wittmacanthus stanleyanum*). 350 x 453mm (K).

This is just one example of a plant whose scientific name was dedicated to the Earl of Derby. It was named by one of Britain's most distinguished plant collectors, Sir Robert Hermann Schomburgk (1804-1865). The first specimens were collected from Roraima, British Guiana (now Guyana), in South America in 1843 and it was described in 1844. The type specimen is preserved at Kew.

The hand-coloured engraving is by Henry Sowerby (1825-1891), who at the time was the assistant librarian at the Linnean Society. The engraving has a printed dedication to the 'Rt. Hon. Lord Derby'.

The following year, in 1845, Sir William Hooker reported on the flowering of a new *Gardenia* which Lord Derby had helped to introduce to Kew Gardens. On the 24th of February, Hooker wrote with the news that 'yesterday I went to the Garden & to my great surprise & delight found two more flowers open upon the Gardenia. I immediately cut one of them & ordered it to be put into a small tin box. I trust your Lordship will be pleased with the flower & since it was by your Lordship's exertions that the plant became known, that you will permit it to bear the name of *Gardenia Stanleyana*'. This plant was given the name *Gardenia Stanleyana* by John Lindley in 1845; this is now considered to be a synonym of the species *Randia maculata* De Candolle.

Hooker also named *Clematis Stanleyi* after Lord Derby in 1843, remarking that the plant 'deserves to bear the name of that noble-man Lord Derby'.

JE

[1]*Journal of Botany, British & foreign* vol. 3: 622. [2]Hooker to Derby from Kew, 24th February 1845 (LVRO 1/82/30) Hooker described this plant more fully in a letter sent the previous day (1/82/29). It was 'a handsome .. shrub .. about 4 feet high sending out horizontal branches near the top .. flower .. white within mottled with deep brown & purple'. [3]*Icon. Pl.* t. 589.

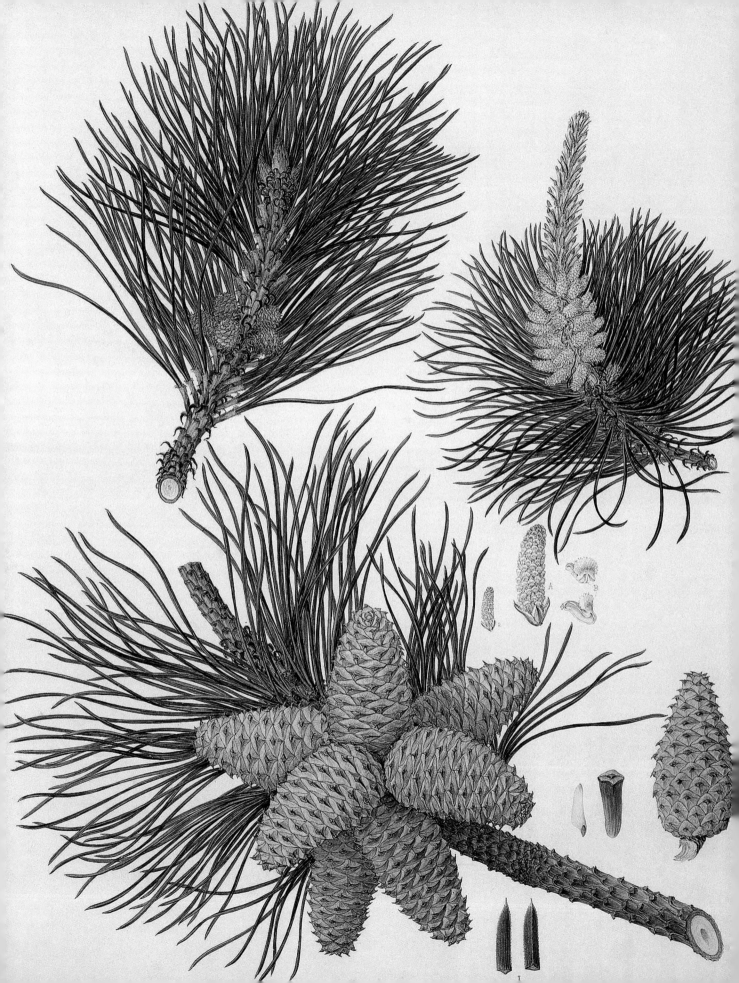

THE 13TH EARL OF DERBY'S
BOTANICAL AND HORTICULTURAL LIBRARY

JOHN EDMONDSON

The botanical and horticultural books, prints and drawings amassed by the 13th Earl of Derby form a collection unparalleled within privately held collections in England. The only remotely comparable group of botanical drawings (which was compiled during the 20th century) is the fine collection of Henry Rogers Broughton, 2nd Baron Fairhaven (1900-1973), which is now in the University of Cambridge's Fitzwilliam Museum.[1]

For the purposes of this catalogue, it has only been possible to select a few examples from the many gems of this extraordinarily diverse library. This chapter will therefore provide merely an overview of the collection, and draw attention to its quality. A short passage will highlight the Earl's growing passion for horticulture in later life.

While still a young man, Edward Stanley started to acquire botanical drawings. Some were purchased at the sale of part of a library formerly in the possession of Henry Noel, 6th Earl of Gainsborough (1743-1798). These included drawings by James Bolton of Halifax (c.1735-1799), a self-educated botanical artist and naturalist.[2]

The source of many of the botanical drawings at Knowsley is unknown, but the provenance of some can be traced by reference to auction lot numbers, dates and prices which Lord Derby sometimes noted in pencil on the reverse of the sheets. Part of his large and outstanding collection of botanical drawings by Georg Dionysius Ehret (1708-1770), purchased from Philipe in London between 11-13 May 1814, originated from the estate of Ralph Willett (1719-1795) of Merly, Dorset. Ehret composed many paintings while enjoying Willett's hospitality on his country estate.

Ehret's principal patron, Dr Christoph Jacob Trew (of Nurenberg, Germany) published several volumes of drawings by his enormously talented protégé, for example *Plantae Selectae*, which contained images of 'natural examples from London in curious [interesting] gardens'.[3] Ehret tended to compose several versions of a particular painting; some of the original Ehrets at Knowsley are extremely similar to of those used for *Plantae Selectae*. An album of Ehret's drawings once in the possession of the 13th Earl, dating from around 1732, was recently acquired by Liverpool Museum; these were prepared during Ehret's early career as a botanical artist and are evidence of his precocious talent.[4]

Another part of the Ehret collection at Knowsley was acquired from the sale of the library of Sir Ashton Lever (1729-1788) of Alkrington (near Manchester), who was the founder of the famous Leverian Museum.[5] The Lever drawings acquired by Lord Derby in 1806 were of hothouse plants, mainly succulents.

The second largest component of the Knowsley Ehret collection was acquired at 'Mr W. Wilson's Sale' on 22nd April, 1808. The largest part, however, seems almost certain to have come from the vast collections of John Stuart, 3rd Earl of Bute (1731-1792) who was the unofficial director of the Royal Botanic Gardens at Kew. Lord Bute built a botanic garden at Luton Hoo, Bedford where he also kept a magnificent collection of botanical drawings. Peter Collinson described Lord Bute as 'the only great man that encourages ingenious men in painting botanical rarities'.[6]

Above The German-born artist Georg Dionysius Ehret (1710-1770), self-portrait (Chelsea Physic Garden Trust).

Opposite Watercolour, heightened with body colour, on paper. Inscribed 'Pinus rigida' and signed 'Ferd. Bauer del.'. See Catalogue entry 75 (K).

137

The Austrian-born botanical artist Francis (Franz) Bauer was engaged by Sir Joseph Banks as botanical artist at Kew. Along with his younger brother Ferdinand, he prepared many of the illustrations for Lambert's monograph of the genus *Pinus*. Pencil & chalk drawing by William Brockedon, 1834 (By courtesy of the National Portrait Gallery).

As a patron of many of the botanical artists whose work is represented in the Knowsley collections, Lord Bute could be aptly described as providing the foundation for Lord Derby's botanical library. Bute himself is represented at Knowsley by a fine copy of his extraordinary and very rare nine-volume book, entitled *Botanical Tables*.[7] Only 12 copies of this work, which was 'composed purely for the amusement of the fair sex' and dedicated to Queen Charlotte, were ever produced.

Another artist closely associated with Lord Bute was Peter Brown (fl.1751–1799). Brown painted many plants from living specimens at Kew, and at least one of his original paintings at Knowsley (the drawing of *Cotyledon orbiculata*) has an exact counterpart in the library at Kew. Another of Bute's protégés was Simon Taylor (1742–c.1796). Taylor's work closely resembles that of Ehret in style and format. Lord Derby acknowledged this by having the drawings of both artists bound together, in a series of twelve large folio albums with the plants grouped roughly in botanical order.

Another rare published work at Knowsley for which some of the original drawings also exist in the 13th Earl's library is *Flora Londinensis*, by the London apothecary and botanist William Curtis. The Knowsley copy is bound in six fascicles as issued between 1775 and 1798. The early parts of this flora include many plates engraved from the drawings of William Kilburn (1745-1819).[8] Kilburn, a designer and artist, the son of a Dublin architect,[9] was commissioned by Curtis to prepare many of the 432 plates for his book. Amongst a volume of original drawings purchased by Lord Derby are some signed by Kilburn that, curiously, seem to have been copied from the published plates.[10]

Another set of Knowsley originals closely associated with a published botanical monograph are the conifer drawings by the exceptionally talented Austrian artists Ferdinand Bauer (1760-1826) and Francis Bauer (1758-1840).[11] These drawings form part of the original work for *A description of the genus Pinus*, published in 1803 by Aylmer Bourke Lambert (1761-1843). The sixty drawings range from pencil studies of individual cones, to complete illustrations.

Lambert possessed an important series of botanical drawings and an extensive private herbarium. At the sale of Lambert's collections in 1842, several albums were

purchased by the 13th Earl – most notably the so-called 'Lambert Drawings' of birds and plants from Port Jackson, Australia, composed by various (probably convict) artists.[12] Some of the plant drawings in these volumes have botanical names added by Sir James Edward Smith, founder of the Linnean Society of London,[13] and some formed the basis of illustrations in Smith's *A specimen of the botany of New Holland*. Lambert also corresponded with Edward Stanley on horticultural matters and they exchanged specimens, such as the 'famous golden potatoes from Peru' which Lord Stanley obtained from Lambert in 1833.[14]

One of the London nurseries which propagated and distributed newly introduced plant material from Australia and other recently explored areas was the Vineyard Nursery in Hammersmith, founded by James Lee (1715-1795) and developed in partnership with John Kennedy (1759-1842). Lee's daughter Ann (1753-1790) had access to these botanical riches and under the tuition of Sydney Parkinson (official artist on Cook's voyage of 1768 and a protégé of Sir Joseph Banks) she developed an attractive style of flower painting.[15] A large body of her work is preserved at Knowsley.

The botanical drawings so far mentioned are dated mainly from the second half of the eighteenth century, and – with the exception of the Lambert Drawings and Ehret's *Deliciae Botanicae* – were composed in England (albeit in some cases by German-born or Austrian-born artists). An equally important component of the botanical library at Knowsley is the work of Dutch and French artists, dating from the seventeenth and early eighteenth centuries. Most notable of these are the works by Nicolas Robert (1614-1685), the original creator of the famous series known as *Velins du Roi* which is preserved in the Museum d'Histoire Naturelle in Paris. The Robert drawings at Knowsley are watercolours on vellum. They are unsigned, and some were once thought to have been composed by the German-born Flemish natural history artist Maria Sybilla Merian.[16]

Another French artist featured in the 13th Earl's library is Claude Aubriet (1665-1742), who succeeded Robert as *peintre du roi* and was trained by the leading French botanist of that period, Joseph Pitton de Tournefort (1656-1708). Aubriet was thus able to combine his superb skill at flower painting with botanical accuracy. This combination of skills is rare in botanical artists, and perhaps one which was actively sought by the 13th Earl.

The Aubriet drawings in the Knowsley library, which are bound into a volume with the title *'Trente plantes peintés sur velin d'aprés nature'*, show mainly commonly cultivated plant species. They include a manuscript note by a former owner, M[onsieur] D. Pajot of Dons-en-Bray which describes their rarity and perfection.

A third French botanical artist whose work is represented at Knowsley is Pierre-Joseph Redouté (1759-1840). He is best known for his published works *Les Liliacées* (1802-c.1816), *Les Roses* (1817-1824) and *Choix des plus belles fleurs et des plus beaux fruits* (1827-1833). Redouté's books are greatly sought after and highly prized; his original drawings are extremely rare and the fact that Lord Derby acquired some of them is noteworthy.

The Earl of Derby also collected the work of early Dutch botanical artists, mostly composed in the seventeenth and early eighteenth centuries. Some (such as Jan and Maria Moninckx) worked only in the Netherlands; others (such as Alida Withoos and Jacob van Huysum) also sought patronage in England. One of the most intriguing artists represented in the library at Knowsley is John [or Johann] Augustus Simson, a German artist. He may have worked in Holland for George Clifford, an Anglo-Dutch merchant who was the patron of both Carl Linnaeus and Georg Ehret. Simson's drawings of cacti and succulents (e.g. *Stapelia*[17]) are some of the most striking works in the Earl of Derby's collection.

One of the most exotic elements in the Knowsley botanical art collection is the large series of drawings of garden and economic plants, painted on thin, delicate paper by unknown oriental artists and bound in exotically designed leather bindings. Recently, a volume formerly in the 13th Earl's library was acquired by the Liverpool Museum. It includes 85 drawings, mainly of plants introduced to Chinese gardens from other parts of the world, but also some of the plants native to China which are particularly characteristic of these gardens (such as the Camellias). The patron who commissioned these drawings may have been John Reeves (1774-1856), who worked as a tea inspector for the British East India Company in Canton and Macao.[18]

A little-known collection of paintings of American origin is an album prepared by Thomas Davies, a British Army officer based in America at around the time of the War of Independence. This includes such characteristically North American plants as *Dionaea muscipula* (the Venus fly-trap), which Davies painted as early as 1763 but whose scientific name was only published by Linnaeus in 1767.[19]

Another famous American artist, William Bartram (1739-1823), was responsible for sketching a plan of his father's garden in Kingsessing, near Philadelphia. This sketch, enclosed in an annotated and interleaved volume formerly in Peter Collinson's library, is a foundation document of American garden history.[20] This volume of Collinson's also demonstrates Mark Catesby's importance. Catesby (1682-1749) made expeditions to Virginia and Jamaica between 1712 and 1719. His second expedition, sponsored by James Sherard (1666-1738), the owner of a fine garden in Eltham, took Catesby to Carolina, Florida and the Bahamas and he later wrote and illustrated a book on the subject.[21] Most of Catesby's original paintings are now in the Royal Library at Windsor, but some can be found tipped into Peter Collinson's copy of the printed book, with characteristic annotations and pasted-in ephemera.

Evidence that Edward Stanley had a particular interest in the North American flora can be gauged from the support he offered to William Roscoe, founder in 1802 of the Liverpool Botanic Garden, for a plant-collecting expedition by the Cheshire-born botanist John Bradbury (1768-1823) to the upper Missouri River.[22]

Bradbury, an artisan naturalist, came to Liverpool as an assistant in the museum of William Bullock, who provided him with training in taxidermy. Lord Stanley agreed to meet one third of the cost of the expedition. Bradbury's wife, writing to Roscoe in September 1810, informed him that her husband had established 'his garden within three miles of St. Louis' and had 'already sowed about 150 species of American trees, shrubs and plants; he feels confident of being able to introduce a number of plants of 'real utility'.[23]

Derby's interest in North American plants may have been stimulated by his near neighbour, Thomas Nuttall of Nutgrove Hall, St. Helens. Before his return to England Nuttall had been Professor of Botany at Harvard University and was author of *The genera of North American plants* and the *North American Sylva*; he is also revered in American ornithological circles.[24]

As he grew older, the 13th Earl became increasingly interested in horticulture, particularly orchids; he grew many of these in his conservatory at Knowsley. After 1835, when Lord Derby acceded to the Earldom and took over responsibility for the Knowsley estate, considerable funds were expended on horticultural improvements. Although the aviary and menagerie were his principal concern, he also made significant alterations to the gardens. Evidence for the huge amount of tree planting on the estate instigated by the 13th Earl can be found in the account books of the Caldwell Nursery of Knutsford,[25] one of the leading horticultural suppliers in north-west England. Horse Chestnuts (*Aesculus hippocastanum*) were notably purchased in large quantities.

Edward Stanley's increasing interest in horticulture can be gauged by the extensive correspondence he had with the botanist Sir William Hooker, which began in January 1831. Hooker, then Professor of Botany at the University of Glasgow, wrote to advise Lord Stanley that Thomas Drummond, his plant collector in North America, was willing to accept orders and instructions for bird skins. Their correspondence soon turned to orchids; Hooker was willing to publish illustrations in the *Botanical Magazine* of 'any new orchidaceous plant that may flower at Knowsley'.[26] The Hooker correspondence shows that Edward Stanley provided considerable sums of money in support of plant collectors working in South Africa, North and South America and Australia. Joseph Burke (1812-1873) was a long-serving collector of both zoological and botanical specimens, whom Lord Derby sent on an expedition to the Transvaal, South Africa from 1839 to 1842. During Burke's travels, several new species of Stapeliads were discovered, some of which were published and illustrated in Hooker's journal *Icones Plantarum*.

Lord Derby's assistance in supporting such expeditions led to an exchange of specimens between Knowsley and Kew. For example, Hooker sent Lord Derby living specimens of *Drimys winteri* (Winter's Bark) and *Nothofagus forsteri* (Forster's Southern Beech), which had lately been collected by his son Joseph in Tierra del Fuego. Sir William advised Derby that they 'ought to do well in the open air with us, & they will prove highly ornamental'[27] Derby reciprocated by sending Hooker a mate for his widowed Peahen, whose distress had caused Hooker much concern.

Another collector responsible for the introduction of new plant species to Britain under Lord Derby's patronage was Thomas Whitfield, who collected in Sierra Leone and the Gambia from 1841-1849. At this time, the early stage of Kew's revival, such collectors made an important contribution to the tropical plant holdings at Kew. Hooker expressed his gratitude to Lord Derby for a shipment of plants in the following terms:

The first official Director of Kew Gardens, Sir William Jackson Hooker (1785-1865) entered into a lengthy correspondence with the 13th Earl of Derby on botanical and horticultural matters. They collaborated in sending collectors to South Africa and North America, and plants introduced by Lord Derby were grown at Kew. (By courtesy of the National Portrait Gallery. NPG P354).

'You have the satisfaction of having introduced to our Gardens on one and the same day three of the most remarkable plants that have ever come to Europe & I have to send your Lordship my best thanks for putting the Royal Gardens in possession of each of them'.[28]

One of these was the Vegetable Ivory palm *Phytelephas macrocarpa*, whose hard white fruits provided an acceptable substitute for ivory and were used in the manufacture of buttons and trinkets.

Lacking a comprehensive catalogue of the living plants at Knowsley from this period, we can only piece together some fragmentary evidence of the contents of Lord Derby's conservatory from jottings in his notebooks. He clearly appreciated orchids, tree ferns, cycads and flowering trees and shrubs, and was also interested in plants which might provide cover for the livestock in his aviary and menagerie. The 13th Earl's enthusiasm for introducing living plants from the native habitats of his captive breeding stock indicates a vision much in advance of the philosophy of modern zoos, which try to provide appropriate settings for their animals. In this respect, as in so many other walks of life, Lord Derby showed great far-sightedness and this contributed to his success with the captive breeding of so many birds and mammals.

In conclusion, the 13th Earl of Derby's collection of botanical art, and horticultural notes and correspondence, is of great range and quality and tells us much about the man who compiled it. As a scientist and patron, Lord Derby appreciated the importance of plants both in the wild and in cultivation and was fully prepared to deploy his wealth to support those who undertook pioneering botanical explorations of unknown ecosystems. For a man whose primary scholarly interests lay in zoology to have amassed such a remarkable collection of botanical art and books is a tribute to his many-faceted character.

[1]Grant 1952. [2]Edmondson 1995: 21-24. [3]Schnalke 1995. [4]Calmann 1977: 21-22. [5]See page 45.
[6]Edmondson, J.R. 'Peter Collinson' in Fitzroy-Dearborn *Encyclopedia of Gardens and Garden Design* (in press, to be published 2002). [7]Stuart 1785. [8]For an account of Kilburn's career see Butler 2000.
[9]*Gentleman's Magazine*, March 1832: 222-224. [10]For example *Sedum anglicum*, (K). If these Kilburn drawings at Knowsley had been the originals from which the published illustrations were derived, the images would be (but are not) reversed in the printed plates. [11]Lack 2001: 80-91. [12]See Catalogue entries 8, 14, & 84.
[13]Gage & Stearn 1988: 13-21. [14]Lambert to Stanley, undated, and 7th March 1833 (LVRO 1/102/1-2). According to Professor Jack Hawkes (in litt. 2001) these were probably *Solanum stenostomum* subsp. *goniocalyx*, or possibly *S. tuberosum* subsp. *andigena*. Neither would have grown in England, as they would have failed to adapt to the long day-length of northern European summers. [15] Wilson 1961. [16]Confirmed as Robert, not Merian, by Dr Sam Segal. [17]See Catalogue entry 68. [18]Elliott 1994: 14-15. [19]Nelson & McKinley 1990: passim. [20]I am grateful to Amy Meyers (Huntingdon Library and Botanic Garden) for confirming that the sketch was substantially the work of William Bartram. See Catalogue entry 71.
[21]Catesby 1729-1747; see also Meyers in McBurney 1997: 11-27; Armstrong (in press) and Catalogue entries 12 & 13. [22]Stansfield 1951. [23]Mrs Bradbury to Roscoe, Cork, 1810 (LVRO, Roscoe Papers series 10: 394). [24]Nuttall 1818 & Nuttall 1842-49. For comments about Nuttall's importance to ornithology, see endnote 18 on page 51. [25]Stock book, Cheshire County Record Office. [26]Hooker to Derby, Glasgow, 16th September 1837 (LVRO 1/82/2). [27]Hooker to Derby, Kew, 19th May 1843 (LVRO 1/82/10). [28]Hooker to Derby, Kew, 10th September 1844 (LVRO 1/82/19).

The Old Greenhouse at Knowsley, built by the 13th Earl of Derby (Huyton Library, Knowsley).

65. SNAIL FLOWER

Family Fabaceae (peas)

Watercolour on paper by Herman Saftleven, depicting a Snail Flower *Phaseolus caracalla*. Signed and dated 'HS. F. 1684, den. 25. October'.[1] 250 x 347mm (K).

The Snail Flower is named after its buds, which are coiled like a snail's shell. It is a fragrant species from tropical South America, related to the Scarlet Runner Bean (*Phaseolus coccineus*) which is a popular garden plant.

Herman Saftleven (1609-1685) was born in Rotterdam, Netherlands and moved to Utrecht in 1632, where he made a name as an engraver. As a young man, he mainly painted landscapes, townscapes and farmhouse interiors. From 1680 onwards, during the last years of his life, he composed over a hundred watercolours based on the plants and flowers in Agnes Block's world-famous botanical garden, 'Vijverhof' at Nieuwersluis (between Amsterdam and Utrecht).[2] This painting by Saftleven was probably the first drawing ever made of the Snail Flower and must have been one of his last works, as it is dated less than two and a half months before his death.[3]

Agnes Block (1629-1704), who commissioned Saftleven to paint this plant, corresponded with curators of botanic gardens all over the world in order to obtain and exchange plants, and was particularly keen on newly-discovered species. She commissioned the best Dutch artists to make hundreds of drawings.

SS

[1]The painting was commissioned by Agnes Block, who inscribed on the verso 'Coracalla vel Phaseolus Americanus perennis, flore cochleato odorato, van dezelve [from the same]. 1684'. It was sold by her heirs in 1705 to William Wilson and then sold again by King & Lochee, London on 22nd April 1808, lot no. 1690. [2]Saftleven composed at least 111 flower drawings for Block, according to an inventory by Valerius Röver (1686-1739), lord mayor of Delft, who bought some of them. Eight of these are found at Knowsley, together with one more which is not included in Röver's inventory. [3]A similar drawing of the Snail Flower by Saftleven is also dated 1684 (private collection; Schulz 1982: 487-488, fig. 234).

66. TOBACCO
Family Solanaceae (potatoes)

Watercolour (heightened with body colour) on vellum, painted by Claude Aubriet and depicting *Nicotiana tabacum*. Inscribed: 'Tabac'. Annotated (?by Edward Stanley) 'Nicotiana – Tobacco – Linns. Cl. 5' (a reference to Linnaeus' artificial system of flowering plant classification). 450 x 310mm (K).

The French botanical artist Claude Aubriet (1665-1742) was a distinguished court painter at the Jardin du Roi in Paris, established by King Louis XIII in 1635.[1] Michel Adanson (1727-1806) later named the genus *Aubrieta* for him. The French tradition of painting garden plants was established by Gaston d'Orleans and it was he who engaged Nicolas Robert (1614-1685), whose work is also represented in the Earl of Derby's collections.

Tobacco was first introduced into cultivation in Central and South America (where most of the 67 species of *Nicotiana* are native) in the Pre-Columbian era and its use was first discovered by European explorers in the 15th century. Sir Walter Raleigh is credited with having first brought it to Europe. The specimen painted by Aubriet was almost certainly cultivated in the Jardin des Plantes in Paris. The painting, of a large-leaved cultivar, possibly of the kind used for manufacture of cigars, includes a detached lower stem leaf, a flowering raceme and a detail of the fruit and seeds, all drawn to the same scale. The shadows cast by the two upper leaves onto the larger leaf add to the verisimilitude of this drawing.

JE

[1]Lack 2001: 44.

67. VARIEGATED STAPELIA
Family Asclepiadaceae (milkweeds)

John Simson, who painted four of the pictures included in this section, was a flower painter from Ludwigsburg, near Munich.[1] His signature is sometimes abbreviated to 'Johs' ('Johannes').

This plant was among the earliest of the succulents from the Cape of Good Hope to be brought back to Europe. It was first figured in Joannus Bodaeus van Stapel's edition of the works of Theophrastus in 1644. The species is widespread in Cape Province, down to Cape Point, and is the most southerly of all stapeliads. William T. Aiton called it the 'Variegated Stapelia' in his *Hortus Kewensis*[2] and recorded that it was introduced to Britain by the Earl of Portland in 1690.

The Variegated Stapelia is a near-hardy plant in cultivation under glass in Britain, and is hugely variable in flower size, colour and patterning and in details of the corona and other organs. Many variants have been preserved in cultivation. This variability has led to a surfeit of scientific names, now mostly consigned to synonymy or treated as varieties or hybrids. Although attractive and spectacular, it is usually avoided as a house plant because of the malodorous flowers. Robert Thornton immortalised it as 'the maggot-bearing Stapelia'[3] in reference to this fetid odour, which resembles fresh carrion and deludes flies into laying their eggs on it.

Orbea variegata is a popular subject with artists, and there is another version at Knowsley by Georg Ehret, dated 1743.

GR

[1]Fecht 1887. [2]Aiton 1810-1813. [3]Thornton 1807.

68. HAIRY STAPELIA
Family Asclepiadaceae (milkweeds)

Watercolour and body colour on vellum, depicting the Hairy Stapelia *Stapelia hirsuta*, signed: 'John Augustus Simson, 1739'. From a bound volume entitled 'Original drawings, fruit and flowers'. 390 x 510mm (K).

According to Aiton's Hortus Kewensis this was the second earliest stapeliad to be introduced into cultivation in Europe, having been first imported in 1710.[1] In 1714 it was introduced from Holland to Britain by Richard Bradley, who inaccurately called it, 'The larger thick-leav'd Cape Fritillary'.

Like *Orbea variegata*, which was also illustrated by Simson in a similar format,[2] this is a widespread and variable African species. The flower is from 6-12 cm in diameter and ranges from pure deep purple to cross-striped with cream, or totally yellow. All flowers have the characteristic silky hairs, which give the plant its name; these make them very carrion-like in appearance. All the varieties are of striking beauty, despite the smell of 'unemptied dustbins', as one writer put it.

Stapeliads are credited by the Zulus with various medicinal properties; to cure hysteria, earache, numbness, as an emetic and (after burning to ash) for general pain relief when rubbed on the body. They are also reputed to ward off lightning.

GR

147

[1] Aiton 1789. [2] See Catalogue entry 67.

Family Amaryllidaceae (daffodils)

Watercolour and body colour on vellum, depicting the Amaryllis *Hippeastrum phoeniceum*, annotated 'Lilio-narcissus' and signed 'John Augustus Simson, 1739'. 382 x 509mm (K).

This was one of the most popular bulbous plants under cultivation in Europe during the early 18th century. A native of the West Indies, it needs to be raised in a stove or heated conservatory that replicates the conditions of the humid tropics. It is quite possible that Amaryllis plants were grown by the 13th Earl of Derby, who had good hothouse facilities on his estate. One of the Edward Lear watercolours now at Knowsley, which he may have painted there, also depicts an Amaryllis.[1] These plants were often the subject of botanical illustrations because of their beauty and elegant form.

This drawing was selected for the exhibition by the eminent English botanist Professor William T. Stearn (1911-2001) during a visit to Knowsley Hall in 1999. It is one of eight paintings by Simson (four of which are included in the exhibition), that are bound in an album entitled 'Original drawings, fruits and flowers'. The volume also includes 42 flower paintings by Schouten and nine by Jan van Huysum.

JE

[1] 'Amaryllis stria[ti]folia. Brazil'. Undated, Lear Box 1, no.1.

70. TURK'S CAP or MELON THISTLE CACTUS
Family Cactaceae (Cacti)

Watercolour, heightened with body colour, on vellum, of Turk's Cap *Melocactus curvispinus* subsp. *caesius*. Annotated 'Echinoleus' and signed 'J[ohn] A[ugustus] Simson pinxit 1739 ad vivum'. From a bound volume entitled 'Original drawings, fruit and flowers'. 384 x 509mm (K).

It is a quirk of history that the first specimens of globular cacti to reach Europe from the New World in the sixteenth century were among those least easy to cultivate and preserve. Mature melocacti, even when dug up with plenty of root and transported by air, never survive for long, and it was many years before horticulturalists realised that raising these plants from seed is a much better way of acclimatising them. It is likely, therefore, that the illustrated specimen (which is displayed in a Delftware pot) was grown from seed.

The genus *Melocactus*, which includes about 33 species,[1] is remarkable in growing a terminal inflorescence which telescopes into a cap of spines and bristles. From this cap emerge small tubular flowers, followed by elongated (usually red) berry-like fruits. Seedlings grow rapidly, given sufficient warmth, and can begin to form this cap from the age of five to ten years, after which growth of the plant ceases.

The Turk's Cap (or Melon Thistle) Cactus has fascinated collectors since it was first discovered. It is one of the most variable and widespread of the melocacti, with three recognised subspecies. The plant figured belongs to subsp. *caesius*, which has a glaucous body and long straight spines and is found from the Caribbean to coastal Colombia and Venezuela.

GR

149

[1]Anderson 2001.

Ink and pencil sketch by William Bartram inscribed: 'A Draught of John Bartram's House and Garden as it appears from the River 1758'. Bound into an album of natural history drawings and prints once owned by Peter Collinson. 261 x 419mm (K).

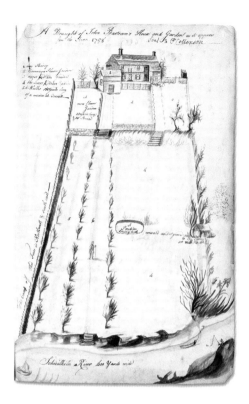

John Bartram (1699-1777) was a Quaker farmer, nurseryman and botanist.[1] In 1728 he bought a farm at Kingsessing, on the banks of the Schuylkill River in Pennsylvania. Bartram was the first native-born American botanist to make a major contribution to the scientific knowledge of the flora of the eastern part of North America. His most lasting achievement was to assist the London Quaker merchant Peter Collinson (1694-1768) to introduce many new species of trees, shrubs and herbs into cultivation in English gardens.[2]

Bartram's garden, where plants were propagated before being shipped to England, can justifiably be described as the first Botanic Garden in North America. His increasing fame as a plant and seed collector from about 1742 eventually let to his appointment as 'King's Botanist' by George III. Many of John Bartram's choicest introductions were first grown at the Royal Botanic Gardens, Kew or in Peter Collinson's own garden.[3]

This sketch of Bartram's garden was composed in 1758 by his son William (1739-1823), who was himself a naturalist and artist of considerable note. It was sent by John Bartram to Peter Collinson and later acquired by Aylmer Bourke Lambert (1761-1842). The 13th Earl of Derby purchased it, as part of Peter Collinson's album, in 1843. William Bartram's sketch is an extremely valuable historical document, because of the detailed record it provides of the garden's layout and the functions of the various compartments. This garden is currently being restored to its former glory by the Historic Bartram's Garden Trust and this drawing has provided vital evidence of its original design.

JE

[1]Berkeley & Berkeley 1992. [2]Dillwyn 1843. [3]Edmondson 2002.

The first painting shows a Rosa Mundi, an old cultivar derived from the French Rose *Rosa gallica* and the Wood Cranesbill, which is native to Europe and West Asia. The second painting also shows a quasi-natural scene, with European plants. The Horned Poppy is native to the coasts of Europe, where it commonly grows on sand dunes and is also sometimes found in gardens.

Thomas Robins the Elder (1716-1770) of Bath, is best known for his drawings of country houses and rococo garden scenes. He also composed botanical watercolours and painted flower sprigs, sometimes in a landscape or an unusual cornucopian setting, for instance with a bird. In this respect Robins was influenced by the Dutch artist Jan van Huysum (1686-1749). Robins and his son, Thomas Robins the Younger (1743-1806), were also clearly influenced by the famous artist Maria Sibylla Merian (1647-1717) to whom both these paintings were once mistakenly attributed.[1]

SS & IW

[1] The first painting is incorrectly inscribed 'MM'; the second 'M Merian'.

Two watercolours, heightened with bodycolour, on paper.

Left Rosa Mundi *Rosa gallica* cv. *Versicolor*; Wood Cranesbill *Geranium sylvaticum*; an unidentifiable lizard and extremely fanciful representations of three tropical butterflies (possibly based on: bottom right, Plain Tiger *Danaus chrysippus*; top right, sulphur butterfly *Catopsilia* sp. or *Belenois* sp.; top left: a blue satyrid *Caeruleuptychia* sp. 441 x 315mm (K).

Right Yellow Horned Poppy *Glaucium flavum*; Earth-nut Pea *Lathyrus tuberosus*; Bearded Tit *Panurus biarmicus*; a rodent robbing a nest; an unidentifiable lizard and fanciful representations of three tropical Lepidoptera (possibly based on: top, a blue satyrid *Caeruleuptychia* sp.; middle, tiger moth *Euplagia* sp.; bottom left, a sailor butterfly *Pantoporia* or *Neptis* sp. 444 x 316mm (K).

151

73. PIG'S EAR
Family Crassulaceae (houseleeks)

Watercolour and body colour on vellum, depicting Pig's Ear *Cotyledon orbiculata* and signed 'P. Brown', undated. Bound in a volume of botanical paintings together with work by Thomas Davies. 286 x 225mm (K).

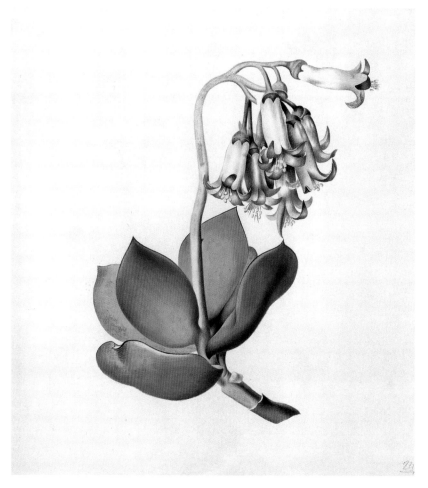

During the reign of George III, Peter Brown (fl. 1750-1790) was court painter to Frederick, Prince of Wales until his untimely death in 1751, and then to the Queen Mother, Princess Augusta. Brown was one of a group of late 18th century artists whose style was clearly influenced by that of Georg Ehret and much of his work was carried out under the tutelage of the Earl of Bute, who was then the *de facto* director of the Royal Gardens at Kew.[1]

Cotyledon orbiculata has been the commonest species of succulent plant in cultivation since its introduction from southern Africa in 1690 by a Mr. Bentick, of whom little is known. Even earlier, in 1664, Pig's Ear had been recorded in the form of a woodcut in J.B. van Stapel's edition of the works of Theophrastus. It is an extremely variable plant, sometimes found in dwarf form but often growing into a shrub up to a metre tall, with narrowly orbicular leaves. It flowers readily and is thus very popular with succulent plant enthusiasts. The precise instructions for cultivation which Miller gave in his *Gardener's Dictionary* of 1768 are still valid today.

GR

[1]King 1985: 62-74.

74. RED FIVE-CORNERS
Family Epacridaceae (Epacris family)

Watercolour on paper, of a Red Five-corners *Styphelia tubiflora*. Inscribed: 'New South Wales' and signed ' Thomas Davies delin.'. From a bound volume of original drawings, many by Davies. 250 x 378mm (K).

Thomas Davies (1737-1812) was a colonel in the British Army, who was stationed for many years in North America during and after the War of Independence. His official work was as a topographic artist, recording battle scenes and landscapes, especially waterfalls.[1] However, he also specialised in much more intimate botanical works on vellum, in a style reminiscent of his near contemporary James Bolton (1735-1799). Due to their exceptional rarity, examples of Davies' botanical drawings are not well known.[2]

Paintings by Davies at Knowsley number more than forty drawings on paper and vellum and range in date from 1763 to 1810. Some of the earliest were evidently composed in the vicinity of New York; one is captioned 'Wild Aster, New York' and another shows the insectivorous Venus' Fly Trap *Dionaea muscipula*.

Davies never visited Australia, so this painting of an Australian plant must have been based on cultivated material. The genus *Styphelia* was first discovered after the first European settlers arrived in Australia in 1788 as part of the First Fleet. The Surgeon General of the penal colony, Dr John White, is known to have collected herbarium specimens of *S. tubiflora* from the vicinity of Port Jackson (Sydney), where it grows as an undershrub on sandstone. These specimens were sent back to England and examined by Sir James Edward Smith, who described the species in 1795.

JE

[1]Blunt & Stearn 1994. [2]Davies is not, for instance, cited in Desmond 1994.

75. PITCH PINE & CEMBRAN PINE
Family Pinaceae (pines)

Right Watercolour, heightened with body colour, on paper. Inscribed 'Pinus rigida' and signed 'Ferd. Bauer del.'. Pl.19 from a bound volume of watercolours composed for Aylmer Bourke Lambert's *'A descripion of the genus Pinus'* (1803), purchased by the 13th Earl of Derby in c.1842.[1] The original of plate 18 of Lambert's work. 415 x 557mm (K). See enlargement on page 136.

Far right Watercolour, heightened with body colour, on paper. Inscribed: 'Pinus cembra' and signed 'Ferd. Bauer del.'. Pl.25 from the same bound volume. The original of plates 23 & 24 of Lambert's work.[2] 400 x 540mm (K).

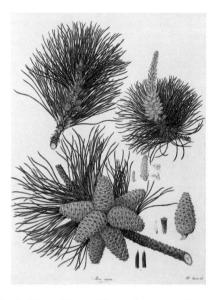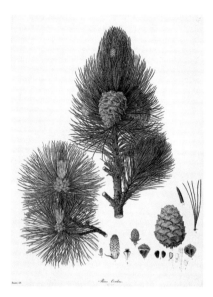

Pitch Pines *Pinus ridiga*, whose needles are borne in bundles of three, are native to eastern North America and were introduced to cultivation in Europe in 1759. They grow rapidly and can reach 25-30m in height.

Cembran Pines *Pinus cembra*, whose needles are in bundles of five, were first introduced to cultivation in Europe in 1746 from their natural habitat in the Alps and Siberia. Lambert noted that the flowers 'have a more beautiful appearance than in any other species of pine, being of a bright purple'.[3] Despite its rather limited geographical range in Europe, the wood is much used by Tyrolean wood-carvers to make souvenirs.

Three Austrian brothers, Ferdinand, Franz and Joseph Bauer, were all noted botanical artists - the last in his own country, the first two also in England. Their father worked as a court painter to the Prince of Liechtenstein, but Lukas Bauer died in 1762 and his sons learned their art the hard way, being employed at the monastery in Feldsburg, Austria to help produce the *Codex Liechtenstein*. Ferdinand Bauer (1760-1826) then came to England and later accompanied Robert Brown on Matthew Flinders' circumnavigation of Australia between 1801 and 1805. Towards the end of Ferdinard Bauer's life he contributed many of the illustrations for Lambert's monograph of the genus *Pinus*.

Goethe heaped praise upon Ferdinand Bauer for the artistry displayed in this work, saying 'It is a real joy to look at these plates, for Nature is visible, Art concealed'.[4] Franz Andreas Bauer (1758-1840) also worked in England, but was much less of a traveller than his younger brother. At least four of the drawings amongst the Knowsley originals for Lambert's work are signed by Franz Bauer; one is dated 1801. This album of drawings at Knowsley may help to identify which artist composed the originals for each of Lambert's published engravings.[5]

JE

154

[1]Sotheby 1842. [2]Renkema 1928: 20. [3]Lambert 1803-1807: 34-35. The 13th Earl possessed a copy of the 1832 edition of Lambert's work, but this is no longer in the library at Knowsley. [4]Rix 1989: 120. [5]See Renkema 1928: 10-30.

76. DANE'S BLOOD
Family Ranunculaceae (buttercups)

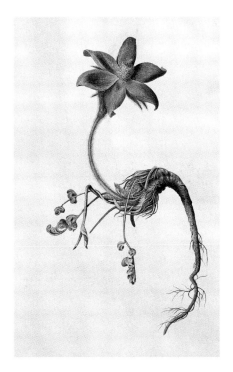

Watercolour on paper, by Georg Dionysius Ehret, annotated 'Anemone pulsatilla'. From a leather-bound volume of original paintings by Ehret entitled 'Deliciae Botanicae', previously in the possession of the 13th Earl of Derby. 210 x 330mm (LM 2001.32).

The English names of *Anemone pulsatilla*, Dane's Blood or Pasque Flower, refer to its limited occurrence on grassy chalk and limestone ridges where, allegorically, the plant sprang up at spots where the blood of Danish warriors had been spilt, and to the time of its flowering, which falls around Easter.

Deliciae Botanicae, or 'Botanical Delights', the title of the volume in which this and 322 other drawings are bound, aptly describes this collection of the early work of Europe's best known 18th century botanical artist, Georg Dionysius Ehret (1710-1770). The album was originally known as *Herbarium vivum pictum*, or 'Pictures of living plant collections'. Prepared during Ehret's apprenticeship, the paintings consist of a mixture of wild flowers of southern Germany, common garden plants, and a few exotics such as *Dracaena draco* (Dragon's blood), a native of the Canary Islands, and *Oryza sativa* (Rice).

The paintings were originally commissioned by the apothecary Johann Wilhelm Weinmann of Regensberg, but were eventually sold through Ehret's patron Dr C.J. Trew to the Nuremberg physician Johann Wilhelm Widmann. It is not known how they came into the possession of the 13th Earl of Derby.

One can appreciate the self-confidence which led Ehret to uproot himself from his native Germany and travel abroad to seek his fortune as a botanical artist, when one sees the precocious quality of his early work. Only one other painting exists in a public collection from this early Ehret period – a *Corallodendron* dated 1732,[1] which 'shows the same manner of work and an equally high quality' as the Knowsley volume.[2]

JE

---

[1] Natural History Museum, London. [2] Calmann 1977: pl.18 (opposite p.36 and p.22).

77. COFFEE
Family Rubiaceae (Bedstraws)

Body colour on vellum, signed: 'G.D. Ehret p[inxit]'. Inscribed ['Arabian Jasmine, with chestnut leaves, flowers white, strongly scented, whose fruit we call COFFY in medicinal parlance']. Seven floral dissections, each annotated by the artist. 600 x 480mm (K).

On stylistic grounds this work must date from the 1760s. The painting, of the branch of a Coffee bush *Coffea arabica*, shows both flowers and fruit, including a partly shrivelled leaf which is reproduced with Ehret's characteristic fidelity. By this period coffee was being grown as a conservatory plant.

A painting of *Jasminum arabicum* was listed in the description of the 1771 sale of the late Georg Dionysius Ehret's effects, along with another 15 drawings.[1]

JE

156

[1]*A catalogue of the curious collection of paintings of plants, shells, fossils, butterflies etc. of that eminent artist and botanist, Mr George Dennis Ehret, deceased; which (by order of the executors) will be sold by auction by Mr Langford and Son at their house in the Great Piazza, Covent Garden, on Wednesday the 24th of this instant, April 1771, and the three following days*. London: Langford & Son (1771): see Lot 75 on Day 2.

78. PAWPAW
Family Caricaceae (pawpaws)

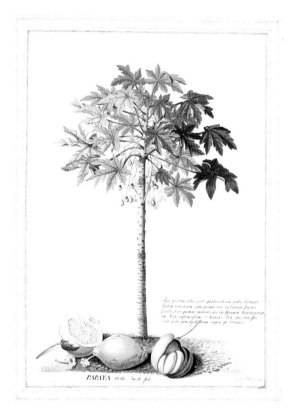

Body colour on vellum, signed: 'G.D. Ehret p[inxit] 1742'. Inscribed: 'Papaya mas. Boerh. Ind.'. Annotated by the artist '*Haec planta alta erat quatuordecem pedes, diametri septem unciarum cum prima via in Europa fructus ferret, et eos quidem matures diem XXX Januari Anno MDCCXLII in horto instructissimo Dr. Baronis Petri* ... [this plant grew forty feet tall, [the stem] seven inches in diameter, bore fruit for the first time in Europe, which ripened on the 30th day of January in the year 1742 in the very interesting garden of Baron Petre]. 590 x 470mm (K).

The Pawpaw or Papaya *Carica papaya* is cultivated throughout the tropics for its edible fruits and also as a source of the enzyme papain, which is used for tenderising meat. There is tenuous evidence that the fruits were imported into Britain in the seventeenth century; Van Dyke's portrait of the children of King Charles I includes a fruit which appears to be a Pawpaw.[1]

Georg Ehret's painting commemorates the great achievement of Robert Petre, of Thorndon Hall, Essex, in being the first person to succeed in growing ripe fruit of the Pawpaw (a native of the New World tropics) in his hothouses. Baron Petre, who tragically died of smallpox later the same year that the painting was composed, was an enthusiastic horticulturist who collaborated with Peter Collinson and others in the introduction of many new plants into cultivation in England. Petre's stoves (hothouses) were the largest in size and number in England, and his Great Stove stood 30ft high at its apex.[2] Credit for this horticultural 'first' should also be given to the skilful James Gordon (c.1708-1780). He later became one of London's leading nurserymen, but was working as Baron Petre's gardener in 1742.

The artist, Georg Ehret, undertook many commissions for noble patrons in the course of his successful career as an illustrator of botanical subjects but only this painting is associated with Baron Petre. Ehret felt it sufficiently important to be reproduced in *Plantae et Papiliones Rariores*.[3]

JE

[1]Royal Collection, Windsor. [2]Clutton & Mackay 1970: 34. [3]Ehret 1748, pl.3.

Hand-coloured engraving,
in *Plantae et Papiliones
Rariores*, by Georg Dionysius
Ehret, Heidelberg, 1748;
710 x 542mm (K).

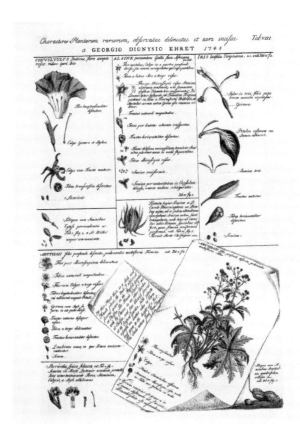

Ehret started publishing this work in 1748, when his English career as a botanical artist began to falter and just before he began, in 1749, 'to give instruction in painting of plants and flowers to the highest nobility of England'.[1] Twelve plates in this series had been published by 1750, when he took up an appointment as gardener and instructor at the Oxford University Botanic Garden. A copy of Ehret's final plate, of the Cape Jasmine *Gardenia jasminioides*, is also at Knowsley.

This, Ehret's first major publication, was well received, partly because it served to demonstrate the artificial system of plant classification which had been developed by Carl Linnaeus, Ehret's botanical mentor. Many of the plants in *Plantae et Papiliones Rariores* were of American origin, reflecting the upsurge in new plant introductions which Ehret's friend Peter Collinson had done so much to promote. These included economic plants such as Cocoa and Pawpaw, as well as some virtuoso plants of horticulture.

This plate, whose full title is *Characteres Plantarum rariorum, observatae delineatae et aeri incisae*, was published in 1748 as number 8 in the series. Deliberately conceived as a record of the careful labours of the botanical artist, the plate shows numerous floral dissections of species more fully illustrated in other plates of the series. These include *Hibiscus cannabinus* ('Ketmia'), *Iris versicolor* ('Iris latifolia') and *Mollugo verticillata* ('Alsine procumbens'). The legume in the bottom right hand corner is indeed a Peanut.

JE

[1]Ehret 1896: 57.

158

80. DUMBCANE
Family Araceae (arums)

ARUM caule geniculato, Canna Indica foliis, summis
labris degustantis nudos reddens. Sloan. Cat.

Body colour on vellum,
signed: 'G.D. Ehret', dated
1760 and inscribed: 'Arum
seguinum caule geniculato,
Cannae Indicae foliis, summis
labris degustantes nudos
pallens'. From bound volume
(no. 5) of 'Drawings of natural
history', mainly by Georg
Ehret. 356 x 459mm (K).

This drawing is of dual interest in that it shows both a plant reputed to have been used as a punishment for verbal offences by slaves and an insect pest of sugar plantations. The West Indian *Dieffenbachia seguine*, aptly known as Dumbcane, contains a highly toxic juice that paralyses the vocal chords. The grasshopper may have been collected by Dr James Grainger, who resided in the West Indies from 1759 to 1763 and later published a poem which includes references to the pests of sugar cane.[1]

Each summer Georg Ehret was accustomed to spend a period in Merly, Dorset as the guest of Ralph Willett, a wealthy landowner whose father acquired sugar plantations at St. Christopher's (St. Kitt's) in the West Indies. Willett owned a notable library, which along with his extensive collection of original drawings was sold by his descendants in 1813 and 1814.[2] This painting may originate from this sale, or could be the *'curious Arum'*, listed in the catalogue of the sale of the late G.D. Ehret's effects in 1771.[3]

JE

[1]Kevan 1977: 195 (*The Sugar Cane*, 1764). [2]Also see Catalogue entry for Costus. [3]*A catalogue of the curious collection of ... George Dennis Ehret ... which ... will be sold by auction ... on ... 24th ... April 1771, and the three following days.* Langford & Son, London: see Lot 58 on Day 1, 'a curious Arum'.

81. COSTUS
Family Zingiberaceae (gingers)

Body colour on vellum, signed 'G.D. Ehret pinxit 1762' and inscribed 'Costus officinarum Dal. Pharm. 366'. Annotated by Lord Stanley 'Philipe, 11 May 1814, Lot 16 – Merly Library. To send to Mr Roscoe'. 330 x 650mm (K).

Georg Ehret composed several paintings of Costus (*Costus arabicus*). The first was one of the 200 paintings commissioned, at a guinea each, by the royal physician Dr Richard Mead, one of Ehret's most valuable early patrons. The painting now at Knowsley was commissioned later by Ehret's friend Ralph Willett (1719-1795), of Merly, Dorset, who left it to his cousin; the painting was eventually sold to Lord Stanley by the dealer Philipe on 11th May 1814.

Like many of the ginger family, *Costus* contains a pungent oil in its root which has medicinal uses, though the plant is mainly grown for ornament. The genus *Costus* is native in the tropics of both the New and Old World; *C. arabicus* is probably native to India. The pencil note 'to send to Mr Roscoe' is evidence of Lord Stanley's friendship with William Roscoe, the Liverpool based monographer of the gingers[1] and founder of Liverpool Botanic Garden in 1802. The garden's stove house was full of orchids and gingers.

The butterfly shown in Ehret's painting is the common species *Morpho menelaus*, found in Surinam and Guyana. Its inclusion may have been inspired by Maria Sybilla Merian's *Metamorphoses Insectarum Surinamensium* (1705), which similarly portrays economically useful plants and insects together.

JE

[1]Roscoe 1824-1828.

82. AMARYLLIS
Family Amaryllidaceae (daffodils)

Amaryllis Formosissima.

Watercolour, heightened with body colour, on vellum, inscribed: 'Amaryllis formosissima … Lis St. Jacques, originaire au Mexique' and signed: 'P.J. Redouté pinx.'. Bound in an album of original paintings entitled: 'Les Liliacées, par P.J. Redouté, peintre de fleurs de S.M. l'Imperatrice et Reine; dessinateur en titre de la Classe de Physique et Mathématique de l'Institut et du Museum d'Histoire Naturelle'. 330 x 480mm (K).

This effulgent species of Amaryllis, *Sprekelia formosissima* (a native of Mexico and Guatemala) is a spectacular plant with crimson sepals and a specific name that translates as 'very beautiful'. It was first illustrated in the *Botanical Magazine* in 1788.[1]

The botanical artist Pierre-Joseph Redouté (1759-1840) was the second of three artistically talented brothers, born in the Ardennes of southern France. In his youth he travelled and studied botanical drawings in several countries, and was particularly inspired by the work of Jan van Huysum in Amsterdam. Redouté was invited to London in 1787 and there contributed many of the plates for Charles l'Heritier du Brutelle's *Sertum Anglicum* (1788). On the eve of the French revolution Redouté returned to Paris to work for Marie Antoinette. Despite these royal connections, he survived and later was employed by Joséphine Bonaparte in developing Malmaison as an unrivalled centre for the introduction, description and illustration of plants new to European horticulture.

The public acclaim that greeted his greatest work, *Les Liliacées*, was due in part to the superb quality of the engravings, yet the delicacy of his original work can also be appreciated. Most surviving original works by Redouté are among the 'Vélins du Roi' at the Museum National d'Histoire Naturelle in Paris; privately held examples are rare. The 13th Earl of Derby was most fortunate to have acquired this set of Redouté drawings.

JE

[1]Curtis 1788, vol.2, Plate 47.

83. SILK COTTON TREE & INDIAN SHOT
Families Bombacaceae (baobabs) & Zingiberaceae (gingers)

Right Watercolour, heightened with body colour, on Chinese paper (made from *Cannabis sativa* fibre), depicting the Silk Cotton Tree (or Kapok). Inscribed 'Bombax ceiba'. 430 x 340mm. From a bound volume of original botanical paintings once in the collection of the 13th Earl of Derby. 340 x 430mm (LM 1999.36.1).

Far right Watercolour, heightened with body colour, on Chinese paper as above, depicting Indian Shot. Inscribed 'Canna indica'. From bound volume as above. 325 x 383mm.

The Silk Cotton Tree *Bombax ceiba* is the source of the valuable plant fibre known as Kapok which until recently was the conventional stuffing material for life jackets. The red flowers are edible and are supposed to have aphrodisiac properties.[1] Indian Shot *Canna indica* is an ornamental plant closely related to Arrowroot, and is widely cultivated. Its rhizome contains an easily digestible form of starch and the seeds can be used as beads.

These two plates are from an album of 85 delicately painted botanical drawings, some with butterflies and other insects added in the style of Georg Ehret. The volume dates from the late 18th or early 19th century. The subjects of the paintings are mostly of decorative and economic plants which are native to China and widely cultivated in oriental gardens – for example Okra, camellias, Madagascar Periwinkle, Japanese quince, Lotus and Tiger Lily. The drawings are very similar in style to those commissioned by John Reeves (1774–1856) while he was working as an inspector of tea at Canton and Macao.[2]

The book from which these paintings have been temporarily removed has a contemporary green stippled morocco binding, with an interlacing pattern of gilt tooling and bears the Eagle & Child bookplate of the Earls of Derby. It was purchased by the Liverpool Museum in 1998.

JE

[1]Mabberley 1987: 74. [2]Elliott 1994: 98.

These are just two of the botanical paintings from a series of 370 watercolours in two bound volumes, a collection which was acquired by Lord Derby at the sale of Aylmer Bourke Lambert's library in 1842.[1]

The first shows a Port Jackson Grass-tree, though it is not an accurate painting and so cannot be more fully identified. Grass-trees can reach several metres in height and have fire-blackened trunks - hence their other name, 'black-boys'. The long, stiff, leathery leaves arise in clusters at the tip of the shoots and from these tufts emerge lance-like flowering stalks, which can also be several metres tall. The individual flowers are small, and thousands are closely packed into each of these spikes. The Grass-tree was an important plant to the aboriginal peoples of Australia, and also to the early European settlers who arrived with the 'First Fleet' in 1788. The Latin name *Xanthorrhoea* alludes to the yellow gum which could be extracted from the trunk and used as a natural glue or as varnish.

The First Fleet surgeons, who became desperate for medicines once the penal colony was established at Port Jackson, investigated the therapeutic properties of Grass-tree gum. Dr John White, the Surgeon-General, and his assistant, Dr. Dennis Considen both claimed credit for discovering the gum could be used as a medicine. White remarked that it was 'good pectoral medicine, and very balsamic',[2] while Considen called it 'the balsam … of New South Wales'.[3]

The second painting shows a Triggerplant, most probably the Narrow-leaved Triggerplant, *Stylidium lineare*, a small herb that blooms in the southern hemisphere spring (as the inscription on the painting indicates) and is only found in New South Wales. Triggerplants have remarkable flowers, each with a sensitive, catapult-like 'trigger' mechanism that aids pollination. When touched by an insect, the 'trigger' jerks backwards, hitting the insect and pasting pollen onto its back. This painting was certainly known to the English botanist Sir James Smith. He also commented that:

'We learn … that Mr. Baver [Ferdinand Bauer] has observed a striking instance of irritability in one of the species which flowered at Kew, the column of the stamens, when touched, throwing itself backward into a curved form with great quickness. We find the column in that posture in several drawings and dried specimens sent by Dr. White from Port Jackson, New South Wales, from which our only knowledge of the two species we are about to describe is derived.'[4]

ECN

[1]Two of the zoological paintings are also included in the catalogue (see pages 60 and 66). [2]White 1790: 236. [3]D. Considen to Joseph Banks, 'Port Jackson, No. 18, 1788'; letter published in Historical records of New South Wales 1892, 1: 220-221. [4]Smith 1806: tab.66.

Watercolour of a Grass-tree *Xanthorrhoea* sp., by one of the anonymous 'Port Jackson' artists, with details of the seed and flower, inscribed 'Xanthorrhoea Hastile'. From botanical volume 1 of the bound albums known as the 'Lambert Drawings'. 188 x 315mm (K).

Watercolour of a Triggerplant *Stylidium* sp., by one of the anonymous 'Port Jackson' artists, with details of the 'trigger' and inscribed: 'October. The Natural size. Is found in dry sandy soil'. From botanical volume 2 of the bound 'Lambert Drawings'. 195 x 315mm (K).

female or young male.

Stanley Parrakeet   *Platycercus icterotis* (Temm.)   Swan River.

The Original of Plate 24 of Lear's Illustrations of Psittacidæ.

EDWARD LEAR, NATURAL HISTORY ARTIST

ROBERT McCRACKEN PECK

Of the many notable visitors to Knowsley during the 19th century, no artist or writer is more closely associated with the estate than Edward Lear (1812-1888). In about six years from the early 1830s, Lear created a stunning visual record of the exotic birds and mammals there. He also began to compose the endearing limericks and other illustrated nonsense verses for which he is so well known today. The 13th Earl of Derby's patronage would eventually enable Lear to move on to a life of travel and landscape painting abroad (see page 175), but not before he had established himself as one of the leading natural history artists of the time.

Although the earliest surviving record of personal contact between Edward Lear and Lord Stanley dates from February 1831,[1] when Lear was launching an ambitious publishing project (the *Illustrations of the Psittacidae*), in letters written later in life Lear recalled his patronage as having begun earlier.[2]

Lear was raised by his eldest sister Ann, with whom he lived until he moved to Italy in 1837. His sister taught him to draw and paint; Lear's childhood paintings of exotic birds, set in imaginary tropical or desert landscapes, hint of the life he would ultimately create for himself as a scientific illustrator and topographical artist.[3] As a boy, Lear earned a meagre income drawing what he called 'uncommon queer shop-sketches ... colouring prints, screens, fans ... [and] making morbid disease drawings for hospitals and certain doctors of physic' in London.[4] By the time he met Lord Stanley, Lear's artistic focus had moved from lifeless subjects to the animals owned by the Zoological Society of London. At first Lear merely created small line drawings for E.T. Bennett's *The gardens and menagerie of the Zoological Society delineated* (1830-1831) but later, working in a larger format and different medium, he made plates for more scholarly scientific publications.[5] After two years, Lear decided he could secure a greater income and establish a broader reputation as an artist by publishing a book of his own. He chose as his subject the most colourful, exotic and popular group of birds he could think of - the parrots.

In June 1830, Lear formally applied to the zoo's council for permission 'to make drawings of the Parrots belonging to the Society'. Lord Stanley chaired the meeting at which his application was approved.[6] Lear used the zoo's museum collection at Bruton Street as well as painting living birds in their gardens at Regent's Park, and travelled elsewhere to find additional species.[7] He made dozens of pencil and watercolour studies of his subjects. When satisfied that he had captured both the physical appearance and characteristic postures of the living birds, Lear drew them again (on lithographic stones) to create the plates for his book. These were printed and then professionally coloured with reference to the pigments in a set of 'pattern plates' Lear had prepared. The book was issued in parts by subscription, and Lord Stanley lent prestige and influence to Lear's efforts by allowing his name to be attached to Lear's roster of patrons.[8]

Lear included at least two birds from Lord Stanley's collection in his monograph, the Stanley Parakeet and the Red-capped Parakeet (now known as the Red-capped Parrot *Purpureicephalus spurius*). Seeing his birds in print may have inspired Lord Stanley to commission Lear to paint more of the species he had in captivity. *Illustrations of the family of Psittacidae, or parrots* earned Lear immediate respect and admiration; England's leading ornithologist, Prideaux John Selby, pronounced Lear's parrot plates 'beautifully coloured & I think infinitely superior to Audubon's in softness and the drawing as good'.[9]

Opposite Lear's watercolour of a 'female or young male Stanley Parakeet Platycercus icterotis (Temm) [the Western Rosella]. Swan River. The Original of Plate 24 of Lear's Illustrations of the Psittacidae', painted in September 1831. The name *Platycercus Stanleyi* ('Stanley Parakeet') was published by Nicholas Vigors in 1830, but he subsequently realised his name applied to a bird which had been named *Platycercus icterotis* in 1820 (K).

A sheet of sketches by Lear, of the Hwamei Laughing Thrush & other birds (several parrots and a heron) (Houghton Library, Harvard University, Cambridge, MA, USA). The completed version is at Knowsley.

Within 24 hours of issuing his first two plates, Lear was nominated to associate fellowship of the Linnean Society of London. This was an exciting and heady time for Lear. Despite his modest background and meagre education, he found himself, aged 18, associating with some of the most sophisticated, cultured and wealthy people of his time. Despite this, the young artist had great difficulty recouping the expense he had incurred in his publishing venture: 'The tardy paying of many of my subscribers renders it but too difficult to procure food and pay for publishing at once' he complained to a bookseller.[10] He had hoped his book would be larger, but financial constraints caused him to terminate the project after issuing only 42 plates. Lear busied himself instead in producing plates for books by John Gould, William Jardine and Prideaux Selby. This consumed almost every minute of his time. 'I am up to my neck in hurry and work from 5 a.m. till 7 p.m. without cessation,' he wrote to a friend.[11]

In fact, Lear's largest commission during this period was from Lord Stanley, who offered an open-ended invitation for Lear to paint the birds and mammals in his museum and those living in the aviary and menagerie at Knowsley. Lear's role was to create a visual record of the species (living or dead) that had been the most difficult to obtain, or were considered particularly important, by Lord Stanley. Subjects such as the Stanley Crane were obvious choices. For every finished painting he created, Lear made one or more sheets of life studies. These he often saved for his own future reference.[12]

One such study, dated 'Knowsley, June 24 1835', reveals Lear's working methods. The subject is a bird which Lear called Garrulax sinensis or 'Indian Crying Thrush' (Hwamei Laughing Thrush *Garrulax canorus*). Lear augmented a detailed rendering of his primary subject with marginal posture studies of other birds, and made notes to himself about how to capture the illusive colours of the living thrush. At the top of the page he wrote 'this bird must be more graceful' and 'make the head smaller'. He also instructed himself to make the 'eye greener', the tail area 'brighter', the legs a 'pale shiny flesh-horn colour', the throat 'more olive-mottled' and the 'plumes very silky'. Lear's final version of the painting, which incorporates all of his own instructions, is at Knowsley.

Two watercolours by Lear of a 'Tyrse Argus' (the African Softshell Turtle *Trionyx triunguis*), 'Brought home alive by Mr Whitfield'; a) 'lower side', b) 'upper side', the original of the plate in *Gleanings* (K).

While Lear was sometimes required to paint preserved specimens, he much preferred to study and draw live subjects. 'I am never pleased with a drawing unless I make it from life', he declared.[13] Sometimes he incorporated vignettes of characteristic behaviour into his portraits of birds and mammals, as if to reinforce their vitality. The Lear painting of Orinoco Geese at Knowsley, for instance, shows several of the birds in full puffed-up mating display, a posture which Lear also used in one of his cartoons.[14]

In an unusual double portrait of a soft-shell turtle, Lear depicted the animal from two perspectives. In one pose the overturned turtle kicks wildly to right itself and protect its fleshy, pink underbelly. In the second, the turtle appears to be diving for safety. A more animated pair of reptilian portraits may never have been made. Lear, however, was not happy with them and explained to Edward Stanley that, even though James Hunt (a groundsman at Knowsley) 'held [the turtle] for me for two whole mornings … I have had very great trouble in getting the drawings to look satisfactory: even now, only the under side of the trionyx is what I really like'.[15]

From Lear's earliest natural history painting in the Knowsley collection (a Chestnut-belted Gnateater *Conopophaga aurita*, dated 1830) to the latest (a series of dove studies dated May and June 1837), one can see a dramatic progression from artistically adequate to extraordinary and then a gradual decline in the quality of his work as Lear grew weary of the repetitive nature of his subjects. During the best years of his natural history painting - 1832 to 1837 - Lear's watercolours show a total mastery of both his subjects and his medium and a thorough grasp of avian anatomy and feather structure.

It is perhaps not entirely coincidental that Lear's improvement as a natural history artist coincided with his first prolonged visits to Knowsley, for the visibility and prestige of Edward Stanley's patronage, and the access to living models, must have given the young artist an enormous boost. Even in 1831 Lear was being paid as much as £3 per painting by Lord Stanley, for whom he was drawing 'very frequently'.[16] Nevertheless, it took Lear some time to adjust to living and working at one of the grandest estates in England. Despite the large number of people

A sheet of Lear cartoons and doodles, including a group of parrots perched on a robed figure, a family with their pet dogs, a view of parkland (probably at Knowsley) and the pencil outline of a Blue-rumped parrot, *Psittacus cyanurus*. The final version is at Knowsley. The fragment of yellow parrot is from the preliminary sketch for the lower Golden Parakeet plate illustrated on page 55 (Houghton Library, Harvard University, Cambridge, MA, USA).

employed by Edward Stanley ('between 20 + 30 servants wait at dinner' Lear noted)[17] and the perpetual presence of his many house guests, relatives and friends, Lear at first felt isolated and out of place in the social hierarchy that controlled life at Knowsley. 'I think my stay here will make me burst to have some fun' he wrote during one of his working visits to the estate; 'Consider, I have no creature of my own grade of Society to speak to'.[18] Sometimes he drew cartoons on the edges of his bird paintings and invented eccentric stories to entertain the children of the household, or to relieve the tension he felt working in such a formal place.

Edward Stanley's position in society and his role as employer initially assured a degree of formality in his relationship with Edward Lear, but the personalities and shared interests of the two men would eventually lead to a closeness that transcended the normal boundaries of the time. Their early meetings seem to have been businesslike, but after Lord Stanley became Earl in 1834 and began to spend more time at Knowsley, he saw more of the young artist he employed. Lear, still fulfilling painting commitments for John Gould and others, shuttled between London and Liverpool on a regular basis. He kept in close contact with Lord Derby in both locations, noting the Earl's generous spirit in a letter:

'Really his extreme kindness is quite extraordinary. He takes opportunities continually of showing it + is without partiality - a perfect gentleman in every respect'.[19]

In another letter he wrote:

'Lord D - I must say - has behaved with very great kindness: two or 3 things while he was in town were particularly marked - such as at the Gardens + Zoological Meetings - shaking hands with me before all the great bodies + in calling + sitting for a long half hour at 28 Southampton Row [Lear's home in London]. These attentions - little in themselves - have a great effect when coming from people of rank - to us small fry of artists - + it is very praiseworthy of noblemen to make use of such means to bring young beasts forward one step in life'.[20]

168

A sheet of watercolour and pencil sketches by Edward Lear, including a series of sketches of the Stanley Crane; the completed version can been seen in Catalogue entry 53. The sheet also shows a very yellow Military Macaw *Ara militaris* (Houghton Library, Harvard University, Cambridge, MA, USA).

This same letter records that Lear was soon made to feel at home at Knowsley, moving from the housekeeper's dining room to that of Lord Derby's own family in 1835. Following an extended visit in 1836, Lear noted his change in feelings about life at the estate:

'I never remember passing so happy a consecutive 6 weeks as I did this year at Knowsley. The breaking up of the party was a regret to all - and knowing that I could not meet with better fun or better friends elsewhere - I did not set out [on a long-anticipated sketching trip] *with all the alacrity with which a tourist ought to begin his journey'.*

At the end of that year, Lear was invited to share Christmas dinner with Lord Derby and his family. Then, in an even more remarkable gesture of friendship, Lear was extended an open invitation to come to Knowsley 'when I please, without being asked'.[22] In just a few years, Knowsley had become a second home to Lear, where he had become a proxy member of the Earl's large family and wide circle of friends. By 1837 Lear was enjoying Lord Derby's hospitality on a carriage trip from London to Liverpool, an occasion that afforded the opportunity to extend their unusual friendship. Lear recounted the experience in a letter a few days after it occurred:

'At five past 4 o'clock [we] left London in a chariot drawn by four horses, accompanied by 2 custodians [?] + 2 domestics + containing Lord Derby, myself, 6 cloaks, one jerboa [a small rodent] - 3 pigeons - 20 or 30 books - some bread + biscuits - a roast fowl + a bottle of wine …' [23]

169

Lemur rufus, Audebert.   *Madagascar.*

The Original of the plate in the 'Gleanings'.

Lear may have taken advantage of such an opportunity to talk to the Earl about his growing desire to progress beyond natural history painting. Troubled by poor eyesight from an early age, Lear found the close work required for scientific illustration particularly taxing. He was also beginning to tire of the repetitive nature of the paintings he was being commissioned to produce. While developing his skills as a lithographer under the direction of Charles Hullmandel in London, Lear had come into contact with several artists whose extended painting trips to Europe and the Middle East whetted his own appetite for travel and ignited a long-held ambition to become a landscape artist.[24]

Although it was in Lord Derby's best interest to keep Lear in England and working on natural history projects, he recognised Lear's need for personal and artistic growth. Ultimately, he and a number of his friends and relatives would underwrite a two-year study trip to Italy for Lear (see pages 175 to 183), but first the Earl helped Lear explore a very different travel plan.

Since 1826, Lord Stanley had enjoyed a cordial relationship with the American artist John James Audubon (1785-1851), who had come to Liverpool in that year to seek support for an ambitious publishing project. Lord Stanley subscribed to Audubon's massive book *The Birds of America* and Audubon, in return, arranged to procure specimens of American birds and mammals for the Earl's museum, aviary and menagerie. Lear had met Audubon several times, often at the Zoological Society of London.[25] Audubon admired Lear's work so much that he bought a copy of *Illustrations of the Psittacidae*, despite the high price of the book and his own severely limited financial situation.

It is not clear whether it was Edward Lear or Lord Derby who first developed the idea that Lear might accompany Audubon on a natural history and painting expedition through the United States, but in 1835 they jointly approached him with such a proposal. Audubon, always eager to please his patrons, found himself in an awkward situation. While wishing to accommodate Lord Derby's request, he did not want to have Lear's company imposed upon him for a working expedition. Audubon must have viewed 'our young friend, Mr. Lear' not only as an encumbrance to his own travels, but also as a potential rival in the increasingly competitive market of ornithological illustration. In a carefully worded letter to Lord Derby, Audubon professed his 'pleasure' at the idea of having Lear join him, but then went on to enumerate the difficulties such a journey would entail. None of the three men ever mentioned the idea again.

Audubon could not have played his hand better, for Lear's health, never robust, was now suffering from the cold and damp of the British climate. The very medical conditions that argued against his staying in England also argued against his accompanying Audubon on a rigorous trek through North America. Lear's doctor urged him to find a warm, dry, climate in which to live and work. Rome, with its Mediterranean climate and thriving artists' colony, seemed the perfect choice. With financial backing from Lord Derby and '30 friends of very different families', Lear travelled to the Eternal City in the autumn of 1837.[26]

As he embarked on this new phase of his artistic career, Lear left behind an impressive list of scientific publications and a large number of superb natural history paintings. Lord Derby alone owned more than one hundred of Lear's bird and mammal portraits. He eventually published seventeen of these in the first volume of *Gleanings from the menagerie and aviary at Knowsley Hall* (Gray 1846a), some nine years after Lear's departure. The plates for *Gleanings* were transcribed from Lear's original watercolours by another artist, J. W. Moore. They were then

Opposite Lear's watercolour of 'Lemur rufus' (the Rufous Lemur *Eulemur fulvus rufus*), painted in December 1836, which was published as Plate 3 in volume one of Gray's *Gleanings* (K).

printed in sets of one hundred each by the lithographic firm of Hullmandel & Walton. Each plate was hand-coloured by professional colourists, who matched the subtle tones in Lear's originals with extraordinary skill.

The 'Whiskered Yarke', 'Piping Guan', 'Eyebrowed Rollulus', 'Eyed Tyrse' and several of the other species depicted in this privately published folio boasted common names which one might expect to find in the writings of Lewis Carroll or Lear himself, but the meticulous accuracy of the plates and the detailed descriptions of each bird and mammal (written by John Edward Gray of the British Museum in London) leave no doubt that *Gleanings* was intended to be a serious scientific publication. While choosing paintings to include in the book, Gray was struck by the superiority of Lear's work to that of other artists who had been given comparable commissions by Lord Derby. Originally the Earl had wanted to combine Lear's illustrations with those of Benjamin Waterhouse Hawkins (1807-1889), an experienced artist who had been hired to paint most of the larger animals living at Knowsley. Gray argued against this idea as he thought that Lear's drawings were so good, they 'might make Hawkins' look worse than they really are if mixed together'.[27] Gray advised instead that the artists' work be published 'in two separate works of equal rank and appearance, one coming out a year after the other' and Lord Derby agreed. The edition of *Gleanings* featuring Lear's plates now ranks, along with Lear's *Illustrations of the Psittacidae*, as one of the rarest and most desirable colour plate books of the nineteenth century. Three of Lear's books were published in 1846; *Gleanings*, *Illustrated excursions in Italy* and *The book of nonsense*. The concurrent publication of these three very different books tangibly illustrates the many-tiered nature of Edward Lear's life.

Ironically, it was Lear's whimsical nonsense verses, originally written and illustrated to entertain the 13th Earl of Derby's young relatives, which ultimately overshadowed Lear's contributions to the art of both natural history and travel. Lear was at first embarrassed to be associated publicly with such frivolous writings, fearing that they might undercut his credibility as a serious artist. To ensure anonymity, he used the pseudonym Derry-Down-Derry ('who loved to see little folks merry') when publishing the first collection of his 'nonsense'.[28] No matter how hard Lear tried to distance himself from it, however this was the side of his creative genius that resonated with the public and permanently attached itself to his reputation.

While the watercolours he made at Knowsley and during every other period of his long career look effortless, the process of putting pigment on paper was always a struggle for Lear. It was also his all-consuming passion. At the time of his death in San Remo, Italy, Lear had composed more than 7,000 watercolours of his travels in Europe, the Greek isles, the Middle East and India, about 2,000 studio watercolours, more than 300 oil paintings, almost 400 natural history paintings, five illustrated travel books, two books of natural history illustration and more than 100 other published lithographs documenting birds, mammals, and reptiles from various parts of the world.[29] 'Strange', he mused, '… that what to me is always painful and disagreeable work, painting, should in a couple of months, create a work which not only gives pleasure to its possessor at present, but may continue to do so to hundreds of others for a century or more'.[30] Stranger still, he must have thought, that the limericks and doodles that came to him so easily would do the same.

Lear spent six decades earnestly recording the physical world and its colourful inhabitants, but it was the landscape of his imagination that would have the greatest and most lasting appeal. The Victorian artist and critic John Ruskin declared Lear's

Book of nonsense 'the most beneficent and innocent of all books yet produced' and placed Lear first in his list of one hundred authors.[31] A half century later, the poet W. H. Auden celebrated Lear's genius with a poem about his lonely but triumphant life; '… and children swarmed to him like settlers'. The poem concluded 'He became a land'.[32]

[1]From a mainly political diary of Lord Stanley's (K). [2]Lear to Chichester Fortescue, 31st July 1870 (Noakes 1988: 224). In this letter Lear refers to beginning his life at San Remo, "with the same Knowsley patronage I began life with at 18 years of age" (i.e. 1830). A letter of 1851 (Strachey 1907: 17-18) hints that he first went to Knowsley in 1829. [3]Lear's notebook of 1829 (National Library of Scotland), and his childhood album (Houghton Library, Harvard). [4]Comment 'By Way of Preface' in *Nonsense songs and stories* 1888. [5]For example, *The zoology of Captain Beechey's Voyage* (dated 1839, but Lears' pictures are much earlier). [6]Council minutes for 16th June 1830. [7]Lear also acknowledged that, amongst others, he had used birds in the collection of Lord Stanley and John Gould. [8]Stanley was 18th of Lear's 110 subscribers. [9]Selby to William Jardine, 10th January 1831, Cambridge University Library. [10]Lear to Charles Empson, 1st October 1831 (Noakes 1988: 14). [11]Lear to George Coombe, 19th April 1833 (Frederick Warne Archives). [12]Many of these preliminary sketches are in the Houghton Library at Harvard, or the Blacker-Wood Library at McGill University in Montreal. [13]Lear to Empson, 1st October 1831 (Noakes 1988: 14). [14]See page 20 and Catalogue entry 31. [15]Lear to Lord Derby, 2nd June 1836 (Noakes 1988: 21). Both turtle paintings are at Knowsley. [16]Lear to Empson, 1st October 1831 (Noakes 1988: 14). In contrast, John Gould was much later paid just £1 each for 'original sketches' of birds (Gould to Lord Derby, 3rd March 1843, LVRO 1/67/12). [17]Lear to Mrs George Coombe, 20th July 1835 (Frederick Warne Archive). [18]Lear to Mrs Coombe, 24th June 1835 (Warne Archive). [19]Lear to George Coombe, 24th June 1835 (Warne Archive). [20]Lear letter fragment, undated (Warne Archive). [21]Lear to Mrs Coombe, 24th August 1836 (Warne Archives). [22]Lear to Mrs Coombe, 3rd January 1837 (Warne Archives). [23]Lear to Mrs Coombe, 19th April 1837 (Warne Archive). [24]Lear particularly admired the Middle Eastern paintings of his friend, the landscape artist Daniel Fowler (Letter fragment, 1835? Warne Archives). [25]Lear was actually closer in age to Audubon's son Victor Gifford Audubon (1809-1860) and the two became life-long friends. [26]Lear to Mrs Coombe, 3rd March 1837 (Warne Archive). [27]Gray to Derby, 14th February 1844 (MM/8/K/3: 173-5). [28]Lear finally admitted authorship in the third edition, published in 1861. [29]Noakes 1985: 10. [30]Chitty 1988: 165. [31]*The Pall Mall Gazette* for 15th February 1886. [32]W. H. Auden in *Edward Lear* 1939, reprinted in Noakes 1985: 203.

Edward Lear

14

nel Luglio 1840

EDWARD LEAR IN ITALY 1837-1848

EDWARD MORRIS

Opposite Pencil portrait of Edward Lear by Wilhelm Marstrand, 1840 (By Courtesy of the National Portrait Gallery, London).

Edward Lear's chosen profession was that of landscape painter, not nonsense poet, travel writer or animal illustrator. 'Genus homo! I aint. I'm a landscape painter & I desire you to like me as sich [sic], or not at all', he wrote to his great friend Chichester Fortescue, three years after his return from Italy.[1] He made his decision in 1836 or early 1837, at the age of twenty-four. Constable and Turner were still alive and English landscape painting was pre-eminent throughout Europe. Allowing for his talent for self-mockery, Lear took his chosen career very seriously, travelling over much of southern Europe and beyond in search of scenery and producing around ten paintings and hundreds of drawings every year, despite finding the actual process of painting difficult and unrewarding. He even enrolled at the Royal Academy Schools in 1850, believing that an intense study of the human figure was useful for a landscape artist already thirty-seven years old:

> '… hard study beginning with the root of the matter, the human figure, which to master alone would enable me to carry out the views and feelings of landscape I know to exist within me'.[2]

Two years later Lear took instruction from Holman Hunt and struggled for some years with the Pre-Raphaelite principle of working directly from nature. Despite poor health and failing eyesight he continued to paint and exhibit his landscapes on a large scale well into his seventies. Lear achieved neither great critical acclaim nor financial success – 'misfortune in the exhibition of his pictures pursued him', as his friend, the artist W.P. Frith, put it – but this never deterred his dedication to landscape painting.[3]

For the launch of his new career in 1836-1837, Lear was indebted not only to his own sense of vocation but also to Lord Derby, who helped to pay for his prolonged stay in Rome between 1837 and 1848. There was a long tradition by which aristocratic patrons paid for promising young artists to study in Rome. In 1826 Lear's great friend Penry Williams, notable as a painter of landscapes and scenes from everyday life, had been sent to Rome by his patron Sir Joseph Bailey. Bailey, later Lord Glanusk, had already bought some of the young artist's landscapes and now stipulated that, in return for establishing him in Rome, Williams should send home to Bailey some, or all, of his Italian paintings.[4] The condition was not unreasonable, although Williams tried to escape from it, and similarly Lear felt for many years that Lord Derby had a first call on his Italian output. In 1838 Lear wrote to his sister Ann that he was planning to send some paintings to Lord Derby because 'I consider always the money advanced to me as only paid beforehand for pictures', and of his first six paintings, all completed in 1840, three went to Derby or his family.[5] In fact it is most unlikely that Lord Derby imposed any such specific condition; he was more interested in natural history than in landscape painting and was not a patron of contemporary art except in that context. Lear had graduated from being his servant to being his friend, and he paid for Lear's Roman trip out of kindness towards a dear and faithful friend embarking on a new career. Lear's gratitude was unbounded. In a letter to Derby of 5th June 1839, referring optimistically to his future as a landscape painter, Lear noted that he was 'progressing in my profession, however slowly, and not less grateful for the kindnesses which have enabled me to look forward to more pleasing prospects than I once thought of'.[6] In 1851 he wrote to Chichester Fortescue:

175

Oil on canvas of 'Civitella di
Subiaco' by Edward Lear,
1847 (The Clothworkers' Company,
London).

'You suppose rightly that I felt Lord Derby's death; I have not felt anything so much
for many many years – 22 years ago I first went to Knowsley, & have received nothing
but kindness from him and his family ever since'.[7]

Derby's son and grandson continued to buy Lear's landscapes right up to 1884,
only a few years before his death, not really because they wanted them but rather
because Lear's welfare and career as a landscape painter had become a family
obligation and duty. In 1870, Lear wrote again to Fortescue after persuading
Derby's grandson, the 15th Earl, to commission a landscape:

'So I begin my San Remo life with the same Knowsley patronage I began life with
at 18 years of age. I had some strong and particular reasons for making the request I
did, – and to no-one else could I have made it, or would I have made it'.[8]

Lear's work for the Stanley family had a particular value in the context of his
artistic development. He was not content to remain a watercolourist, painting
highly accomplished but small, simple and unpretentious views of local scenery in
the style of most English professional watercolourists (and some oil painters). Like
some other British nineteenth century artists Lear was determined to progress from
illustrator to watercolourist and then up to oil painter, working on ever more
pretentious subjects as he advanced in techniques. He aspired to the grand manner
of Turner, with sublime and demanding compositions on a large scale, inspiring
elevated emotions and profound thought. In his early Italian years Lear learnt how
to paint in oil, and his watercolours acquired increasing sophistication, with that
subtle combination of expressive ink outline and flat washes of carefully related
colours which was to characterize his best mature work. With greater access to old

master paintings and to the expertise of fellow artists, and in response to the grand and dramatic features of the countryside around Rome, his compositions became more elaborate and his command of space and of recession into depth more assured. Examples can be seen in his *Civita Castellana*, painted for Lord Derby's cousin, James J. Hornby, in 1844 (see Catalogue entry 95), and in his *Civitella di Subiaco* of 1847, developed from a smaller painting of 1843 for the same patron. His *Acropolis of Athens, Sunrise; Peasants assembling on the Road to Piraeus*, painted for Lord Derby (probably at Lear's own suggestion, but not finished until after the 13th Earl's death), contrasts the monumental ancient grandeur of the Acropolis - isolated on its hill and dramatized by the sunrise behind it - with the picturesque everyday life of local peasants. It was probably Lear's first large scale painting with such an ambitious programme. Artist and patron discussed in detail the composition, the figures and the fall of light in order to emphasize 'the poetic identity of the place', as Lear put it.[9] The 13th Earl of Derby's son, Lord Stanley, winner of the Chancellor's prize for Latin verse at Oxford and translator of Homer, contributed to the discussion, and in 1853 Lear painted for him a large picture of another grand subject, *Windsor Castle*, no less rich in historical associations. Lear must have been very familiar with the most important masterpiece then hanging at Knowsley, Nicolas Poussin's *Landscape with the Ashes of Phocion*, in which the great French artist has constructed a noble and solemn landscape reflecting in its mood and composition the grave and portentous events it depicts.[10] These great and elevating historical landscapes, however, took Lear months to paint and proved hard to sell when there was no Derby commission. Pre-Raphaelitism imposed new and very different principles of composition and of naturalism, which unsettled Lear. Sadly,

Oil on canvas of 'The Acropolis of Athens, sunrise; peasants assembling on the road to Piraeus' by Edward Lear, 1850–1852 (Museum of the City of Athens, Athens).

177

he eventually had to depend too much on carefully arranged and highly finished watercolours, often painted with mechanical precision.

Edward Stanley did more than encourage Lear's ambitions for grand historical landscape with commissions and advice. While Lear was staying at Knowsley between 1831 and 1837, working on animal illustration for him, Lord Stanley and his family introduced him into that level of society in which classical erudition and artistic awareness were widely cultivated. In 1831 Lear, the poorly educated son of a dysfunctional, downwardly mobile middle class family, admitted to 'being but very little used to company or society' but once at Knowsley, where Derby treated him as a guest rather than as a servant, he saw 'half the fine people of the day' and was quietly pleased that the Earl of Wilton 'always asked me to drink a glass of champagne with him at dinner'.[11] These were the years in which the 13th Earl's son, Lord Stanley, was establishing his political career (which culminated in three terms as Prime Minister) and in which Knowsley was building its reputation as one of the great 'political' country houses. These connections later greatly assisted Lear in finding subscribers in England for his volumes of lithographs of Italian landscapes. It must also have been this familiarity with aristocratic life which enabled Lear to develop while in Italy his exceptional talent for close friendships with young men belonging to a social class much higher than his own. These friendships with Chichester Fortescue (later Baron Carlingford and an important Liberal statesman), with Thomas Baring (later Earl of Northbrook and Viceroy of India) and with many others, were enormously useful to Lear professionally and emotionally. Most dated from his Italian years. Lear could never depend on the market to sell his landscapes; he had to rely on friends. It was one of the great attractions of Italy to young Englishmen that social class and distinction, which dominated London life, counted for much less in Rome. English visitors could form friendships reflecting their tastes and inclinations rather than their positions in society. Lear taught drawing in Rome, and the son of an English nobleman could easily tour Italy with his drawing master, but not Scotland nor the Lake District.

Nonetheless artists could still not be members of the exclusive English Club in Rome and there were other problems, even for Lear. One of his pupils was J.J. Proby, who arrived in Rome in 1846 to study art. They toured Sicily and Calabria together in 1847, and Lear attributed the cause of a sharp row with Proby to his ignorance of the rank of his companion, who was heir to the Earls of Carysfort.[12] The rift was soon healed, thanks to Lear's easy charm and social assurance. These qualities must also have been very helpful to Lear in selling his paintings and drawings which, apart from teaching, were his main source of income. In Rome, artists sold their work not through public exhibitions but by means of visits by wealthy visitors to their studios, where the right level of persuasiveness, tact and amiability could make or mar a sale. This was a sales technique which Lear learned in Rome and then practiced all his life. In Rome, between 1837 and 1848, Lear could easily find customers and pupils among the enormous number of English tourists with the leisure and inclination to learn and buy art. Cholera epidemics in Italy between 1834 and 1837 had discouraged visitors, but during the Roman 'season' of 1837-1838, Macaulay reported that:

'Rome is full of English. We could furnish exceedingly respectable Houses of Lords and Commons. There are at present twice as many coroneted carriages in the Piazza di Spagna [known by then as the 'ghetto degli Inglesi'] as in St James's Parish'.[13]

Lear wrote to Ann, a month earlier, that half the English peers were in Rome.[14] In January 1839 Samuel Palmer estimated that there were about 1500-2000 English tourists in Rome – out of a total population of less than 150,000.[15] The leisurely eighteenth century grand tour (which lasted years) had been replaced by shorter breaks on a much larger scale, as a result of better communications. By late 1838 Lear had seven pupils who would expect to pay as much as 10 shillings for an hour's tuition, and by 1839 teaching had become his main occupation (although he was eventually able to reduce this commitment). Among these pupils was Coutts Lindsay, whose Grosvenor Gallery exhibitions forty years later would play a very important part in the Aesthetic Movement.[16] In 1839 Gladstone, the future Prime Minister and notable patron of the arts, called at Lear's Rome studio and noted in his diary that Lear 'draws beautifully'.[17] By 1843 Lear was listed in Murray's indispensable *Handbook to Central Italy* as 'an English artist of great promise', with a flattering note on his published lithographs of Rome and its surroundings.[18] In 1847 Georgiana Duff Gordon, then visiting Italy with her mother (the formidable and influential Lady Duff Gordon), introduced Lear to G.F. Watts with whom she may have been in love.[19] Georgiana and Watts dined with Lear at his flat in Rome, and Lear took Georgiana's sister out sketching in the Campagna. Although Lear had little sympathy later with Watts's intensely symbolic art, this and other chance encounters demonstrate the richness and diversity of Lear's life in Rome. Indirectly, Rome provided Lear's most exalted introduction, for it was his lithographs of Rome and its surroundings that persuaded Queen Victoria that Lear should improve her drawing skills. It may have been the 13th Earl of Derby's son, then her Colonial Secretary, who first suggested that she should subscribe to the lithographs, for one volume was dedicated by Lear to him.

In Rome, Lear was looking not only for patrons but also for the companionship of fellow artists. In England, as an overworked animal illustrator based for much of his working life at Knowsley, he had little opportunity to meet and learn from other painters. English naturalist artists, most notably Constable, were strongly hostile to the eighteenth century tradition of study in Rome, particularly for landscape painters. However, many artists still made the journey (often as mature professionals rather than as young students) and sculptors were particularly attracted by the availability of well-trained Italian assistants. Artists' models were inexpensive, easy to hire and showed a natural grace of posture and uninhibited display of emotion useful to the artist. Flats incorporating a studio were amazingly cheap and many were purpose built. Lear paid £2 10 shillings monthly for his but Samuel Palmer's rent in 1839 was only £1 10 shillings. In 1837 William Collins could have had Claude's old house, which Lear painted in 1850, but he found it too dirty and the landlord too disreputable.[20]

Like their patrons, the artists increasingly tended to stay for shorter periods. A list of British painters living in Rome at various times between 1837 and 1848 would include Penry Williams, William Collins, Samuel Palmer, George Richmond, G.F. Watts, E.M. Ward, Henry O'Neill, A.W. Elmore, Charles Coleman, Joseph Severn, Ford Madox Brown, E.W. Cooke and G.H. Mason. They generally attended the British Academy in Rome for practice in drawing, frequented the same cafés, lived in the same streets, walked in the same areas and went together to the annual artists' festival. Lear wrote to the ornithologist John Gould in 1839:

'I know all the English artists – who are universally kind to me … & our little supper parties in winter, & our excursions in spring and autumn are very lively and agreeable'.[21]

Lear also knew some members of the large international community of artists in Rome. The city was still a major artistic and literary centre and he might even have met Nikolai Gogol, who wrote the best chapter of his masterpiece *Dead Souls* in a miserable inn frequented by tourists in the hills between Albano and Genzano during the winter of 1837-8. Lear was especially fond of Wilhelm Marstrand, a Danish painter whose pencil portrait of Lear of 1840 shows a charming, eager, sensitive and wistful young man, quite different from the rather disillusioned and withdrawn figure of later portraits.

There were also a few disadvantages. Artists resident in Rome could not become associates or members of the Royal Academy – although an exception was made for John Gibson. The transport of paintings back to England was risky, slow and costly, as well as subject to customs duties. During the summer months Rome was too hot and the risk of malaria too great, but artists could stay at inns in the picturesque villages scattered around the safer and cooler surrounding hills for only about 19 shillings per week, including all meals.[22] Indeed it was not primarily the great monuments of antiquity and of the Renaissance that appealed to Lear, but rather the countryside - which then spread right up to and around them, for Rome was still a small city, about the same size as Leeds in the 1840s. Landscape artists had long regarded the Roman Campagna, the countryside around Rome so rich in classical associations and remains, as the greatest inspiration and subject for their art. There Claude and Poussin had invented classical landscape in the seventeenth century, and by the mid-nineteenth century many of their paintings were in British collections. It was also there that Richard Wilson had created English ideal landscape in the eighteenth century. In 1825 David Wilkie wrote to William Collins, the landscape painter, trying to persuade Collins to join him in Rome:

'Here everything is seen clearer than in England – the sky is bluer, the light is brighter, the shadows stronger and colours more vivid than with you'.[23]

The great Romantic poets were also generally impressed. For Wordsworth the Campagna was 'that sad and solemn district' – even if Shelley at first only found it 'a flattering picture of Bagshot Heath'.[24] Figure painters were exhorted by the great critic William Hazlitt not to study ancient sculpture in the city, but rather 'to make studies of the heads and dresses of the peasant girls in the neighbourhood, those goddesses of health and good temper'.[25] An international school of artists, led by the Swiss, Léopold Robert, soon developed in Rome. They specialized in the romantic world of the brigand, the herdsman and their women in their picturesque costumes, seen against the brilliant and evocative landscape of the Campagna. Charles Eastlake, Joseph Severn, Thomas Uwins and many other English artists came to Italy in order to study high art but actually concentrated on these highly marketable subjects.

Lear's close friend Penry Williams was the leading English member of this international group. His genre paintings sold more easily to tourists than Lear's landscapes, so Lear began to add small, characteristic figures to his landscapes, sometimes with Williams' assistance. Lear's wish to study figure painting in part reflects this commercial reality, but Williams' greatest contribution to Lear's art was to introduce him to the countryside of central and southern Italy. Lear was immediately intoxicated by its beauty, and descriptions of it in his letters and books reveal both a deep sensuous attachment and a scientific observation in his attitude to its enormously rich and varied landscape, flora and fauna. Here is a typical example from one of his letters, written to his sister in the first summer after his arrival in Italy:[26]

> 'All the way up this road you see profusions of aloes in bloom, Indian figs (cacti) of an immense size, Indian corn, figs, oranges and pomegranates full of scarlet blossom … … You walk constantly in a beautiful path like a park walk through a wood of young chestnuts where the cuckoos and nightingales are innumerable, and indeed all the walks about this part of the country are more like pleasure grounds than roads, and I am only describing one in a hundred … … All along most of the paths are fountains of most delightful water, and the wild flowers are really superb, red lilies, larkspur, roses, myrtles and thousands of other plants cultivated by us grow here wild on all the rocks, and the butterflies and all sorts of insects are beautiful'.

Lear's descriptions of the more desolate and empty Campagna, with its rocks, lines of distant hills, intense and vivid colours, exotic animals and sense of loneliness, are even more haunting and evocative. The diversity, abundance and cheapness of Italian food and drink in the better country inns provoked another catalogue of delight in the same letter to Ann:

> 'Now what do you think I live for? Today for instance we had coffee & eggs at 5, at 12 beautiful macaroni soup, boiled beef and mutton cutlets, strawberries, cherries and a bottle of wine each, & at supper macaroni & an omelette, wine and oranges, to which you are to add lodging & now guess … actually 2/8 [about 13 pence] of our money daily'.

Lear was no less delighted by the picturesque costumes and social customs surviving in remote areas of southern and central Italy, particularly Calabria and the Abruzzi, which he was among the first artists to visit. Despite all his efforts, Lear never overcame his deficiencies in drawing the human figure and he only very cautiously introduced people into his paintings, even employing Penry Williams to draw them into some of his Italian lithographs. However, many of Lear's own figure drawings do survive, including sketches in a letter of about 1841 to Lord Derby, showing how some Italian women carried their babies in cradles secured on their heads.[27] Lear described the everyday life of these unsophisticated people in the text of his Italian travel books with all the zeal of an ethnographer. He was by no means the first artist to show more interest in Italian contemporary life than in ancient architecture and sculpture, but he studied the subject from the evidence of his own eyes and conveyed his findings in spontaneous anecdotes and lively conversations.[28] Similarly Hector Berlioz and other composers had collected popular music and folk songs in the villages east of Rome before Lear, but Lear was among the first to integrate them into illustrated travel books for the general public and he soon had imitators, most notably J.M. Jephson in Brittany.[29] When later Lear travelled to even more primitive regions in the Eastern Mediterranean, his enthusiasm for strange and ancient habits and dress, first kindled in Italy, was all the greater.

Lear had greatly enjoyed his sketching tour in the Lake District in 1836, despite the wretched weather, but Italy was a different world. It was his experiences there which made him the dedicated traveller of later years and he looked back on his journey to Italy in 1837, and on his early Italian years, as the happiest in his life. In Corfu in 1862 he wrote:

Detail from Lear's 'The Acropolis of Athens', see page 177. (Museum of Athens, Athens).

'There is everywhere a flood of gold & green & blue. This, & the breeze blowing freshly now and then, remind me of days before … … . On Swiss & Como hills in 1837, in the first years of Rome & Amalfi life, 1838, 1839 – the long Civitella sojourns – 1839-40 … … I do not suppose that kind of happiness can ever come back but by unexpected & unsought snatches'.[30]

Lear left Italy in 1848, to avoid revolution and civil war. In 1858, rather at a loose end, he returned to Rome but the spell was broken and he hated it. Rents were much higher, the visitors coming to the public days at his studio to inspect and buy his watercolours were 'queer and rude and vulgar', the cafés were filthy, the weather was terrible, the artists were narrow minded, the social life was insufferable, Rome was a prison, his servant hated it too. Only out in the Campagna was Lear happy.[31]

[1]Strachey 1907: 18. [2]Strachey 1907: 13-14. [3]Frith 1889: 30. [4]Webley undated: 17-38. [5]Letter to Ann Lear, 29th October 1838 (Bowen unpublished, typescript 33); Strachey 1907: 311; one of these three paintings was in the Earl of Derby Sale, Christie's, London, 27th May, 1909, lot 34. [6]Letter to Derby, 5th June 1839 (LVRO 1/106/3). [7]Strachey 1907: 17-18. [8]Noakes 1988: 224. [9]Noakes 1988: 109-114. [10]Poussin's painting is now in The Walker, Liverpool. [11]Noakes 1988: 15; Lear 1907: xix-xx. [12]Oppé 1934, 2: 133; Noakes 1968: 79; see also Proby 1938. [13]Trevelyan 1876, 1: 466. [14]Letter to Ann Lear, 29th November 1838 (Bowen unpublished, typescript 34). [15]Lister 1974, 1: 265. [16]Lister 1981: 49; Webley undated: 75. [17]Foot 1968, 2: 547. [18]Murray 1843: 459. [19]Gaja 1995: 96. [20]Noakes 1988: 33; Palmer 1974, 1: 258; Collins 1848, 2: 91. [21]Noakes 1988: 48. [22]Letter to Ann Lear, 11th May 1838 (Bowen unpublished, typescript 19). [23]Collins 1848, 1: 260-1. [24]Wayne 1954: 226; Angeli 1911: 49. [25]Hazlitt 1873: 321-333. [26]Letter to Ann Lear, 10th June 1838 (Bowen unpublished, typescript 24). [27]Undated letter to Derby (LVRO 1/106/9). [28]See Wells unpublished (56 ff) and Graham 1820. [29]Jephson 1859. [30]Lear's Diary, 10th May 1862, quoted in Noakes 1985: 141. [31]Lear's diary, December 1858-May 1859 (Mss Houghton Library, Harvard University). See Noakes 1968: 165-70.

Landscapes by Edward Lear

EDWARD MORRIS

There is no firm indication of provenance of the Knowsley collection of Edward Lear watercolours, as Lear supplied watercolours and drawings to the 13th, 14th and 15th Earls of Derby. However, all the watercolours illustrated here have early dates, so were probably gifts to the 13th Earl of Derby by Lear.

85. A VIEW OVER THE PARK

Lear probably first visited Knowsley in 1831 and this rather summary watercolour may record his first impressions. It must also be one of the first landscapes he ever attempted. Lear spent most of the years between 1831 and 1837 at Knowsley making illustrations of the animals in Lord Derby's living collections and museum, and it was during this period, with the encouragement of Lord Derby, that he decided to become a landscape painter.

A view over the park, Knowsley. Watercolour, inscribed: 'Oct. 31. 1831 Knowsley'. 76 x 127mm.

Opposite Detail of *Sunset at Knowsley* (see overleaf).

Study of trees at Knowsley. Pencil and gouache, inscribed: 'Knowsley. 11. July. 1836'. 349 x 514mm.

Lear's delight in the twisted forms and varied surfaces of these oak trees anticipates his later artistic treatment of the olive groves of Italy. In the background at the left can be glimpsed the façade of Knowsley Hall. Another similar pencil drawing of twisted oak trees at Knowsley dated 1839 is in a private collection.[1]

[1]See Harrison 1995: 10, No.4. There is a photograph in the Witt Library (London).

Lear toured Ireland and the Lake District sketching landscapes in 1835 and 1836, gaining some relief from the painstaking precision and minute detail required for his zoological illustrations. His new freer and more imaginative style is clearly visible here, although the Knowsley landscape must have seemed rather featureless after the Lake District. A more detailed view of the same gently undulating area (with what is probably Parbold Hill in the background), dated 4th July 1835, was sold at Sotheby's London in 1991 (14th November, lot 155).

Sunset at Knowsley.
Watercolour, inscribed:
'Knowsley. Oct 30. 1836'.
114 x 179mm.

88a. *Knowsley Hall.* Pencil and gouache, inscribed: 'Knowsley. Sept. 1. 1835'. 216 x 362mm.

88b. *Knowsley Hall.* Pencil, inscribed: 'Knowsley. Sept. 5. 1835' [or 1833?]. 254 x 349mm.

The east front, built in this form by the 10th Earl in the early eighteenth century, appears in the upper drawing. The lower shows the west front, dating from the same period, with (at the right) the oldest part of the Hall, partly rebuilt by John Foster around 1820. These two drawings reflect the carefully balanced, well detailed and sharply drawn picturesque style usual in country house views in this period but very rarely employed by Lear. They may have been intended as gifts for Lord Derby (or his family) or as preliminary drawings for lithographs. There is at Knowsley a third very similar drawing by Lear of the south front from which, with some variations, he did make a lithograph.[1] Three more distant and more sketchy views of Knowsley Hall by Lear, dating from 1834, are now at the Yale Center for British Art, New Haven.[2]

[1]Reproduced in Falchi & Wadsworth 1997: 286. [2]Inv. Nos. B. 1997.7.15–17; see Wilcox. 2000: 49.

Lear arrived in Italy in 1837. For most of the following 11 years he was based in Rome but travelled extensively over central and south Italy, making innumerable drawings and sketches as he went. These four drawings and watercolours, together with the next eleven, were apparently made in late May and June 1843 on sketching tours north of Rome. Here Lear was gathering material for the second volume of his *Illustrated excursions in Italy* of 1846, which he dedicated to Lord Derby's son. Mount Soratte (or Soracte) can be seen from Rome, which is some twenty miles to the south. It was described by Horace: 'Seest thou how Soracte stands glistening in its mantle of snow'[1] and by Byron:

> '… All, save the lone Soracte's heights display'd / Not now in snow, which asks the lyric Roman's aid / For our remembrance, and from out the plain / Heaves like a long-swept wave about to break / And on the curl hangs pausing …'[2]

Mount Soratte could be climbed from Civitella Castellana and the path to the summit went through the village of Sant'Oreste on its south-eastern slopes. Murray, in his 1843 *Handbook,* commented: 'A great part of the mountain is beautifully wooded and numerous fine landscapes will afford agreeable occupation to the artist'.[3]

The watercolour is a 'finished' work of a type that Lear would have sold to his patrons.[4] It would have been painted in his studio, using as a guide the more sketchy and linear drawings which Lear had made on the spot in front of the view in question. These rough drawings themselves were often further elaborated in his studio with the addition of ink, watercolour and more detail, all derived from the colour and topographical notes Lear wrote on the original drawings.

89a. *Mount Soratte.* Watercolour, signed: 'EL.', inscribed: 'Soracte'. 104 x 201mm.

[1]Horace (Quintus Horatius Flaccus, 65-8 BC), *Odes,* Book 1, ode 9: 2. [2]Byron: 4. 74-75. [3]Murray 1843: 245 & 1850: 284. [4]A small oil version of the watercolour, with a different foreground and left-hand side, was with Agnew's in 1988.

89b. *Mount Soratte.* Pencil, inscribed: 'Soracte. 25 May 1843'. 157 x 255mm.

89c. *Mount Soratte.* Pencil, inscribed: 'S.Oreste 25 May 1843'. 163 x 255mm.

89d. *Mount Soratte.* Pencil, inscribed: Soracte, 25 May 1843. 164 x 255mm.

90. MADONNA DEL SORBO

90a. *Madonna del Sorbo.* Pencil and watercolour, inscribed: 'Madonna del Sorbo. June 3. 1843'. 241 x 361mm.

90b. *Madonna del Sorbo.* Pencil, inscribed: 'Madonna del Sorbo. 3.June.1843'. and with colour and topographical notes. 244 x 359mm.

The view of this convent in Lear's *Illustrated excursions in Italy* was taken from the side not shown in these drawings. In the book Lear described the convent as 'one of the most lonely and picturesque within a ride of the capital'.[1] It is about 15 miles south-west from Mount Soratte. There is a Lear watercolour, dated 3rd June 1843, in the Northbrook Albums in the Liverpool City Libraries (vol. 4: 40), which is very similar to these drawings. Lear made another painting of this subject for the Hon. Mrs. Greville-Howard in 1845.[2]

[1]Lear 1846, ii: 37, plate 21. [2]Strachey 1907: 312.

191

91a. *Orvieto.* Pencil and watercolour, inscribed: 'Orvieto. June. 10 1843' and 'an acqueduct of yellow stone'. 367 x 210mm.

91b. *Orvieto.* Pencil, pen, ink and watercolour, inscribed: 'June. 12. 1843 Orvieto'. 335 x 231mm.

Murray's *Handbooks* of 1843 and 1850 describe the scene in Lear's first watercolour thus:

> '*The first view of Orvieto is one of the finest scenes imaginable; the plain of the Paglia is surrounded by hills of picturesque and broken outline and from the midst of the plain rises the immense rock on which the city is built, completely isolated … as we descend the hill into the fertile plain of the Paglia which may be seen winding in the distance the fine forms of the mountain and the magnificent aspect of the city … presents a panorama of the most striking interest*'.[1]

Orvieto is about 60 miles north of Madonna del Sorbo. In the left foreground of this watercolour is the romanesque Abbey of Saints Severo and Martirio.[2] A larger version, with a different foreground but also dated 1843, was sold at Christie's, London in 1980 (18th November, lot 198). There are two Lear drawings, and one watercolour, of Orvieto (dated 10th and 12th June 1843) in the Houghton Library at Harvard University.

192

[1]Murray 1843: 155 & 1850: 165-9. [2]For the identification of this, and many other topographical details throughout this section we are deeply indebted to Mario Marcone and Ettore Pallante.

92. CAPRAROLA

92a. *Caprarola.* Watercolour and pencil, inscribed: 'Caprarola. 14. June.1843'. 107 x 186mm.

92b. *Caprarola.* Watercolour and pencil, 120 x 239mm.

Caprarola is about 40 miles south of Orvieto. On the left is the famous sixteenth century Palazzo Farnese, designed by Vignola. These two watercolours show Lear developing the composition of his lithograph of Caprarola for his *Illustrated Excursions*. He noted: 'Caprarola is now uninhabited though tolerably well kept in repair. During the last century (1714) the son of James II remained here for some time, as did his grandson in 1740'.[1] Lear made a painting of Caprarola for Thomas Bell in 1846.[2]

[1]Lear 1846, ii: 27, plate 15. [2]Strachey 1907: 312.

93a. *Corchiano.* Pencil, inscribed: 'Corchiano. 18.June.1843'. 162 x 255mm.

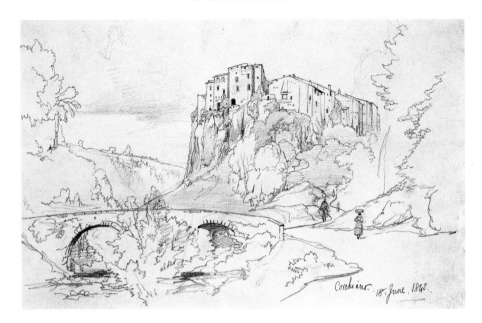

93b. *Corchiano.* Pencil, inscribed: 'Corchiano. 18.June.1843' and with colour notes. 166 x 256mm.

Lear must have used these two drawings for his lithograph of Corchiano in his *Illustrated excursions*, to which they are very similar. In this book Lear remarked on Corchiano: 'I know very little concerning this place, whose chief interest lies in its pictorial capabilities'.[1] He probably used the same two drawings as a basis for a watercolour sold at Sotheby Parke Bernet, New York in 1981 (19th March, lot 188). Murray commented: 'Near [Gallese] is the miserable village of Corchiano occupying the site of an Etruscan town the name of which is lost'.[2] In fact the name was probably Fescennium, which Murray wrongly attributed to Gallese. The river Fratte runs through Corchiano, which is about 10 miles east of Caprarola.

[1]Lear 1846, ii: 29, plate 16. [2]Murray 1850: 228.

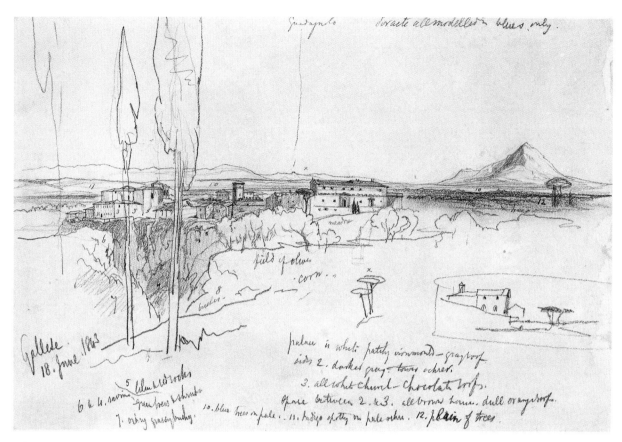

This drawing is very similar to the lithograph of Gallese in Lear's *Illustrated excursions*. He described the lithograph thus:

> '*The annexed drawing is taken from the garden of the Capuchin monastery above the town; the view over the Campagna, with Soracte on the right and the Sabine hills in the distance, is very beautiful.*'

As for Gallese itself it was 'a small and picturesque town beautifully situated on the edge of a ravine between the Tiber and Monte Cimino'.[1] Gallese is about 5 miles north east of Corchiano.

[1]Lear 1846, ii: 31, plate 17.

Gallese. Pencil, inscribed: 'Gallese 18. June.1843' and with numbered colour notes which refer to numbers on the drawing itself. 171 x 254mm.

95a. *Civita Castellana*.
Pencil and watercolour,
inscribed: 'Civita
Castellana 19. June.
1843' and with colour
and topographical notes.
250 x 492mm.

Civita Castellana is about 10 miles south of Gallese.

The first drawing includes at the right the Citadel, partly designed by Antonio da Sangallo the Elder in the early sixteenth century and notorious in Lear's day as the prison of many of the Pope's liberal opponents, some of whom were released during Pius IX's amnesty of 1846. The area was also famous for its Etruscan remains. Both drawings show the town's precipitous surroundings. Murray in 1843 wrote:

> 'The ravines, which almost insulate the town, and the fine scenes commanded by the higher ground extending over the Campagna and embracing the plain of the Tiber and Soracte will afford occupation for many successive days to the archaeologist and the travellers who carry sketchbooks'[1]

Civita Castellana had also fascinated Camille Corot, who made numerous sketches and paintings of it in 1826 and 1827, with viewpoints similar to those used by Lear.[2] Even earlier, in the 1780s, Pierre-Henri de Valenciennes, author of a very influential book on landscape and perspective, sketched there alongside other French artists.

An oil painting done by Lear for James J. Hornby, similar to the right hand side of the first drawing and dating from 1844, was sold at Christie's London in 1972 (28th January, lot 98) and more recently at Sotheby's, London in 1997 (9th July, lot 94). Hornby was the Vicar of Winwick and the father of Robert A. Hornby, who paid part of the cost of Lear's journey to Italy in 1837. The Hornby family were close friends and relations of the Stanley family. Another painting by Lear, broadly corresponding with the first drawing and of the same date and size as the Hornby painting, was sold by the executors of Sir Philip Shelbourne at Christie's London in 1994 (4th November, lot 93).

95b. *Civita Castellana*. Pen, ink and watercolour, inscribed: 'June 19. 1843. Civita Castellana' and with topographical notes. 240 x 302mm.

197

[1]Murray 1843: 243 & 1850: 280-3. [2]Galassi 1991: 179-195.

Magliano. Pencil, pen, ink, gouache and watercolour, inscribed: 'Magliano. August. 23. 1843'. 276 x 426mm.

In the late summer and autumn of 1843 Lear made a second tour of the Abruzzi with his friend Charles Knight, gathering material and drawings for the first volume of his *Illustrated excursions*, which he dedicated to Lord Derby. This and the following six watercolours were made on this tour. The Abruzzi, away from the towns, were then a very primitive, remote and mountainous part of Italy (although their western borders are only about 70 miles east of Rome) and Lear was one of the first artists to discover them.

Magliano dei Marsi is near the large town of Avezzano, about 80 miles east-north-east from Rome. Lear arrived in Magliano on 22nd August and stayed there for three days. He described it as 'a most neat and thriving little town, containing fifteen hundred inhabitants, placed on an isolated eminence below the towering Monte Velino, and commanding views over the whole of the Campi Valentini'.[1] A few years earlier than Lear, Keppel Craven also noted that it was 'remarkable for its flourishing appearance and the number of large and even elegant villas that surround it'.[2] This watercolour is nearly identical to the corresponding lithograph in Lear's *Illustrated excursions*, which has travelling peasants and mules added into the foreground.[3]

[1]Lear 1846, I: 69. [2]Craven 1838, I: 191. [3]Lear 1846, I: plate 16.

Lear described the scene thus:

'The Church of San Pelino (a building worth the attention of architects of which the only notice I can find relates to its restoration by a Bishop Giovanni in 1081) stands by the side of these ruins [of ancient Corfinium], and, together, they form a group whose grand and solitary character cannot fail to strike the traveller.'

This watercolour is very closely related to the lithograph of San Pelino in Lear's *Illustrated excursions* but the lithograph has two figures and a rather different foreground.[1] Lear composed another painting of San Pelino, also in 1843, for Lord Wenlock.[2]

[1]Lear 1846, I: 32, plate 11. [2]Strachey 1907: 312.

San Pelino. Pencil, pen, ink, gouache and watercolour, inscribed: 'San Pelino. Pentima, Septembr. 18. 1843'. 310 x 490mm.

Isola. Pencil, pen, ink and
brown wash, inscribed: 'Isola.
Septrbr. 30. 1843.' and with
colour and topographical
notes. 445 x 318mm.

Isola del Gran Sasso is about 35 miles north of San Pelino and is famous for its
views of the Gran Sasso mountains to the south-west. Lear commented: 'It is an
exceedingly pretty place and immediately above it rises the single pyramid of
Mount Corno, the Gran Sasso, a most noble background'. The lithograph of Isola
in Lear's *Illustrated excursions* seems to have been based on this drawing.[1] Keppel
Craven also praised the setting but noted that the village was dominated by small
factories.[2] Lear composed another painting, *Isola di Monte Corno, Abruzzi,* for a Miss
Westcomb in 1843.[3]

[1]Lear 1846, I: 108-9, plate 28. [2]Craven 1838, I: 92-5. [3]Strachey 1907: 312.

Aquila is the principal city of the Abruzzi and of exceptional historical interest. With this in mind, Lear described his first sight of the city thus: 'Even now, the castle overlooking all, the Cupola of San Bernardino with various Campanili and Palazzi of a delicate coloured stone throw an air of magnificence over the first approach'.[1] Keppel Craven noted that Aquila had seventy churches and monasteries, 'which, as may be imagined, are far beyond what may be required by so limited, however devout, a population'.[2] Lear has here drawn the city from Mount Luco to the west, with the valley of the river Aterno between him and Aquila. Aquila is about 18 miles south-west from Isola.

Aquila. Pencil, pen, ink, watercolour and gouache, inscribed: 'Aquila. October. 4. 1843' and with colour and topographical notes. 277 x 432mm.

[1]Lear 1846, I: 40. [2]Craven 1838, ii: 205.

Tufo. Pen, ink, watercolour and gouache, inscribed: 'Tufo. 12. October. 1843'. 432 x 322mm.

Tufo Alto and Tufo Basso are on the way from Aquila to Rome, about 25 miles south-west from Aquila. Before the unification of Italy they were near the frontier between the Kingdom of Naples and the Papal States. Lear stayed with his friend Baron Coletti, a landowner with a house there, from 11th to 16th October 1843. He spent the time 'rather idly' and 'in the fine mornings sketched the town from the chestnut-feathered hill opposite the house'. Tufo, he said, was 'a clean little town in the valley'.[1] This view was taken from the road to Pietrasecca.

[1]Lear 1846, I: 118-9.

The first watercolour shows the medieval castle of Passerano from the south, with behind it the Tiburtini, Lucrétili and Cornicolani mountains looking from right to left. The second watercolour shows the same castle from the north. Passerano is about 15 miles east of Rome, near Gallicano. A watercolour in the Northbrook Albums in the Liverpool City Libraries (vol.1: 4) and a drawing in the Houghton Library at Harvard University, dated 20th October 1843,[1] show views similar to those in the exhibited watercolours.

[1]Reproduced in Hofer 1967: pl. 18.

101a. *Passerano*. Pen, ink, watercolour and gouache, inscribed: 'Passerano. 20. October. 1843' and with colour and topographical notes. 174 x 392mm.

101b. *Passerano*. Pencil, watercolour and gouache, inscribed: 'Passerano. 20. October. 1843.' and with colour and topographical notes. 198 x 398mm.

203

Villa Cesi. Pen, ink and watercolour, inscribed: 'Villa Coesia, November. 27. 1843'. 151 x 341mm.

This, and the following four watercolours, were probably made by Lear during day excursions from Rome during the winter of 1843-1844. The Villa Cesi is on the Via Palombarese near Montécelio. In the distance on the left stands Monte Gennaro, which can easily be seen from Rome, about 15 miles to the south-west.

This is the Casale della Cervelletta (or Cervaretto), about six miles east of Rome on the River Aniene (or Anio) and the Via Collatina. The Ponte Mammolo is the ancient bridge (many times rebuilt) at which the Via Tiburtina crosses the river on the way to Tivoli. This area is now dominated by factories.

Cervaretto. Pen, ink and watercolour, inscribed: 'Cervaretto. From Ponte Mammolo. 28. November. 1843'. 160 x 340mm.

Via di Porta Nomentana.
Watercolour, inscribed: 'Via
di Porta Nomentana.
Decembr. 23. 1843'.
238 x 405mm.

The Via di Porta Nomentana was a Roman road running north-east from the Porta
Pia (or Nomentana). During the Roman Empire it was flanked by palaces, villas
and gardens. Lear has painted here the so-called Sedia del Diavolo, one of the many
ancient tombs along the road, which is now surrounded by the Nomentana suburb
of Rome. The tomb was painted several times by Richard Wilson in the late
eighteenth century. The contrast between its ancient grandeur and its desolate
condition and setting in the eighteenth and early nineteenth centuries suggested a
general sense of melancholy at the decay of Roman greatness.

As late as 1881 Lear painted a watercolour of this scene for sale; it was sold at
Christie's, London in 1988 (25th November, lot 106). He made at least two
paintings entitled *Via Nomentana*, one for S.W. Clowes in 1854, but they may have
had quite different compositions.[1] He generally avoided painting well-known
antiquities and ancient buildings in favour of more contemporary scenes or pure
landscape.

[1]Strachey 1907: 314, 318.

This is the medieval Torre di San Eusebio, situated on the river Aniene about nine miles east of Rome. There are two further Lear drawings of this subject, both dated 13th February 1845, in the Houghton Library at Harvard University.

105a. *Torre*. Pencil, pen, ink and watercolour, inscribed: 'Torre January 9. 1844'. 189 x 289mm.

105b. *Torre*. Pencil, pen, ink and watercolour, inscribed: 'Torre. 9. January. 1844'. 149 x 307mm.

106a. *Civitella*. Pencil, pen, ink, watercolour and gouache, inscribed: 'Civitella 20 August. 1844' and with topographical and colour notes. 327 x 312mm.

Civitella di Subiaco and the neighbouring village of Olevano were probably Lear's favourite haunts in the hills near Rome. Olevano was also particularly favoured by the many German landscape artists in early nineteenth century Rome.[1] The composer Hector Berlioz visited Civitella in 1832 in search of folk music and found it 'a wretched foul-smelling place', but he liked the inn and noted: 'The extraordinary formation of the rocks, piled fantastically on one another, has a particular attraction for artists; a painter friend of mine stayed there for six months'.[2] Lear's two watercolours do indeed concentrate on the rock formations, the first in close up and the second as a distant view of the village.

Civitella, now a part of Bellegra, is situated high in the Sabine Mountains, about 35 miles east of Rome. Lear and James Uwins, nephew of the artist Thomas Uwins, visited the village in May 1838 on their way to Naples, and Lear returned to Olevano with Penry Williams in October of the same year. Williams was a painter of scenes from everyday life; he had lived in Italy for some years before Lear's arrival in 1837 and had originally recommended Civitella to Lear. In July 1839 the artist Samuel Palmer and his wife Hannah met Lear there during their Italian honeymoon. They admired his flute playing at an artists' ball in the village.[3] A watercolour of 1839 by Samuel Palmer in the Whitworth Art Gallery, Manchester, shows a distant view of Civitella, like the second of these two watercolours by Lear, but it was drawn from a different angle.

Earlier in the same year George Richmond, who was (like Palmer) a follower of William Blake seeking artistic and spiritual inspiration in Italy, came to Olevano after meeting Lear in Rome.[4] Lear was back in the village in October 1840 and, with a friend, in August 1844; at 800 metres above sea level he was safe from malaria even during the hottest months of the summer.

In later life Lear looked back with nostalgia on 'the long Civitella sojourns' and on the 'Civitella days of old when one sate [sic] from noon to 3 in August and July listening to the songs coming up from the great silent depths below the rock'.[5] One of Lear's first oil paintings was a view of Civitella of 1840 painted for the 13th Earl of Derby. In 1843 Lear painted the subject again for James J. Hornby, Vicar of Winwick and brother-in-law of Lord Derby and then yet again on a large scale in 1847 (see illustration on page 176). In 1853 Lear painted *Civitella di Subiaco, looking south* for his very close friend Chichester Fortescue, and two years later William Nevill bought *Civitella di Subiaco, Sunrise* (now in Worcester Art Museum, Massachusetts) complete with a quotation from Tennyson, Lear's favourite poet.[6] There are many drawings and watercolours by Lear of Civitella in the Houghton Library at Harvard University, but none date from his 1844 visit. There is a Lear watercolour of Civitella in the British Museum,[7] dated 20th August 1844, but with a quite different composition from those in the exhibited watercolours. Lear considered using a distant view of Civitella for his proposed set of illustrations to Tennyson's poems, which eventually were neither printed nor published.[8] This view was itself based on an early lithograph of 1841.[9]

106b. *Civitella*. Pencil, pen, ink, watercolour and gouache, inscribed: 'Civitella. 21. August. 1844'. 144 x 290mm.

[1]Riccardi 1997: 12-81. [2]Cairns 1970: 213. [3]Lister 1974, I: 356. [4]Lister 1981: 49. [5]Noakes 1985: 140-141. [6]Strachey 1907: 311-314. [7]No. 1929-6-11-66. [8]Pitman 1988: 97-101. [9]Lear 1841: Plate 5.

THE 13TH EARL AS AN ART-COLLECTOR

XANTHE BROOKE

The 13th Earl's purchases were made primarily from two auctions of major private collections. In 1816, when he was still Lord Stanley, he bought over 50 art works (mainly sixteenth and seventeenth-century drawings) from the large collection of William Roscoe, the Liverpool attorney, banker and sometime Whig M.P. Stanley shared with Roscoe a scholarly and practical interest in botany. His purchases may have been a form of financial (and moral) support to the bankrupt Roscoe, a close political ally of the 12th Earl. Whatever Edward Stanley's reasons for buying from Roscoe's sale, he certainly bought judiciously. Along with highly finished drawings such as that by Jan Brueghel the Elder, he bought several drawings attributed to Titian, his followers and Rembrandt.

The second sale to attract the 13th Earl's attention was the vast collection of Horace Walpole (1717-1797) in 1842. It was from this sale that the Earl acquired masterpieces of the art of portrait miniature by Nicholas Hilliard and Isaac and Peter Oliver. He also bought from that sale a select group of early sixteenth-century portraits by artists from the Netherlands. Lord Derby obviously shared with Walpole, but on a much smaller scale, an interest in historical portraits and self-portraits.

Those few works not bought from these auctions were either acquired through family connections or, like the Van Laer painting and Anne Damer's sculpture of dogs, probably attracted the Earl for their affectionate and amusing portrayal of animals. The 13th Earl was probably also the purchaser of some of the very fine items of furniture still at Knowsley, such as the two cabinets on pages 232 and 233.

Opposite A selection from the 13th Earl of Derby's collection of miniatures, from left to right.

Top row Self-portrait by **Isaac Oliver**.

Queen Henrietta Maria, probably by **David des Granges.**

Portrait of Peter Oliver's wife, Anne by **Peter Oliver.**

Middle row A Lady Called Frances Howard, Countess of Essex and Somerset by **Isaac Oliver**.

Portrait of Sir Robert Walpole by **Christian Friedrich Zincke.**

Portrait of Robert Devereux, 2nd Earl of Essex by **Isaac Oliver.**

Bottom row Self-Portrait of **Peter Oliver.**

Portrait of an unknown lady by **Nicholas Hilliard**.

Portrait of Drake aged 42, by **Nicholas Hilliard**

Watercolour on vellum, pasted onto the back of a piece cut from a playing card. Portrait of Drake aged 42, painted by Nicholas Hilliard in 1581. Inscribed in Latin: *Ætatis Suæ* 42, *Año Dñi*: 1581. 28mm (NPG. Inv. 4851. By courtesy of the National Portrait Gallery, London).

Lord Derby bought most of his miniatures in 1842, at the sale of the contents of Horace Walpole's home, Strawberry Hill.[1] Walpole's collection of art, antiquities and memorabilia was exceptional. He was fascinated by portraits and personal effects of famous British people and Lord Derby - with his select collection of miniatures, his album of autographed letters and portraits, and such items as a lock of Mary Tudor's hair - appears to have had the same interests. Some of the miniatures have since been sold,[2] and the first seven included here are now in public collections.

107a. SIR FRANCIS DRAKE

This miniature was painted about the time that Drake, having returned from his voyage around the world laden with booty plundered from Spanish colonies in the Americas, was knighted by Queen Elizabeth I. Nicholas Hilliard (1547-1619), who like Drake came from Devon, must have thought the idea of portraying Drake - one of England's heroes and a favourite of the Queen - so soon after his triumphant return would be an attractive and potentially lucrative proposition. Hilliard has captured in this portrait the ruddy face and cheerful character described by both Drake's friends and enemies.

Hillard began painting portraits in lockets at the age of 13 and obtained patronage at the French court in the 1570s. However, his finest work was achieved in the 1580s and in 1584 he was given the monopoly of painting Queen Elizabeth's portraits. He was the first English artist to achieve international distinction as a portraitist and, even after the death of Elizabeth I and the accession of James I, he retained his connections at court.

XB

107b. PORTRAIT OF A LADY

Bodycolour on vellum, laid onto card. Portrait of an unknown lady by Nicholas Hilliard, painted between 1605 and 1610. 51 x 43mm

(YCBA. B 1974.2.51. Yale Center for British Art, Paul Mellon Collection, USA. Photograph: Bridgeman Art Library).

While this miniature was in Horace Walpole's possession, not only was it incorrectly attributed to Isaac Oliver, but the woman portrayed was identified as Princess Elizabeth (1596-1661), daughter of James I and later Queen of Bohemia. In fact, the sitter does not closely resemble the subject of contemporary portraits by Hilliard and Oliver that are known to depict the Princess as a child.[3] With her reddish wavy locks and high forehead, she looks far more similar to another woman painted by Hilliard between 1605 and 1610.[4] This is thought to have been Lady Elizabeth Stanley, third daughter of Ferdinando, 5th Earl of Derby. The 13th Earl would not have been aware of this possibility when he purchased the miniature.

XB

Watercolour on vellum, laid onto card. Self-portrait by Isaac Oliver, painted about 1590. Previous to Walpole's possession was in the collection of Thomas Barrett of Lee Priory, Kent. 64 x 51mm (NPG. Inv. 4852. By courtesy of the National Portrait Gallery, London).

This self-portrait, showing the artist as a fashionable young man, was evidently executed early in Oliver's career[5] – yet already displays the consummate skill in capturing an almost three-dimensional likeness for which he later became renowned. Oliver was Horace Walpole's favourite miniaturist; he wrote that 'This picture alone would justify all I have said of him. The art of the master and the imitation of nature are so great in it that the largest magnifying glass only calls out new beauties'.[6]

Isaac Oliver (1558/68-1617), a French Huguenot refugee whose family fled France in about 1568, was trained as a miniaturist by Nicholas Hilliard but later exceeded his master in technique and became a rival. Oliver gained the patronage of the 2nd Earl of Essex[7] in 1596, which marked his rising reputation. His work was much admired at the Court of James I, particularly by the Queen, Anne of Denmark, who appointed him to her household in 1605. This appointment enhanced Oliver's fortunes at the Jacobean court and he went on to become limner (miniature painter) to Henry, Prince of Wales. In 1606 Oliver was naturalized as a British citizen.

XB

107d. A LADY CALLED FRANCES HOWARD, COUNTESS OF ESSEX AND SOMERSET

Watercolour and bodycolour on vellum, laid on card. Signed 'I O' [Isaac Oliver]. Portrait of a lady, datable to about 1595–1600. Diameter 130mm (V & A. P12-1971. V & A Picture Library).

This impressive miniature, in its splendid contemporary gilt wood frame, carved with scrolls, flower heads, foliage swags and trailing sprays, is one of the finest works produced by Isaac Oliver. It shows all of Oliver's virtuosity in handling the watercolour pigment to describe the ornate encrusted jewels around the woman's neck and on her clothes, and to capture the filmy wired gauze which floats around her head.

Horace Walpole, who purchased this miniature from the collection of James West (c.1704–1772) in February 1773, believed that it portrayed the notorious Frances Howard (daughter of Thomas Howard, 1st Earl of Suffolk). In 1613 she procured the annulment of her first arranged marriage to the 3rd Earl of Essex, in order to marry her lover Robert Carr, Earl of Somerset. With her second husband, she was temporarily imprisoned for the poisoning of Sir Thomas Overbury (a friend of Essex), who had attempted to prevent the second marriage. Whether or not the lady in this miniature is in fact Frances Howard (who in 1600 would have been ten years old), the ownership of a portrait of such a scheming historical figure would have appealed to Walpole, always a great fan of waspish gossip and salacious anecdote.

XB

Bodycolour and grey ink on vellum, laid on card, by Isaac Oliver, datable to about 1600. 51 x 42mm (YCBA. B. 1975.2.75. Yale Center for British Art, Paul Mellon Collection, USA. Photograph: Bridgeman Art Library).

This is an unfinished portrait of one of Queen Elizabeth I's 'favourites', Robert Devereux (1566-1601) who charmed his way to prominence and popularity in the late 1580s while still in his twenties. Essex's greatest feat was to lead the military campaign which defeated the Spanish fleet and briefly captured the Spanish town of Cadiz in 1596. However, he was less successful as governor-general of Ireland in 1599 where, having failed to defeat the Earl of Tyrone's rebel army, he made a temporary truce. He was dismissed from office for making a 'dishonourable treaty' and for having returned to London without royal approval. Essex then compounded his impetuous misbehaviour by conspiring to overthrow the Queen's councillors, whom he believed were intriguing against him. As a result he was tried for treason and executed in February 1601.

Oliver's portraits of the tall handsome Essex, whose patronage marked the artist's rising reputation as a miniaturist, were extremely popular, judging from the number of examples that have survived. These were either replicas by his own hand, or studio versions and later copies.[8] The fact that Essex's beard is painted directly over the sketch, onto unprepared vellum, suggests that Oliver never meant to finish this particular miniature. Instead it was probably kept in his studio as a study from life, providing the pattern from which all other finished versions derive.

In the first half of the eighteenth century this miniature is supposed to have belonged to Frances, Lady Worseley (c.1673 - 1750) who was one of Essex's descendants.

XB

Graphite pencil and wash on card, by Peter Oliver. Signed in Latin: 'PO se ipse [fe.]' [made by himself]; and on reverse, in English: 'P. Oliver/his Wife'. Datable to about 1625-30. 86 x 67mm (NPG. Inv. 4853. By courtesy of the National Portrait Gallery, London).

According to Horace Walpole, who once owned this pair of portraits, they were drawn on a sheet from the artist's pocketbook. Certainly their size makes it very unlikely that they were ever intended to be worn in a locket or other piece of jewellery, as were many portraits 'in little'. Comparison with other portraits of Peter Oliver suggest that this self-portrait was drawn nearer the middle than the late 1620s.[9]

During the seventeenth-century England had the most continuously active and successful group of portrait miniature painters in Europe. Peter Oliver (c.1594-1647) was the son of Isaac Oliver by his first wife, Elizabeth. Peter Oliver started work, as his father's assistant, between 1610-1617 and very much in his father's style. On his father's death in 1617, he inherited his drawings and unfinished miniatures and soon developed a busy practice at court and in royal circles, painting several portraits of Charles, at that time Prince of Wales. By 1625 Peter Oliver was a member of the household of Charles I, by whom he was commissioned to make miniature copies of Old Master paintings in the King's collection. In 1636 the King granted Peter a substantial annual pension of £200.

Being childless on his death, Peter bequeathed everything to his wife, Anne (1593-1672). Anne, who is shown looking out at the viewer from the reverse of her husband's portrait, was a doughty lady as is perhaps suggested by her tight-lipped and firm gaze. She lived on into her seventies, well into the reign of Charles II, to whom she gave a number of her husband's miniatures in exchange for an increased annual pension of £300. However, when she discovered that the King had given them to his mistresses, she declared that he would never have been given them if she had known they were going to 'such whores, bastards or strumpets'. According to George Vertue (who owned this miniature before Walpole) her pension was immediately withdrawn.[10]

XB

Bodycolour on vellum laid onto gesso-backed card, probably by David des Granges, dated to after 1636. 81 x 69mm (YCBA. B. 1974.2.62. Yale Center for British Art, Paul Mellon Collection, USA. Photograph: Bridgeman Art Library).

Henrietta Maria (1609-1669), the youngest daughter of Henri IV of France, married Charles I in 1625 and bore him nine children between 1629 and 1644. When the Civil War broke out she supported her husband, joining him at the battle of Edgehill in 1643 but fleeing to France in 1644, where she remained in exile until her son Charles II regained the throne in 1660.

This miniature is one of numerous examples that used larger portraits by Van Dyck as their models. It derives from a three-quarter-length portrait that Van Dyck painted for Cardinal Francesco Barberini in 1636,[11] but with a landscape view of Windsor Castle added in the background. The miniature was probably painted in the 1640s by one of the followers of John Hoskins (c.1590-1660), to whom it was attributed when in the 13th Earl of Derby's collection. Horace Walpole, who had previously owned the miniature, attributed it to a Hoskins' follower called Nicholas Dixon (fl.1660-1708). The opinion of modern art historians is, however, that the most likely artist is David des Granges (1611-1671/2).

Des Granges was an Anglo-French painter and engraver, whose earliest dated miniature was painted in 1639. In 1651 he was appointed official painter to Charles II in Scotland and is noted for his many miniature copies of work by both John Hoskins and Van Dyck. In 1671, disabled and unable to support his family, he had to plead for the payment owed for thirteen of his Civil War miniatures and is believed to have died shortly afterwards.

XB

107h. PORTRAIT OF SIR ROBERT WALPOLE

Oval enamel with gold frame, by Christian Friedrich Zincke. 38 x 45mm (K).

By the time he made this enamel in 1744, Zincke (c.1683-1767) was the leading miniaturist in England. He had emigrated from Germany in 1706 and came under the wing of Sir Godfrey Kneller. In 1732 Zincke was appointed Cabinet Painter to Frederick, Prince of Wales. About this time, according to George Vertue, he 'had more persons of distinction sitting to him than any person living'.[12]

Zincke's association with the Prince of Wales (a focus of opposition to government in the reign of George II) may perhaps explain why Sir Robert Walpole, First Lord of the Treasury for twenty-one years until 1742 and figurehead of the early Georgian Whig party, did not pose for him until 1744 when he was effectively retired from politics (he died the following year). Sir Robert had a reputation as the most voracious, if not necessarily the most refined, collector of Old Master paintings in England. These paintings were the basis of his re-decoration of the Walpole family seat, Houghton in Norfolk, in the 1720s and 1730s and also of the artistic education of his son, Horace. Horace Walpole described this miniature, which shows Sir Robert in the Robes of the Garter, as 'very like' his father. The 13th Earl of Derby bought it from the sale of Horace Walpole's effects at Strawberry Hill.[13]

AK

[1]This sale took place long after Walpole's death in 1797. [2] The first seven of those included here were sold at Christies' on 8th June 1971. [3] Victoria & Albert Museum P.4-1937; Royal Collection. [4]Viscount Bearsted collection at Upton House; see Reynolds 1971, no.96. [5]Another self-portrait by Isaac Oliver, also datable to about 1590, is in the Royal Collection. In this, Oliver wears a tall black hat and has a beard as well as a moustache. [6]Dallaway & Wornum (eds) 1849 vol.1: 178. [7]See miniature on page 216. [8]Strong 1969: 116-117. [9]Millar 1963: Cat. 214, pl.93. [10] Ilchester & Hake 1930: 66. [11]Private collection, New York. [12]Turner 1996, 3: 685. [13]Purchased in 1842 for £27.6s.0d.

Painted on wood panel, with a
wax seal on the back showing
a cross above a fleur-de-lys.
Brussels School c.1490-1500.
292 x 210mm (K).

The young man looks up from his book, which is probably meant to be a prayer
book, marking his place with his fingers and gazing as if at somebody to his right.
This suggests that the panel might be the right wing of a small altarpiece – a
diptych or even a triptych. His clothes, a fur-lined tunic and cap, are of the fashion
of about 1490. In style the portrait is similar to another of a young man,[1] by the
anonymous painter of the View of St Gudule, who worked in the court city of
Brussels between 1470-1490. He was a follower of Rogier van der Weyden
(c.1399-1464), who was one of the most renowned artists of the fifteenth century.
It has also been suggested that there are similarities with the work by the circle of
Colyn de Coter, who worked in Brussels between 1480-1525.[2] Coter borrowed
many compositions and figure types from Rogier van der Weyden and his own art
influenced virtually all painting in Brussels during this period. After van der
Weyden died, his sons and grandsons continued his Brussels workshop practice into
the early sixteenth century.

When the 13th Earl of Derby bought this painting it was attributed to Quentin
Massys (1466-1530) who settled in Antwerp in 1490 and for a time worked with
van der Weyden.[3]

Lord Derby purchased the portrait at the 1842 sale of Horace Walpole's
collections. Walpole had inherited it from his father, Sir Robert Walpole (1676-
1745), who during his long period in political office acquired a large and
important art collection.[4]

XB

[1]National Gallery, London (2612). [2]Suggestion made by Lorne Campbell of the National Gallery in
London; letter 2 October 1998. [3]Scharf 1875, cat. no.349: 180. [4]See miniature on page 219.

109. PORTRAIT OF A FRENCH COURTIER

Oil on wood panel, painted about 1536-1540 by Corneille de la Haye, called Corneille de Lyon. 165 x 146mm (K).

This portrait, a figure with an ostrich plume decorating his cap and silhouetted against a lime-green background, is typical of the work of Dutch artist Corneille (early 1500s – c.1574), who made his living as a portrait painter in France. The young man is unidentified but around his neck he seems to wear the insignia of the French royal Order of St. Michael (although it does not hang from the usual collar of cockle-shells). The Order was founded in 1469 and held by the French King and thirty-six of his knights. Two other portraits of the same sitter, also from Corneille's workshop, show him when slightly older, wearing the same clothes as in the Knowsley picture but sporting a thin scrubby beard.[1] He may possibly have been one of the sons of Gaston de Foix III, the Comte de Candale.

Corneille worked in Lyons from 1533, becoming a naturalized French citizen in 1547. It was not unusual for artists from the Netherlands to seek employment in Lyons, which was a wealthy textile town whose market fairs had long established links with the Low Countries. In 1533 Corneille began working as painter to Queen Eleanora of Austria, the French King Francis I's second wife, producing portraits of the royal children and courtiers. After 1536 the French court spent much time in Lyons, anticipating Emperor Charles V's attack on France from across the Italian Alps. According to surviving descriptions of court-life, Corneille once exhibited many of his small portraits of the royal family, and the ladies and gentlemen of the court, in a large room in Lyons. These were presumably either intended for sale, or to encourage visitors to order replicas.[2]

XB

[1]Paris, Musée des Arts Decoratifs inv. 40.216; Musée Jacquemart Andre inv. 411. [2]Campbell 1998: 756.

Pen and wash in blue and
brown inks on paper, drawn
in about 1600 by Jan
Brueghel the Elder. Formerly
in the collection of the 13th
Earl of Derby. 288 x 410mm
(The Walker, Inv. 6352.).

The subject is taken from the passage in the Bible[1] describing the successful
crossing of the Red Sea by Moses and the Israelites, and the dramatic drowning of
the pursuing troops of the Egyptian Pharoah. The troops are presumably drowning
somewhere off the page to the right, which is why many figures in the crowd can
be seen looking and gesticulating in that direction. In the left foreground the
turbaned figure of Moses can be seen opening up a coffin to examine the skull and
skeleton of the Old Testament patriarch Joseph, whose bones the Israelites had
carried with them to the promised land.[2] In the centre, the crowd is resting and
admiring the treasures which they had taken from the Egyptians.[3]

Jan Brueghel the Elder (1568-1625) was one of the most successful and versatile
Flemish artists of his day, specialising in landscapes, flower painting and drawings of
biblical subjects. His subtly detailed and delicately painted surfaces earned him the
nickname 'Velvet' Brueghel. The early death of his equally celebrated father, the
painter of peasant scenes Pieter Bruegel the Elder, meant that his son learned
watercolour painting from his grandmother Mayken Verhulst. This is one of Jan
Brueghel's most fully worked out and finished drawings. He has deliberately used
a blue wash in the background to give the impression of a mountainous landscape
receding into the hazy distance.

This drawing must have been one of Lord Stanley's earliest artistic purchases. He
bought it in 1816 at the bankruptcy sale of William Roscoe,[4] along with a further
48 drawings. His decision to buy these items may have stemmed principally from
a wish to help Roscoe (a distinguished botanist, art collector, fellow Whig
politician and anti-slave trade campaigner) out of financial trouble.

XB

[1]Exodus, XIV. [2]Exodus, XIII verse 19. [3]Exodus, XII verses 35-36. [4]26 September 1816, lot 458.

111. PORTRAIT OF THE DUCHESS OF ORLEANS

Oil on panel, possibly by Theodore Russell. 390 x 315mm (K).

The 13th Earl of Derby bought this portrait at the Strawberry Hill sale of Horace Walpole's effects,[1] as *'A Portrait of Mary Princess of Orange, daughter of King Charles I, a beautiful little picture by SIR PETER LELY'*. An eighteenth-century inscription on the back in French wrongly identifies the sitter as Henrietta Maria, the Consort of King Charles, and adds that the owner of the painting in 1748 was the Duc de Valentinois. Against this inscription Horace Walpole noted, also in French, that the portrait was presented to him during the 1770s by the Prince of Monaco, and that the sitter was not Henrietta Maria but her eldest daughter. A collector of historical portraits and with a particular bent for *femmes galantes*, Walpole was also presumably responsible for the attribution to Lely.

George Scharf, in his catalogue of the pictures at Knowsley,[2] seems to have been the first to suggest that the portrait actually represented Charles I's fifth daughter, Henrietta (1644-1670). She married the brother of Louis XIV of France in 1661, became a major player in Anglo-French politics, and in 1670 died in mysterious and sensational circumstances, probably poisoned on the orders of her husband. Scharf, rejecting the possibility that the portrait was by Lely himself, proposed that it was a copy of one of his works by Charles Jervas. Scharf also noted the strong resemblance to portraits by Van Dyck and this consideration has led to the work's recent reattribution to Theodore Russell (1614-1689), an erstwhile copyist in Van Dyck's studio who struck out on his own after his master's death in 1641. Russell's *oeuvre* is at present too little-known to make this proposal more than tentative, but the portrait's charm and sophistication proclaim it as the work of an artist of considerable quality.

AK

[1]1842; 22nd day, lot 122, purchased for £21. [2]Scharf 1875: 21-22.

223

Painting on a wood panel, on the back of which is a red wax seal with the monogrammed initials 'JG', surmounted by a heraldic animal. Signed in yellow letters in the lower right corner 'P Laer' and dated 1644(?). 222 x 266mm (K).

This image of a blacksmith shoeing a horse is typical of the small, naturalistically painted everyday scenes which Pieter (Boddingh) van Laer (1599 – after 1642?) popularised after he arrived in Rome in about 1625. He soon joined his fellow Dutch and Flemish artists in the 'Schildersbent', a rowdy drinking-club, and whose members gave him the nickname 'Bamboccio' (Italian for 'ugly puppet' or 'doll') because of his odd physique; long legs, short chest and hardly any neck. Van Laer became so closely associated with street-scenes showing men playing card and dice games outside inns, that his nickname was adapted to describe his compositions (*bambocciata*) and those painted by a large group of his predominantly northern followers, who were called the 'Bamboccianti'. Although *bambocciata* were much despised by some Italian artists and commentators, van Laer's work sold well and for relatively high prices.

Van Laer has added a note of tension to this commonplace scene of a horseman concentrating on drinking from his tankard, whilst his horse quenches his thirst at a trough being filled by another rider. In the foreground, the visible tightening of the pale horse's muscles and the glint in its eye, suggest that it might be about to deliver a kick. The 13th Earl of Derby and his horse-loving relatives would no doubt have appreciated such a moment of suspense.

Only about four dated works by van Laer are known, the last painted in 1639 after his return to Haarlem. The date of his death has, until now, been assumed to have been in or just after 1642. Van Laer's Dutch biographer Schrevelius described him setting off on a second trip to Rome in 1642 and never being heard of again, comparing the suddenness of his disappearance to that of the philosopher Empedocles (who committed suicide). The date on the Knowsley painting has previously been read as 1694, which would have made it the work of a 95-year-old artist. However, the triangular top to the third numeral suggests it could instead be a 4, making the date 1644 and thus extending van Laer's life and working period by two years.

XB

113. PORTRAIT OF A BURGOMASTER

Oil on wood panel; inscribed on the letter in the Burgomaster's hand (in French): TOUSJOUR//BIEN//fiN//E[t?]. Painted in the 1660s. 235 x 183mm (K).

The painting is unsigned, but its attribution to Gillis van Tilborgh (c.1625-c.1678) is due to a nineteenth-century inscription on the back of the frame, which reads: 'Portrait by Tilborg bought at Brussels 1818 George Hornby'.[1] Tilborgh began his career in the southern Netherlands but in 1654 he became a member of a painter's guild in Brussels, where he ran a busy studio. His portraits were, in many ways, the prototype of the English eighteenth-century 'conversation piece' - which portrayed families, friends and servants in seemingly spontaneous informal groupings in town-house interiors. However, after 1666, when he was appointed keeper of the picture collection at Terveuren castle, Tilborgh tended to produce interior scenes which showed real or imagined art collections.

This small portrait, presumably of a Brussels citizen and assumed to be a burgomaster or mayor, is given an additional swagger by his pose, nonchalantly holding a folded pair of gloves and with his hand on his hip. A further sense of vanity is added by the notation on the piece of paper he holds: 'always well finished'. This is an apt comment on this immaculately turned out gentleman, dressed simply but finely in black and white; perhaps he was a cloth merchant or even the painter himself?

XB

[1] See Scharf 1875, no.33: 17. George Hornby, from whom the 13th Earl acquired the picture, was his cousin and brother-in-law. The Hornby and Stanley families were closely entwined.

Oil on canvas. 735 x 585mm (K).

Kneller, born in Lübeck (now in Germany) in 1646, came to London at the age of thirty after training in Amsterdam and visiting Italy. Following the death of Peter Lely in 1680 he rapidly became the leading portrait painter at the court of Charles II and remained the dominant figure in English portrait painting for over forty years, until his death in 1723.

This virtually unknown work must post-date a self-portrait of about 1670, in which Kneller portrayed himself as a Dutch art student;[1] his handling here is freer and more assured, even though there remains a strong hint of his Dutch training under Ferdinand Bol in the painting of light and shade on the shirt collar. The facial features are recognisably of the same man but they are now given a more characterful emphasis. To judge from Kneller's apparent age, the portrait cannot have been done much later than the date of his arrival in London (1676). It is strikingly plain and unadorned. A half-unrolled drawing of a male head, at whose cranium Kneller points as if to suggest himself to be an artist of strong reason and intellect, provides the only diversionary note from the strongly lit and vigorously painted figure.

AK

[1]Stewart 1983: 5; Bignamini & Postle 1991: 44.

115. PORTRAIT OF JOHN DRYDEN

Oil on canvas by James Maubert. 730 x 640mm (K).

Horace Walpole, who once owned this painting, wrote in his *Anecdotes of Painters* that Maubert:

> '*distinguished himself by copying all the portraits he could meet with of English poets, some of which he painted in small ovals. Dryden, Wycherley, Congreve, Pope and some others he painted from the life. He died at the end of 1746*'.[1]

Little more is known of Maubert than this. He is recorded as having been a pupil of the Dublin-based Flemish painter Gaspar Smitz (c.1635-1707) but his signed and dated portraits of the 1720s do not look as if they were painted by an old man. The veracity of Walpole's statement that Maubert painted Dryden (1631-1700, Charles II's Poet Laureate) from life may therefore be open to question. If Dryden was in his sixties when he sat for the portrait it is possible, but he appears somewhat younger. A second version of the portrait[2] is traditionally said to have been painted for Jacob Tonson, Dryden's publisher, but this may also have been painted after Dryden's death, as Tonson lived until 1736. That canvas, smaller and less refined in its handling, certainly appears to have been copied from the Knowsley version.

John Dryden is shown informally, in an Indian gown and mules (as worn before dressing) and accompanied by a favourite hound, yet an attempt is also made to situate him historically in a lineage of great authors. The names on the spines of the volumes on his table (clearly legible in the National Portrait Gallery version of the portrait) are Shakespeare, Homer, Virgil, Horace and Montaigne.

AK

[1]Dallaway & Wornum 1849, 2: 672. [2]Now in the National Portrait Gallery.

116. PETER MONAMY
EXHIBITING A SEA-PIECE TO MR WALKER, HIS PATRON

Oil on canvas, by Peter
Monamy and William
Hogarth. An old inscription
on the back of the stretcher,
perhaps datable to the early
nineteenth century, reads:
'The seapieces in this picture were
painted by Monamy of whom is
the portrait in the brown coat …
the other figure is that of Thomas
Walker Esq. who had a fine
collection of pictures out of which
this came. The two figures were
painted by Hogarth …'
610 x 480mm (K).

Peter Monamy (1681-1749) was England's leading marine artist in the period
between the death of Willem van de Velde the Younger in 1707 and the emergence
of Samuel Scott and Charles Brooking in the 1740s.[1] Monamy's work was very
much in the style of Van de Velde, as the signed picture within this canvas reveals.
Thomas Walker, a banker, Commissioner of Customs and Receiver of Rents for the
crown, was a noted collector, particularly of maritime painting. Walker owned
fourteen works by Van de Velde[2] and he probably commissioned this work from
Monamy. However, although the inscription quoted above is ambiguous, close
inspection of the canvas strongly suggests that Monamy's contribution was limited
to the large seascape and that the rest of the work - and its basic conception - was
Hogarth's.

William Hogarth sprang to fame in the late 1720s with a series of paintings
representing scenes from John Gay's *Beggar's Opera*. This work must date from early
in the following decade, when Hogarth became fashionable as a painter of
conversation pieces - pictures of small whole-length figures in domestic interiors,
which were a distinctive new genre in British art. Here, although the figures are
obviously portraits, physical likeness was less important to Hogarth than the
relationship between the two men. A fierce champion of artists' rights, Hogarth
characteristically gives Monamy a social edge; he is elegantly posed and looking
down slightly on his wealthy and important patron.

The painting was once owned by Horace Walpole and was bought by Lord
Derby at the sale of Walpole's possessions at Strawberry Hill.[3]

AK

228

[1]Turner 1996, 21: 832. [2]Ilchester & Hake 1936: 178. [3]Purchased in 1842 for £22.1s.0d; Scharf 1875: 183.

117. TWO SLEEPING DOGS

Terracotta by Anne Damer.
Length 380mm (K).

In the Strawberry Hill sale catalogue of Horace Walpole's effects, this sculpture of a poodle and a spaniel was described as *'A model in terracotta by Lady Anne Damer, very spirited in effect'*. It was sold as part of the decorative furniture of the Great North Bedchamber.[1] Reporting to Lord Derby the following day, his agent Sell wrote that:

> *'Mr. Dawson Damer ran me up to a high price for [the dogs]; but as I knew your Lordship would be disappointed if you did not get one of the Articles, I thought it best to buy them at £32 - which certainly is a high price'.*

He added that the dogs were regarded as much superior to Lady Anne's other two works in the sale.[2]

Lady Anne Damer (1748-1828) was the cousin and protégée of Horace Walpole, who eventually bequeathed to her his house, Strawberry Hill, and its contents. After the suicide of her husband in 1776, Walpole encouraged Lady Anne to regard sculpture as more than an aristocratic amusement and to devote herself to it seriously. This terracotta, dated 1782, was the working model for the marble sculpture of two dogs with which Lady Anne made her debut at the Royal Academy in 1784. She later gave the marble version to her brother-in-law, the Duke of Richmond, and it is now at Goodwood.

The informality and naturalism of this little sculpture is in contrast with the somewhat formulaic neo-classicism of Damer's later portraiture of people - a good example of which is her bust of Elizabeth Hamilton, the 13th Earl's mother, as the muse Thalia. It may have been Anne Damer's evident sympathy and affection for the animal kingdom that attracted Lord Derby to her work. Horace Walpole certainly loved this piece, writing to Mary Berry in 1791 that he had newly decorated the little parlour at Strawberry Hill with Lady Diana Beauclerk's *Gipsies* and Mrs. Damer's *Dogs*, and that he 'defied Italy to produce three such monuments of female genius'.[3]

AK

---

[1] Purchased for Lord Derby on 12th May 1842, on the 16th day of the sale. [2] Sell to Lord Derby, LVRO 1/145/1. [3] Lewis 1865, 1: 302. Perhaps Walpole was including Mary Berry in his three.

a) By Alexander J. Strachen (1774-1850), London, 1802-1803. The mosaic is attributed to Giacomo Raffaelli, Rome, c.1800. 18 ct gold, micromosaic. Diameter 58mm, height 18.4mm.

b) By J.C.Barbe, probably French, c.1810. The pietra dura panels are attributed to Opificio delle Pietra Dure, Florence, c.1800-1810. Gold box inset with panels of pietra dura made from hardstones including marble, lapis lazuli, malachite, agate, jasper, quartz and turquoise. Length 78.2mm, width 55.4mm, height 33mm.

c) By Adrien-Jean-Maximilien Vachette (1753-1839), France, c.1810. Micromosaic, maker unknown, c.1810. Tortoiseshell, gold & micromosaic. Diameter 80mm, height 20.6mm.

d) By Thomas Diller, London, 1830-1831. Micromosaic, maker unknown, c.1830. Silver-gilt, glass cover to micromosaic. Length 84.3mm, width 63mm, height 27.4mm.

Four snuffboxes, from Knowsley. Although these items cannot be directly linked to the 13th Earl of Derby, all were made during his lifetime and are decorated with animals or flowers. It is at least possible that he bought or was given them because of his interest in natural history.

a) A circular snuffbox with fully detachable lid. The box is decorated with engine turning and the lid is inset with a micromosaic panel of two doves drinking from a metal stemmed bowl. The whole panel has a narrow border of grey and white micromosaic.

b) A rectangular snuffbox with a hinged lid. The lid panel depicts a parrot in blues, greens, reds and yellows. The background is of black stone with a small coloured butterfly in each of the top two corners; the sides also are decorated with butterflies. The base panel depicts a bouquet of flowers including a daffodil and narcissus, two other flowers and two buds. The gold edge to each panel is rolled or stamped with a pattern of leaves. There is a shell and leaf thumbpiece.

c) A silver-gilt oblong snuffbox with engine turned decoration to the side panels, base and also to the border surrounding the micromosaic panel. The hinged lid has a foliate decorated thumbpiece. The lid is inset with a panel of a pointer looking towards a pond with a small yellow duckling on it.

d) A circular snuffbox made of tortoiseshell, lined in gold. The detachable lid has a micromosaic panel depicting a fox killing a pheasant, in countryside setting. The gold border surrounding the panel is chased with leaf motifs.

AP

119. PAIR OF TORCHÈRES

Oak veneers and gilt wood.
Made in England, c.1820.
1745 x 440mm (K).

In the early 19th century, torchères of this form provided a fashionable means of lighting grand rooms. The form has its origins in ancient Roman marble candelabra and includes a flat top designed to support a lamp or candlestick. Torchères in the classical style were made popular in France by the designs of Charles Percier and Pierre Fontaine[1] and in Britain by such designers as Thomas Hope, whose work was inspired by the classical marbles in his own collection.[2]

AR

[1]Percier and Fontaine 1812 (repr. 1991): pls. 4, 23, 39, 59. [2]For a comparison between a heavily restored candelabrum in Hope's collection (and now at the Lady Lever Art Gallery, inv. no. LL16) and a design of his own, see Hope 1807 (repr. 1970): pls. 1 & 50.

Ebony veneers, painted copper
and brass. Original made in
Antwerp, c.1665–1680, but
with the addition of early 18th
century handles and some
early 19th century mounts.
740 x 1030 x 365mm (K).

During the 17th century, Antwerp specialised in the production of luxurious
painted cabinets which were exported throughout Europe. The painted decoration
typically featured landscapes, episodes from the Bible or mythological scenes. The
seascapes on this cabinet are in the style of Pieter van den Velde (1634–after 1687),
a marine painter from Antwerp who specialised in naval battle scenes.[1]

The architectural form of the cabinet is inspired by Italian and southern
German baroque cabinets, but the exuberant theatricality of such pieces is
somewhat more muted, as if to suit a more restrained Protestant temperament.
Originally the cabinet would have had doors, which when shut would have
disguised the splendidly decorated interior and presented an unadorned and rather
severe external appearance. Such cabinets were generally used for the storage of
important documents, coins, jewels or other small collections.

Some of the mounts (the rococo revival escutcheons on the plinth drawer and
the concave pediment and the Regency anthemion mount within the pediment in
the centre) are early 19th century, and therefore could have been added by the 13th
Earl of Derby. This cabinet reflects the known taste of the 13th Earl more closely
than any other furniture surviving at Knowsley. The acquisitions he made at the
Strawberry Hill sale of 1842 included two ebony chairs and an ebony table, as well
as an armchair dated 1601 and an oak panel carved with the arms of Henry VII.[2]
Such a taste for ebony and antiquarian items makes it distinctly possible that the
13th Earl also acquired this cabinet.

AR

[1]Compare, for example, paintings illustrated in National Maritime Museum 1988: 411 and in Archibald
1980: pls. 110–111. [2]Strawberry Hill sale catalogue, 1842: 176 lot 79; 191 lot 56; 178 lot 117; 189 lot 36.

121. JAPANESE CABINET

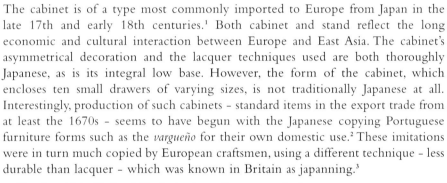

Two views, with doors open
and shut. Lacquered pine and
red cedar with brass mounts
and handles.
Made in Japan, c.1660–1700.
780 x 950 x 520mm.

Chinoiserie stand of ebonised
mahogany, partly gilt.
Made in England, c.1840.
625 x 985 x 565mm (K).

The cabinet is of a type most commonly imported to Europe from Japan in the late 17th and early 18th centuries.[1] Both cabinet and stand reflect the long economic and cultural interaction between Europe and East Asia. The cabinet's asymmetrical decoration and the lacquer techniques used are both thoroughly Japanese, as is its integral low base. However, the form of the cabinet, which encloses ten small drawers of varying sizes, is not traditionally Japanese at all. Interestingly, production of such cabinets – standard items in the export trade from at least the 1670s – seems to have begun with the Japanese copying Portuguese furniture forms such as the *vargueño* for their own domestic use.[2] These imitations were in turn much copied by European craftsmen, using a different technique – less durable than lacquer – which was known in Britain as japanning.[3]

By the 13th Earl of Derby's time, Europeans had access to more accurate information about East Asian architecture and design,[4] but the love of using Chinese and Japanese motifs and objects to create informal and fantastic chinoiserie interiors continued, reaching its apogee in this country in the Royal Pavilion at Brighton in the 1820s. This cabinet's stand, a somewhat heavy amalgamation of late Regency taste with fretwork reminiscent of mid 18th century designs by Thomas Chippendale,[5] can be seen as a product of this continued enthusiasm.

AR

[1]Comparable examples are recorded in the Royal Collection and at Syon Park, Middlesex: see Edwards 1964: 97, fig. 18 and the Victoria and Albert Museum Furniture and Woodwork Collection's picture archive, no. 28061. [2]Impey 1977: 111. [3]The technique is described in Edwards 1964: 327-331 and Huth 1971: 24-26. [4]Chambers (1757) was particularly influential. [5]Chippendale 1754. This stand's fretwork is very similar to the 'Gothick' fretwork of plates XXXIX and CLVI, while its brackets (some now missing) were probably inspired by ones similar to those in plates 50 [sic] and XCIII.

BIBLIOGRAPHY

Aiton, W. 1789. *Hortus Kewensis, or a catalogue of the plants cultivated in the Royal Botanic Garden at Kew*. George Nicol: London.

Aiton, W.T. 1810-1813. *Hortus Kewensis, or a catalogue of the plants cultivated in the Royal Botanic Garden at Kew*. Longman, Hurst, Rees, Orme & Brown: London.

Alexander, E.P. 1985. William Bullock. *Curator* 28 (2): 117-147.

Anderson, E. F. 2001. *The Cactus Family*. Timber Press: Portland.

Angeli, H.R. 1911. *Shelley and his friends in Italy*. Methuen: London.

Archibald, E.H.H. 1980. *Dictionary of sea painters*. Antique Collectors' Club: Woodbridge, Suffolk.

Argyll, Duke of (ed.) 1910. *Intimate society letters of the eighteenth century*. Stanley Paul & Co.: London.

Armstrong, A. (in press). *Forget not Mee and my Garden: selected correspondence of Peter Collinson*. American Philosophical Society: Philadelphia.

Aspden, T. 1873. *Historical sketches of the House of Stanley and biography of Edward Geoffrey, 14th Earl of Derby*. T. Aspden: Preston.

Audubon, J. J. 1827-1838. *The Birds of America*. 4 vols, 435 pls. J.J. Audubon: Edinburgh & London.

Audubon, M. 1897. *Audubon and his journal*. 2 vols. Charles Scribner: New York.

Bagley, J.J. 1985. *The Earls of Derby 1485-1985*. Sidgwick & Jackson: London.

Bailey, C. 1975. *Edward Lear & Knowsley*. Merseyside County Council: Liverpool.

Barnaby, D. 1996. *Quaggas and other zebras*. Basset Publications: Plymouth.

Beckett, J.V. 1986. *The aristocracy in England 1660-1914*. Basil Blackwell: Oxford.

Berkeley, E. & Berkeley, D.S. (eds) 1992. *The correspondence of John Bartram*. Tallahassee Press, University of Florida: Tallahassee.

Bignamini, I. & Postle, M. 1991. *The artist's model*. Nottingham University Art Gallery: Nottingham.

Blunt, W. & Stearn, W.T. 1994. *The art of botanical illustration*. Antique Collectors' Club: Woodbridge, Suffolk.

Bowen, E. (unpublished). *Transcripts of letters from Edward Lear to his sister Ann*.

Bullock, W. 1819. *Catalogue of the London museum of natural history … at the Egyptian Hall in Piccadilly …. sold by auction … by Mr Bullock*. William Bullock: London.

Burkhardt, F. et al. (eds) 1986. *The correspondence of Charles Darwin, 1837-1843*. Cambridge University Press: Cambridge.

Burkhardt, F. et al. (eds) 1987. *The correspondence of Charles Darwin, 1844-1846*. Cambridge University Press: Cambridge.

Butler, P. 2000. *Irish botanical illustrators and flower painters*. Antique Collectors' Club, Woodbridge, Suffolk.

Byron, G.G. 1818. *Childe Harold's pilgrimage*, 4th canto. John Murray: London.

Cairns, D. (ed.) 1970. *The memoirs of Hector Berlioz*. Granada Publishing Ltd.: St. Albans.

Calmann, G. 1977. *Ehret, flower painter extraordinary: an illustrated biography*. Phaidon: Oxford.

Campbell, L. 1998. Anne Dubois de Groer Corneille de la Haye. *Burlington Magazine* 140: 755-756.

Catesby, M. 1729-1747. *A natural history of Carolina, Florida and the Bahama Islands*. C. Marsh: London

Chambers, W. 1757. *Designs of Chinese buildings, furniture, dresses, machines, and utensils*. W. Chambers: London.

Chippendale, T. 1754. *The gentleman and cabinet-maker's director*. T. Chippendale: London.

Chitty, S. 1988. *That singular person called Lear*. Weidenfeld & Nicolson: London.

Clutton, G. & Mackay, C. 1970. Old Thorndon Hall. *Occasional Papers of the Garden History Society* 2: 34.

Cockayne, G.E. 1916. *The complete peerage of England, revised & enlarged by Vicary Gibbs*. The St. Catherine's Press: London.

Collins, W.W. 1848. *Memoirs of the life of William Collins*. Longman, Brown, Green & Longman: London

Cox, M. 1974. *Derby: the life and times of the 12th Earl of Derby*. J.A. Allen & Co.: London.

Craven, K. 1838. *Excursions in the Abruzzi*. 2 vols. Richard Bentley: London.

Cunningham, M. 1993. *The story of The Oaks and Oaks Park*. Sutton Press: London.

Curtis, W. 1788. *Amaryllis formosissima*. The Botanical Magazine 2: pl. 47.

Dallaway, J. & Wornum R.N. (eds) 1849. *Horace Walpole's 'Anecdotes of painting in England'*. Henry G. Bohn: London.

De Lattre, A. & Bourcier, J. 1846. Description de quinze espèces nouvelles de Trochilidées. *Revue Zoologique* 9: 305-312.

Denton, M.L. 1995. *Birds in the Yorkshire Museum*. Yorkshire Museum: York.

Derby, 13th Earl of, 1841. A letter from the President of the Society, the Earl of Derby. *Proceedings of the Zoological Society of London* (for 1840): 33.

Desmond, R. 1994. *Dictionary of British and Irish botanists and horticulturists*. Taylor & Francis: London.

Dillwyn, L. 1843. *Hortus Collinsonianus: an account of the plants cultivated by the late Peter Collinson … arranged alphabetically according to their modern names, from the catalogue of his garden, and other manuscripts*. W.C. Murray & D. Rees: Swansea.

Dobson, W. 1868. *History of the parliamentary representation of Preston*. W. & J. Dobson: Preston.

Draper, P. 1864. *The House of Stanley*. T. Hutton: Ormskirk, Lancashire.

Edmondson, J. 1995. *James Bolton of Halifax*. National Museums & Galleries on Merseyside: Liverpool.

Edmondson, J. R. 2002. *Peter Collinson*, in: Shoemaker C. (ed.). *Encyclopedia of gardens: history and design*. Fitzroy Dearborn: Chicago.

Edwards, R. 1964. *The shorter dictionary of English furniture*. Country Life Books: London.

Egerton, J. 1978. *British sporting and animal paintings 1655-1867*. Tate Gallery: London.

Ehret, G.D. 1748-1759. *Plantae et papiliones rariores depictae et aeri incisae*. G.D. Ehret: London.

Ehret, G.D. 1896. A memoir of Georg Dionysius Ehret. *Proceedings of the Linnean Society of London* (for 1894-95): 41-58.

Elliott, B. 1994. *Treasures of the Royal Horticultural Society: 350 years of botanical illustration*. The Herbert Press: London.

Falchi, R. & Wadsworth, V. (eds) 1997. *Edward Lear*. Lalli Editore: Poggibonsi.

Farrer, W. & Brownbill, J. (eds) 1907. *The Victoria history of the County of Lancashire*. Vol. 3. Archibald Constable & Co.: London.

Fecht, K.G. 1887. *Geschichte der haupt- und residenzstadt Karlsruhe*. Antiquariat der Braunschem Universitätsbuchhandlung: Karlsruhe (1976 reprint).

Fisher, C.T. 1986. A type specimen of the Paradise Parrot, *Psephotus pulcherrimus* (Gould, 1845). *Australian Zoologist* 22 (3): 10-12.

Fisher, C.T. 1988. An unpublished drawing of the pig-footed bandicoot by John Gould and H.C. Richter, with comments on museum specimens. *Australian Zoologist* 24 (4): 205-209 and cover plate.

Foot, M.R.D. (ed.) 1968. *The Gladstone diaries, 1833-1839*. Oxford University Press: Oxford.

Forbes, H.O. 1898. Introductory. *Bulletin of the Liverpool Museums* 1 (1): 1-2.

Foreman, A. 1998. *Georgiana, Duchess of Devonshire*. Harper Collins: London.

Fraser, L. 1850. *Catalogue of the Knowsley collections belonging to the Right Honourable Edward (Thirteenth) Earl of Derby, K.G. (Mammalia)* . Louis Fraser for the 13th Earl of Derby: Knowsley.

Fraser, L. 1852. On new birds in the collection at Knowsley. *Proceedings of the Zoological Society of London* (for 1850): 245-246, pls XXV-XXIX.

Frith, W.P. 1889. *My autobiography and reminiscences.* Richard Bentley & Son: London.

Frost, C. 1987. *A history of British taxidermy.* Lavenham Press: Lavenham, Suffolk.

Fuller, E. 2001. *Extinct birds.* Oxford University Press: Oxford.

Gage, A.T. & Stearn, W.T. 1988. *A bicentenary history of the Linnean Society of London.* Academic Press: London.

Gaja, K. 1995. *G.F. Watts in Italy.* Leo S. Olschki: Florence.

Galassi, P. 1991. *Corot in Italy.* Yale University Press: New Haven, Connecticut.

Garnett, W.J. 1849. *Prize report on the farming of Lancashire.* Royal Agricultural Society: London.

Glover, R. 1973. Knowsley Hall: a tale of lost opportunities. *Marwell Zoo News* 4: 10-11.

Glover, R. 1975. The man who did not go to California. *Historical Publications of the Canadian Historical Association, Edmonton:* 95-112.

Goodwin, G. 1887. *Emanual Mendes da Costa, 1717-1791,* pp. 271-272, in: Stephen L. & Lee S. (eds) *Dictionary of national biography.* Vol. 12. Smith, Elder & Co.: London.

Gould, J. 1833-1835a. *A Monograph of the Ramphastidae, or family of toucans.* 1 vol., 34 pls. John Gould: London.

Gould, J. 1835b. On a new species of Toucan *(Aulacorhynchus derbianus).* *Proceedings of the Zoological Society of London:* 46.

Gould, J. 1840-1848. *The birds of Australia.* 7 vols, 602 pls. John Gould: London.

Gould, J. 1841-1844a. *A monograph of the Macropodidae, or family of kangaroos.* 2 parts, 45 pls. John Gould: London.

Gould, J. 1844b. Characters of new species of mammals and birds transmitted from Australia by Mr. Gilbert. *Proceedings of the Zoological Society of London*: 103-107.

Gould, J. 1845a. On a new species of *Platycercus. Annals and Magazine of Natural History* 15: 114-115.

Gould, J. 1845b-1863. *The mammals of Australia.* 3 vols, 182 pls. John Gould: London.

Gould, J. 1846. Description of six new species of birds. *Proceedings of the Zoological Society of London:* 67-71.

Gould, J. 1849a-1861. *A Monograph of the Trochilidae, or family of humming-birds.* 5 vols., 360 pls. John Gould: London.

Gould, J. 1849b-1883. *The Birds of Asia.* 35 parts, 530 plates. John Gould: London.

Gould, J. 1854. *A Monograph of the Ramphastidae, or family of toucans.* 2nd ed, 1 vol., 52 pls. John Gould: London

Graham, M. 1820. *Three months passed in the mountains east of Rome during the year 1819.* Longman: London.

Grant, M.H. 1952. *Flower paintings through four centuries: a descriptive catalogue of the collection formed by Major the Honourable Henry Rogers Broughton, including a dictionary of flower painters from the XVIth to the XIXth century.* Lewis: Leigh-on-Sea, Essex.

Gray, G.R. 1844-1849. *The genera of birds: comprising their generic characters, a notice of the habits of the genus and an extensive list of species referred to their several genera.* 3 vols., 420 pls. Longmans: London.

Gray, J.E. 1836. On the genus *Moschus* of Linnaeus, with descriptions of two new species. *Proceedings of the Zoological Society of London:* 63-68.

Gray, J.E. 1837. Description of some new or little known Mammalia. *Magazine of Natural History* 1: 577-587.

Gray, J.E. (ed.) 1846a-1850. *Gleanings from the menagerie and aviary at Knowsley Hall.* 2 vols. 13th Earl of Derby: Knowsley.

Gray, J.E. 1846b. Description of the species of *Cephalophus* (H. Smith) in the collection of the British Museum. *Annals and Magazine of Natural History* (1) 18: 162-168.

Gray, J.E. 1847. Description of a new species of antelope from West Africa. *Annals and Magazine of Natural History* (1) 20: 286.

Greenway, J.C. 1967. *Extinct and vanishing birds of the world.* 2nd ed. Dover: New York.

Harrison, C. 1995. *Edward Lear: drawings and watercolours.* Ashmolean Museum: Oxford.

Hazlitt, W.C. (ed.) 1873. *English students at Rome*, pp. 321-333, in: *Essays on the fine arts.* Reeves & Turner: London. .

Hewitson, A. 1883. *History of Preston.* Preston Chronicle: Preston, Lancashire.

Hill, B.J.W. 1948. *Eton medley.* Winchester Publications: London.

Hofer, P. 1967. *Edward Lear as a landscape draughtsman.* Harvard University Press: Cambridge, Massachusetts.

Hooker, W.H. 1843. *Icones Plantarum, or figures with brief descriptive characters and remarks, of new or rare plants, selected from the author's herbarium,* ser. 2, vol. 6, pl. 589. Longman, Rees, Orme, Brown, Green & Longman: London.

Hope, T. 1807. *Household furniture and interior decoration.* John Tiranti & Co.: London (1937 reprint).

Hunt, D. 1992. *A history of Preston.* Carnegie Publishing: Preston, Lancashire.

Hunt, H. 1820. *Memoirs of Henry Hunt Esq. written by himself in his Majesty's jail at Ilchester.* 3 vols. Henry Hunt: London.

Huth, H. 1971. *Lacquer of the West: the history of a craft and an industry 1550-1950.* University of Chicago Press: Chicago.

Hutton, I. 1990. *Birds of Lord Howe Island past and present.* Ian Hutton: Coffs Harbour, New South Wales.

Ilchester, Earl of & Hake H. (eds) 1930-1936. *Vertue notebooks,* vols 1-4. Oxford University Press: Oxford.[6]

Impey, O. 1977. *Chinoiserie: the impact of oriental styles on western art and decoration.* Oxford University Press: London.

Jackson, C.E. 1998. *Sarah Stone. Natural curiosities from the new worlds.* Merrell Holberton: London.

Jackson, C.E. 1999. *Dictionary of bird artists of the world.* Antique Collectors' Club: Woodbridge, Suffolk.

Jephson, J.M. 1859. *Narrative of a walking tour in Brittany.* Lovell Reeve: London.

Joseph, L. 1988. A review of the conservation status of Australian parrots in 1987. *Biological Conservation* 46: 261-280.

Kear, J. (ed., in press). *Ducks, geese and swans of the world.* Oxford University Press: Oxford.

Keeling, C.H. 1984. *Where the lion trod.* Chapter VI: *Knowsley Park (1834-1851).* Clam Publications: Guildford, Surrey.

Keeling, C.H. 2000. *The marvel by the Mersey.* Clam Publications: Guildford, Surrey.

Kevan, D.K.M. 1977. Mid-eighteenth century entomology and helminthology in the West Indies: Dr. James Grainger. *Journal of the Society for the Bibiography of Natural History* 8 (3): 193-222.

King, R. 1985. *Royal Kew.* Constable: London.

Knox, A. G. & Walters, M.P. 1994**.** Extinct and endangered birds in the collections of the Natural History Museum. *Occasional Publications of the British Ornithologists' Club* 1: 1-292.

Lack, H.W. 2001. *A garden for eternity: the codex Liechtenstein.* Benteli: Berne.

Lambert, A.B. 1803-1807. *A description of the genus Pinus, illustrated with figures, directions relative to the cultivation, and remarks on the uses of the several species.* J. White: London.

Largen, M.J. 1987. Bird specimens purchased by Lord Stanley at the sale of the Leverian Museum in 1806, including those still extant in the collections of the Liverpool Museum. *Archives of Natural History* 14 (3): 265-288.

Largen, M.J. 1988. Henry Salt (1780-1827) and the first zoological collection from Ethiopia, including bird specimens still extant in the Liverpool Museum. *Archives of Natural History* 15 (3): 331-355.

Largen, M.J. & Fisher, C.T. 1986. Catalogue of extant mammal specimens from the collection of the 13th Earl of Derby, now in the Liverpool Museum. *Archives of Natural History* 13 (3): 225-272.

Largen, M.J. & Rogers-Price, V. 1985. John Abbot, an early naturalist-artist in North America: his contribution to ornithology, with particular reference to a collection of bird skins in the Merseyside County Museums, Liverpool. *Archives of Natural History* 12 (2): 231-252.

Latham, J. 1781-1801a. *A general synopsis of birds.* 3 vols + 2 supplements. Benjamin White and Leigh, Sotheby & Son: London.

Latham, J. 1790-1801b. *Index ornithologicus sive systema ornithologiae.* 2 vols + supplement. Leigh & Sotheby: London.

Latham, J. 1821-1824. *A general history of birds.* 10 vols. John Latham: Winchester.

Lear, E. 1830-1832. *Illustrations of the family of Psittacidae or parrots.* 42 plates. Edward Lear: London.

Lear, E. 1841. *Views in Rome and its environs.* Thomas McLean: London.

Lear, E. 1846. *Illustrated excursions in Italy.* 2 vols. Thomas McLean: London.

Lewis, T. (ed.) 1865. *Extracts of the journals and correspondence of Miss Berry from the year 1783 to 1852.* 3 vols. Longman, Green & Co.: London.

Lister, R. (ed.) 1974. *The Letters of Samuel Palmer.* Oxford University Press: Oxford.

Lister, R. 1981. *George Richmond: a critical biography.* Robin Garton: London

Llanover, Lady 1862. *The autobiography and correspondence of Mary Granville (1700-1788) 'Mrs Delany'.* Richard Bentley: London.

Mabberley, D. 1987. *The plant book.* Cambridge University Press: Cambridge.

Mathews, G.M. 1930. *Systema avium Australasianarum, a systematic list of the birds of the Australasian region,* vol. 2. British Ornithologists' Union: London.

Maxwell, H. (ed.) 1903. *The Creevey papers: a selection from the correspondence and diaries of Thomas Creevey M.P.,* vol.1. John Murray: London.

McBurney, H. 1992. *Mark Catesby's natural history of America.* Merrill Holberton: London.

Medway, D.G. 1976. Extant types of New Zealand birds from Cook's voyages. *Notornis* 23: 44-60.

Meyers, A. 1997. *Introduction,* pp. 11-27 in: McBurney, H. (ed.). *Mark Catesby's Natural History of America: the watercolours from the Royal Library.* Merrill Holberton: London.

Millar, O. 1963. *Tudor, Stuart & early Georgian pictures on the Royal Collection.* Phaidon: London.

Moore, T.J. 1851. *A catalogue of the menagerie and aviary at Knowsley formed by the late Earl of Derby, K.G.* Joshua Walmsley: Liverpool.

Moore, T.J. 1890. Lord Derby's Museum. *The Liverpool Review:* 10-11.

Moore, T.J. 1891-1892. Opening address on the history of the living collections at Knowsley. *Transactions of the Biological Society of Liverpool* 5: 1-18 (part 1); 6: 1-9 (part 2).

Morgan, P.J. & Brennan, M.T. 1977. Lord Edward Smith Stanley, 1775-1851, XIIIth Earl of Derby: a review of his biological collections and their importance. *Biology Curators' Group Newsletter* 6: 20-28.

Morrell, J. & Thackray, A. (eds) 1984. *Gentlemen of science: early correspondence of the British Association for the Advancement of Science.* Royal Historical Society: London.

Mullet, M. 1972. The politics of Liverpool, 1660-88. *Transactions of the Historic Society of Lancashire and Cheshire* 124: 31-56

Murray, J. 1843. *Handbook for travellers in Central Italy.* John Murray: London.

Murray, J. 1850. *Handbook for Travellers in Central Italy.* 2nd ed. John Murray: London.

Nelson, E.C. & McKinley, D.L. 1986. *Aphrodite's mouse-trap. A biography of Venus's Flytrap with facsimiles of an original pamphlet and the manuscripts of John Ellis, F.R.S.* Boethius Press: Aberystwyth.

Noakes, V. 1968. *Edward Lear: the life of a wanderer.* Collins: London.

Noakes, V. 1985. *Edward Lear 1812-1888.* Harry N. Abrams: New York

Noakes, V. (ed.) 1988. *Edward Lear: selected letters.* Oxford University Press: Oxford.

Nuttall, T. 1818. *The genera of North American plants, and catalogue of the species, to the year 1817.* Thomas Nuttall: Cambridge, Massachusetts.

Nuttall, T. 1842-1849. *The North American Sylva.* 3 vols. J. Dobson, Townsend Ward, Smith & Wistar: Philadelphia.

Oppé, A.P. 1934. *Art,* pp. 101-176, in: Young G.M. (ed.) *Early Victorian England,* vol. 2. Oxford University Press: Oxford.

Orchard, B.G. 1893. *Liverpool's legion of honour.* B.G. Orchard: Birkenhead

Percier, C. & Fontaine, P.F.L. 1812. *Recueil de décorations intérieures comprenant tout ce qui a rapport a l'ameublement.* 2nd ed. C. Percier & P.F.L. Fontaine: Paris.

Phillip, A. 1789. *The voyage of Governor Phillip to Botany Bay.* John Stockdale: London.

Pitman, R. 1988. *Edward Lear's Tennyson.* Carcarnet: Manchester.

Pollard, W. 1871. *The Stanleys of Knowsley: a history of that noble family.* Frederick Warne: London.

Povey, D. 1954. A naturalist's books. *North-western Naturalist* 2 (1): 7-8.

Proby, G. 1938. *Lear in Sicily.* Duckworth: London.

Proby, K.H. 1974. *Audubon in Florida.* University of Miami Press: Coral Gables, Florida.

Proctor, W. 1959. The Preston election of 1768. *Transactions of the Historic Society of Lancashire and Cheshire* 3: 93-116.

Renkema, H.W. 1928. Aylmer Bourke Lambert en zijn 'Description of the Genus Pinus'. *Mededlingen van de Landbouwhoogeschool* 32 (8): 10-30.

Riccardi, D. (ed.) 1997. *Gli artisti romantici tedeschi del primo Ottocento a Olevano Romano.* Electa: Milan.

Ripley, S.D. 1977. *Rails of the world.* David Godine: Boston, Massachusetts.

Ritvo, H. 1987. *The animal estate. The English and other creatures in the Victorian age.* Harvard University Press: Cambridge, Massachusetts.

Rix, M. 1989. *The art of botanical illustration.* Bracken Books: London.

Roscoe, W. 1824-1828. *Monandrian plants of the order Scitamineae, chiefly drawn from living specimens in the Botanic Garden at Liverpool.* George Smith: Liverpool.

Ross, D. 1848. *Sketches of the House of Stanley and the House of Sefton.* Orr: London.

Salt, H. 1814. *A voyage to Abyssinia, and travels into the interior of that country, executed…in the years 1809 and 1810.* F.C. & J. Rivington: London.

Salvin, O. 1860. History of the Derbyan Mountain-Pheasant (Oreophasis derbianus). *The Ibis* 2: 248-253.

Scharf, G. 1875. *A descriptive and historical catalogue of the collection of pictures at Knowsley Hall.* Bradbury & Agnew: London.

Scherren, H. 1905. *The Zoological Society of London.* Cassell & Co.: London.

Schnalke, T. 1995. Natur im bild: anatomie und botanik in der sammlung des Nürnberger arztes Christoph Jacob Trew. *Schriften der Universitätsbibliothek Erlangen-Nürnberg herausgegeben von Konrad Wickert, Erlangen.*

Schomburgk, R.H. 1844. *Calycophyllum stanleyanum. Journal of Botany, British and Foreign* 3: 622.

Schulz, W. 1982. *Herman Saftleven 1609-1685 - Leben und Werke - mit einem kritischen Katalog der Gemälde und Zeichnungen.* de Gruyter: Berlin & New York.

Schulze-Hagen, K. & Geus, A. 2000. *Joseph Wolf.* Basilisken-Presse: Marburg an der Lahn.

Sclater, P.L. 1880. List of certainly known species of Anatidae. *Proceedings of the Zoological Society of London:* 495-536.

Searby, P. 1997. *A history of the University of Cambridge,* vol. 3, 1750-1870. Cambridge University Press: Cambridge.

Shaw, G. 1792-1796. *Museum Leverianum, containing select specimens from the museum of the late Sir Ashton Lever, Kt with descriptions in Latin and English.* 2 vols. James Parkinson: London.

Sholl, A. (unpublished). *The historical development of Knowsley Park; a study of the landscape 1085-1985.* Typescript prepared in 1985 for the Groundwork Trust (copies in the Knowsley Hall and Huyton Libraries).

Simey, M. 1992. *Charity rediscovered*. Liverpool University Press: Liverpool.

Smith, J.E. 1806. *Ventenatia major. Exotic botany, consisting of coloured figures, and scientific descriptions, of such new, beautiful, or rare plants as are worthy of cultivation in the gardens of Britain*. Vol. 2, tab.66. J. Sowerby, London.

Smith, J.E. 1821. *A selection of the correspondence of Linnaeus, and other naturalists, from the original manuscripts*. Longman, Hurst, Rees, Orme, Brown & Green: London.

Sotheby, L. 1842. *Catalogue of the valuable botanical library (689 numbers) of the late Aylmer Bourke Lambert, to be sold at auction April 18th 1842*. Sotheby & Co.: London.

Stanley, E.S. 1814. *Additional remarks on these birds …* app. iv, pp. l-lxii, in: Salt, H. *A voyage to Abyssinia, and travels into the interior of that country, executed … in 1809 and 1810*. F.C. & J. Rivington, London.

Stanley, E.S. 1834. A note on a specimen of a young Sandwich Island goose. *London & Edinburgh Philosophical Magazine and Journal of Science* 5: 233-235 and *Proceedings of the Zoological Society of London*: 41-43.

Stansfield, H. 1951. Plant collecting in Missouri: a Liverpool expedition, 1809-1811. *Liverpool Libraries, Museums & Arts Committee Bulletin* 1(2): 17-31.

Stewart, J.D. 1983. *Sir Godfrey Kneller and the English baroque portrait*. Oxford University Press: Oxford.

Strachey, C. (ed.) 1907. *Letters of Edward Lear to Chichester Fortescue*. T. Fisher Unwin: London.

Strachey, L. & Fulford, R. (eds) 1938. *The Greville Memoirs 1814-1860*. 8 vols. Macmillan: London.

Strahan, R. 1995. *The mammals of Australia*. Reed Books: Chatswood, New South Wales.

Strong, R. 1969. *Tudor and Jacobean portraits*. Her Majesty's Stationery Office: London.

Stroud, P.T. 2000. *The emperor of nature. Charles-Lucien Bonaparte and his world*. University of Pennsylvania Press: Philadelphia.

Stuart, J. 1785. *Botanical tables containing the different familys of British plants distinguished by a few obvious parts of fructification rang'd in a synoptical method*. 9 vols. J. Stuart: London.

Swainson, W. 1840. *Taxidermy, with the biography of the zoologists, and notices of their works*, vol. 119, in: Lardner, D. (ed.) *The Cabinet Cyclopedia*. 133 vols. Longman, Orme, Brown, Green & Longman: London.

Thornton, R.J. 1807. *New illustration of the sexual system of Linnaeus … and the Temple of Flora, or garden of nature*. Robert John Thornton: London.

Toynbee, P. (ed.) 1903. *Letters of Horace Walpole*. Vol. 1. Clarendon Press: Oxford.

Trevelyan, G. 1876. *The life and letters of Lord Macaulay*. Oxford University Press: Oxford.

Turner J. (ed.) 1996. *The dictionary of art*. Macmillan: London.

Urbanski, S.W. (unpublished). *Parliamentary politics, 1796-1832, in an industrialising borough: Preston, Lancashire*. Ph.D. thesis, Emory University, Atlanta, Georgia (1976).

Vigors, N.A. 1826. Descriptions of some rare, interesting or hitherto uncharacterized subjects in zoology. *The Zoological Journal* 2: 234-241.

Vigors, N.A. & Horsfield, T. 1827. A description of the Australian birds in the collection of the Linnean Society. *Transactions of the Linnean Society of London* 15: 170-331.

Vincent, J. (ed.) 1978. *Disraeli, Derby and the Conservative Party: journals and memoirs of Edward Henry, Lord Stanley 1849-1869*. Harvester Press: Hassocks, Sussex.

Wagstaffe, R. 1978. *Type specimens of birds in the Merseyside County Museums*. Merseyside County Museums: Liverpool.

Walmsley, R. 1969. *Peterloo: the case re-opened*. Manchester University Press: Manchester.

Warren, R.L.M. 1966. *Type specimens of birds in the British Museum (Natural History)*, vol. 1. *Non-passerines*. British Museum (Natural History): London.

Waterhouse, G.R. 1841. *Marsupialia or pouched animals*, pp. 45-323, in: Jardine W. (ed.). *The Naturalist's Library. Mammalia*, vol. 11. W. H. Lizars: Edinburgh.

Wayne, P. (ed.) 1954. *Letters of William Wordsworth*. Oxford University Press: Oxford.

Webley, D.P. (undated). *Cast to the winds: the life and work of Penry Williams*. National Library of Wales: Aberystwyth.

Wells, K.M. (unpublished). *The return of the British painters to Rome after 1815*. Ph.D. thesis, University of Leicester (1974).

White, J. 1790. *Journal of a voyage to New South Wales with sixty-five plates of non descript animals, birds, lizards, serpents, curious cones of trees, and other natural productions*. J. Debrett: London.

Wilcox, S. (ed.) 2000. *Edward Lear and the Art of Travel*. Yale Center for British Art: New Haven, Connecticut

Wilson, A. (unpublished). *Culture and commerce: Liverpool's merchant elite c.1790-1850*. Ph.D. thesis, University of Liverpool (1996).

Wilson, E.J. 1961. *James Lee and the Vineyard Nursery Hammersmith*. Hammersmith Local History Group: London.

Woolfall, S.J. 1990. History of the 13th Earl of Derby's menagerie and aviary at Knowsley Hall, Liverpool (1806-1851). *Archives of Natural History* 17 (1): 1-47.

237

INDEX